Libraries, Access and Intellectual Freedom

DEVELOPING POLICIES FOR PUBLIC AND ACADEMIC LIBRARIES

Barbara M. Jones

AMERICAN LIBRARY ASSOCIATION

Chicago and London

1999

While extensive effort has gone into ensuring the reliability of information appearing in this book, the publisher makes no warranty, express or implied, on the accuracy or reliability of the information, and does not assume and hereby disclaims any liability to any person for any loss or damage caused by errors or omissions in this publication.

Cover and text design by Ellen Pettengell

Composition by the dotted i in Janson Text and Novarese using QuarkXPress 3.32 on a Macintosh G3

Printed on 50-pound white offset, a pH-neutral stock, and bound in 10-point coated cover stock by McNaughton & Gunn

The paper used in this publication meets the minimum requirements of American National Standard for Information Sciences—Permanence of Paper for Printed Library Materials, ANSI Z39.48-1992. ♾

Library of Congress Cataloging-in-Publication Data

Jones, Barbara M.
Libraries, access and intellectual freedom : developing policies for public and academic libraries / Barbara M. Jones.
p. cm.
Includes bibliographical references.
ISBN 0-8389-0761-X (alk. paper)
1. Libraries—Censorship—United States. 2. Freedom of information—United States. I. Title.
Z711.4.J66 1999
025.2′13—dc21 99-20937

Printed in the United States of America.

03 02 01 00 99 5 4 3 2 1

In memory and honor of

Paul L. Murphy

Regent's Professor of American History
at the University of Minnesota—
free speech advocate and scholar,
dissertation advisor, teacher and friend.
We miss you.

CONTENTS

APPENDIXES

PREFACE

> Not to be able to come to one's truth or not to use it in one's writing, even in telling the truth having to "tell it slant," robs one of drive, of conviction; limits potential stature; results in loss to literature and the comprehensions we seek in it.
>
> —Tillie Olsen, *Silences*[1]

The July 31, 1998, *Chronicle of Higher Education* is typical of other issues—it contains a major article with direct implications for intellectual freedom in libraries. "Off-Campus Users Swamp College Libraries" describes publicly funded libraries inundated with walk-in users of all ages wanting to take advantage of Internet access at no charge. The dilemma: "The libraries' newfound popularity has left librarians at many public universities wringing their hands. Like their counterparts at public libraries, they are dealing with the downside of open access, which many of them have championed." A Rutgers University at Camden reference librarian provides a representative example:

> . . . the last thing she ever wanted to do was monitor teenagers surfing the Internet or referee their use of e-mail. But last summer, she says, she almost had no choice.
>
> For the summer's first few weeks, she says, the campus's main library became teen central. Packs of camp kids streamed through the doors to use the library's electronic classroom. Others strutted into the reference room on their own, grabbed a seat in front of a computer with access to the Web, and didn't leave for hours.
>
> "On many afternoons, every terminal was in use by a student too young to be a Rutgers student," [the librarian] said during a presentation at a library conference last spring.
>
> The young users' on-line activities rarely included research, she said. . . . On a few nights, the library staff discovered pornographic screen savers on the computers, which they assumed were the work of scheming kids . . .

> The experience led her to write a paper [with a colleague] that will appear in a forthcoming issue of the *Journal of Information Ethics* . . .
>
> "While it is appropriate, even laudatory, for an academic library to offer Internet access to all its users," they write, "it is equally appropriate, probably even necessary, to limit its use and impose guidelines."[2]

The electronic age has given librarians undreamed-of opportunities to reach nontraditional users as well as traditional users who have expanded their research strategies into new frontiers of information gathering. And yet it is proving to be both a blessing and a curse—even for legal experts, who are exploring new territory and don't always have answers for concerned librarians with limited resources. The librarians interviewed for the article raised crucial questions regarding intellectual freedom policy. Similar articles appear almost every week in the *Chronicle*, and the issues, at least in public colleges and universities, are much the same as those in the traditional public community library. These two types of libraries have much in common on the intellectual freedom front.

This book is written to help academic and public librarians make their professional ideals a reality through policies that promote access to information for user communities. If librarians utilize a thoughtful policy process, including good communications skills, even controversial policies have a better chance for wide support and successful implementation. And, contrary to common belief, librarians in publicly funded academic and public libraries have a great deal in common—not only in the library profession, but also in the eyes of the legal system—when it comes to First Amendment litigation. Private academic libraries are not governmental entities; therefore, the First Amendment does not usually apply to actions taken in those libraries regarding collections and services. However, librarians in private institutions will find in this book some strategies, based on library professional ethics, that will help them with their own policies. School librarians' intellectual freedom issues are not specifically covered in this book because the courts have treated their First Amendment problems somewhat differently; however, numerous high-quality sources of information and support can be obtained through their representative American Library Association (ALA) Division, the American Association of School Librarians (AASL).

The 1998–99 American Library Association President Ann Symons adopted intellectual freedom as her presidential theme. I hope that this book will help to maintain the interest and momentum at the end of Ms.

Symons's presidency, and raise librarians' awareness of the complexity and importance of intellectual freedom principles as part of a uniquely American value structure for information access.

I am especially gratified that so many academic librarians have become interested in intellectual freedom issues in recent years, because the profession so needs their support and expertise at this critical juncture. The Association of College and Research Libraries (ACRL) Intellectual Freedom Committee was established in the 1990s, and attendance at their ALA conference programs is approaching standing room only. This has helped dispel the narrow view of intellectual freedom problems as applicable to K–12 and public libraries only. In fact, the most important intellectual freedom cases and issues in recent years have affected academic libraries as directly as, if not more than, any other type of library. As this book will demonstrate, intellectual freedom issues have extended far beyond the more traditional censorship of removing a book from the shelf.

Intellectual freedom principles are embedded in the United States Constitution in the Bill of Rights (appendix A) and in the ethics and values of this country's library profession. It is an important privilege—not a burden—for libraries to provide excellent access to information at the turn of the century, with its explosion of new areas of knowledge and technological innovation. This environment offers unheard-of opportunities for timely information delivery, diversity of opinion and collaborative learning using a broadly accessible universe of information.

In 1992, the *Kreimer* v. *Morristown* court decisions identified publicly funded libraries, for the first time, as "limited public fora." This created an opportunity for librarians to promote library users' right to receive information as legally mandated in such a forum.

At the same time, there is great public and professional concern that when intellectual freedom ideals are translated into real-world library settings, they are too expensive—in terms of time and energy as well as real dollars. Some lament that the information explosion is too "noisy," sexually explicit, violent, homogenized or harmful to children. Many fear that new information technologies will only further what some perceive to be a breakdown of civility and critical thinking. Much Internet content is inaccurate and fungible. It can cross national and county borders without "adults only" or other restrictions, notwithstanding current attempts on the part of some governments to control access. Library collections are thus being developed and managed in different ways today. Library patrons and employees alike are exposed to this vast diversity of information and find much of it offensive. When libraries or other government agencies try to control this information, the danger arises not only of censorship but of invasion of privacy.

Finally, there are more "problem patrons"—reflections of U.S. society's problems and failures in confronting homelessness, mental illness and a host of other issues. As a result, librarians have had to learn when to enforce a library policy themselves, or when to involve the police to enforce a law.

This book is for those academic and public librarians who want to enhance their legal and professional education in order to write good policy. I have tried to address the most frequently encountered problems, pitfalls and ethical dilemmas. Included are reviews of the legal and professional contexts of intellectual freedom. There is also a broad review of public policy theory, using common library problems to illustrate policy enforcement, publicity and review. I hope that my colleagues will be satisfied with my attempt to balance the theoretical and the practical, and to use the "limited public forum" doctrine as a workable descriptor instead of the more traditional split between public and academic libraries.

Interviews with dozens of colleagues suggested that those who are most successful in drafting and implementing intellectual freedom policies have some very helpful skills: approaching problems with an optimistic and a proactive outlook; knowing and involving the major players from the outset; knowing how far to compromise; and identifying common ground values upon which to build. But the bottom line for all is a thorough knowledge and appreciation of intellectual freedom values. Opponents may not always agree, but more often than not they will respect a librarian who stands by professional values as a basis for decision making.

A caveat: This book is not to be used as a legal guide and does not substitute for legal counsel. First Amendment law, especially regarding the Internet, is changing almost weekly now. State and municipal laws vary radically from place to place. Private academic libraries must rely more on professional ethics than on the First Amendment for promoting intellectual freedom, because they are not dependent on public funds for operation. This book will, however, provide historical context and practical guidance for writing good intellectual freedom policies. I hope it will convey my firm belief that librarians need to know what questions to ask their library's attorney, who may not be well versed in specific library-related court cases. This could help avoid costly, time-consuming litigation. When legal action is required, as when the Supreme Court overturned the Communications Decency Act, librarians will know why and how it applies to their operation.

Another caveat: This book does not focus on the myriad of intellectual property issues facing librarians.

I finished this preface in Amsterdam at the International Federation of Library Associations and Institutions (IFLA) annual meeting. This city has been famous for its tolerance of controversial ideas since the seventeenth century. One sees firsthand the results—from the very open expression in the journalistic press, to the vigorous publishing industry, to the excesses of the Red Light District. And this IFLA meeting officially introduced the Committee on Freedom of Access to Information and Freedom of Expression (FAIFE), the newly organized intellectual freedom arm for the international library community. For the first time, librarians worldwide are working together to combat censorship and to promote freedom of expression, despite wide cultural differences. This environment has, indeed, provided me much food for thought in terms of the possible. It is my fervent hope that this book's presentation of intellectual freedom, with its diverse and growing agenda, will inspire librarians to conduct research in this area, to tackle some of the rich interdisciplinary literature on the subject and to write good policy to promote library service. There has never been a more opportune time.

NOTES

1. Tillie Olsen, *Silences* (New York, 1978), p. 44.

2. Lisa Guernsey, "Off-Campus Users Swamp College Libraries, Seeking Access to Web and E-Mail," *The Chronicle of Higher Education* 44 (July 31, 1998): A17.

ACKNOWLEDGMENTS

Thank you to my family for understanding that I had to write this book. My husband, David Dorman, delayed his own research in order for me to finish this labor of love. He also helped me express the technological issues of intellectual freedom in a coherent manner.

I am indebted to my professors at the University of Minnesota for their support during my doctoral studies in legal history, especially Donald Gillmor and the late Paul Murphy. I so wish that Paul were alive to help me celebrate the publication of this book. Thanks also to R. Kathleen Molz, my professor for "Libraries and Public Policy" at the Columbia University School of Library Service some years ago. Her breadth of knowledge and expertise, along with her confident defense of intellectual freedom during very difficult times, has been a great source of inspiration for me.

Thanks, as always, to Judith Krug at the Office for Intellectual Freedom for her encouragement over the years. I feel so privileged to know her and work with her—what a role model for our profession! And to Marlene Chamberlain, my editor, for being so receptive to my proposal and then putting up with my delays. Thanks to Bruce Ennis, Attorney at Law at Jenner & Block in Washington, D.C., not only for his supreme efforts on behalf of ALA at the Supreme Court, but also for his generosity in answering questions at Freedom to Read Foundation meetings both expertly and without "legalese." To James Schmidt, University Librarian at California State University at San Jose, for his academic library perspective, not to mention his tireless work during the FBI Library Awareness days.

Although this book does not necessarily reflect or condone official policy at the University of Illinois at Urbana-Champaign, I have drawn heavily on my colleagues here for two reasons: their proximity, but mostly their professional stature and knowledge of the issues. Though I may not have always agreed with them, I have never ceased to be gratified at how accessible they have been, from the Provost's Office to the Library to the Computing and Communications Services Office (CCSO). The librarians in the Central Public Services Division have provided real-world situations and advice for this book. John Weible in the Library Systems Office patiently demonstrated for me the intricate workings of "anonymous e-mail" and discussed the technicalities of the related privacy issues. Timothy Cole, Systems Librarian for Digital Projects, generously offered to read the section on computer networks and offered many helpful comments that I gladly incorporated. Nancy Romero, Rare Book and Special Collections Cataloging Librarian, took on some of my day-to-day responsibilities. Without her support, I could not have finished this project.

C. K. Gunsalus, Associate Vice Chancellor for Academic Affairs, and Marcia Rotunda, Associate University Counsel, gave me excellent overviews of campus approaches to First Amendment issues. Robert Penka, Acting Director of CCSO, and Robert Foertsch, Senior Research Programmer and campus "point person" for computer security, were incredibly generous with their time, providing me with policy documents (some in draft format) and their candid assessments of the myriad of "interesting" problems they encounter on a daily basis!

I am indebted to Brenda Pacey, Associate Director at the Lincoln Trail Libraries System in Champaign, for her thoughtful intellectual freedom perspectives related to multitype and public library systems. Pam Klipsch, Children's Librarian at the Alton Public Library, has been an ALA Intellectual Freedom Committee colleague for a long time and is just excellent at finding the "common ground" issues on which to build consensus. Also, the Director of the Urbana Free Library, Fred Schlipf, shared with me the importance of the often intangible but essential public relations skills required for successful support of intellectual freedom in public libraries. Frances Jacobson, University High School Librarian, explained how high school students sharing the Internet with a university campus can do so without filters or other means of censorship. Robert Doyle, Executive Director at the Illinois Library Association, shared ILA's success story in working with the Illinois state legislature in recent years.

Especially I want to thank Robert Wedgeworth, University Librarian, whose courageous actions on behalf of intellectual freedom over the years have made a difference in the United States and around the world, and have certainly inspired my own commitment in this area.

I have depended heavily on First Amendment scholar Rodney Smolla, whose writing I admire greatly, especially *Smolla and Nimmer on Freedom of Speech*, 3d ed., vols. 1 and 2 (Clark, Boardman, and Callaghan, 1996).

I must caution that in the process of consulting with such distinguished colleagues, I may have taken a different approach or respectfully taken issue with their perspective on intellectual freedom. Any mistakes are mine alone.

FOREWORD

The publication of this book is a cause for celebration. For far too many years, many nonacademic librarians, and even some academic librarians, considered intellectual freedom to be of concern only to public and school librarians. This book, the first in what I hope is a lengthy list of materials relating to intellectual freedom and the academic world, begins to lay that myth to rest.

Having said that, it is important to note that Barbara Jones has brought together academic and public librarians in this book. Regardless of the type of library, nothing is more important than policy, and policy development is the focal point of this work.

Not only is the subject matter of this publication needed, but the timing is inspired. The role of libraries—bringing together people and the information they need or want—has not changed, but libraries are becoming much more visible and, therefore, are perceived as being much more important in our society. The increased visibility results both from libraries' role in attempting to push back the boundaries of the First Amendment and from our cutting-edge position in the electronic communications revolution.

Through its sister organization, the Freedom to Read Foundation, the American Library Association has been instrumental not only in expanding the First Amendment arena, but also in making libraries an integral part of the First Amendment landscape. Certainly, our challenge of the Communications Decency Act of 1996, and the resultant 9–0 decision of the United States Supreme Court declaring that act unconstitutional, was the hallmark litigative effort. Before that legal action, however, we fought successfully to establish the library as a limited public forum. Although we have not yet litigated the privacy issue, we certainly went toe to toe with the Federal Bureau of Investigation (FBI) when that body attempted to turn libraries into an extension of law enforcement. It took great effort and a long time, but we succeeded in making the FBI aware of the importance of confidentiality in regard to the materials, programs or facilities each library patron uses. The ALA and the Freedom to Read Foundation also have affected other areas of law as they apply to libraries. All of these have been covered, as appropriate, by Barbara Jones.

The second factor that makes the timing of the publication of this book propitious is the evolution of electronic communications. Librarians have been involved with this technology since the very earliest days and, indeed, embrace it as yet another format through which we can bring people and information together. Electronic communication, however, is, in my opinion, the most important revolution in communicating since the invention of the printing press. Libraries have been on the cutting edge since this format first made its public appearance.

To sum up, libraries are changing not what we do, but how we do it. The law, likewise, continues to evolve in order to accommodate a society that is undergoing change. The principles, however, remain the same. Our role, then, is to navigate these changes, protect our principles and values and continue to make sure that our users have the ideas and the information that they need when they need them. We do this with policy. Policies are the guidelines that help us to navigate.

The prerequisite of policy development is to be fully informed about the environment, the issues, the problems and the goals with which the policy deals. Barbara Jones has laid these out. She has then provided the instructions necessary to develop the policies or the guidelines that librarians need today and will need in the future to provide excellent library service based on the precepts of intellectual freedom.

JUDITH F. KRUG
Director, Office for Intellectual Freedom
American Library Association

SECTION I

The "Limited Public Forum" in Academic and Public Libraries

In our view, an application of the Supreme Court's declarations concerning this issue, as well as an examination of the factual similarities and dissimilarities among the cases discussed above and the present one, confirm that the Library constitutes a limited public forum, a type of designated public fora.

—*Richard R. Kreimer* v. *Bureau of Police for the Town of Morristown, et al.*, rev'd and remanded, 958 F.2d 1242 (3rd Cir. 1992)

The "public forum" legal doctrine is a useful framework for analyzing and writing intellectual freedom policy for libraries. This doctrine's evolution in the courts helps explain the unique role and civic responsibility of publicly funded libraries in the United States. At the same time, the public forum doctrine distinguishes public and private libraries in terms of First Amendment obligations. The public forum doctrine was first applied to publicly funded libraries in the 1991–92 *Kreimer* v. *Morristown* cases, which will be analyzed at the end of this section. This complex set of cases is a good model for showing how local library policy is put to the test in the courts, and how legal decisions always have a variety of implications. The public forum doctrine can also be used as a basis for discussing future information policy in the United States—for example, the National Information Infrastructure (NII).

CHAPTER 1

A Legal History of the Public Forum Doctrine

On July 30 and August 1, 1998, Chicago's Newberry Library sponsored the Bughouse Square Debates in Washington Square Park, known as Chicago's oldest existing park and designated as that city's premier free speech forum. That year's topic was "Karl Marx: Dead or Alive?" Anyone was welcome to the soapbox, and the Newberry's Web page assured us, "heckling encouraged."

This program by one of the world's foremost independent research libraries is no accident; it is an integral part of U.S. legal and popular culture. Though First Amendment rights have never been absolute, the designation of those rights to particular public spaces has been a revered American tradition, as demonstrated by historical consensus on this issue in the courts and by the public at large.[1] This consensus is useful "common ground" for reminding public officials and special interest groups of a certain bedrock, enduring level of public respect for freedom of speech in this country—even for unpopular ideas by ordinary people.

In 1939, the United States Supreme Court first discussed the public forum doctrine in *Hague* v. *Congress of Industrial Organizations* (307 U.S. 496). This case affirmed the right of labor union organizers to distribute leaflets, make speeches and march on public property traditionally provided for speech. In so doing, the Court declared unconstitutional a Jersey City, New Jersey, ordinance empowering a "public safety director" to require permits for conducting public meetings or distributing written literature. This ruling opened public parks and certain other public areas to free speech, regardless of topic or point of view. Until the 1980s, in fact, public forum cases referred to *Hague.* The intent of the Court's consistent rulings was to prevent government agencies from excluding certain groups or ideas from expression on public property. Whenever the government opened its property for expressive use, the Supreme Court strictly scrutinized any regulations applied to that expression on that property, to ensure that all groups and ideas had equitable access—even unpopular ideas from unpopular people. It was from this unfettered free speech tradition that Bughouse Square was born.

In the 1960s, probably in response to the extent of civil unrest in the United States over civil rights for African Americans and opposition to the Vietnam conflict, the courts began to modify their public forum analysis. Their intent, still hotly contested by legal historians, was to balance First Amendment rights with the need for social order. Accordingly, the courts began to consider ways to limit access to, and content within, the traditional public forum.

In 1983, beginning with *Perry Educational Association* v. *Perry Local Educators' Association* (103 S.Ct. 948), the courts' decision-making process for the public forum doctrine began to change and a new formula was developed. The courts began to narrow their interpretation of the kinds of public spaces that were designated "traditional public fora"; they added other types of fora that were more limited in their purpose. Only after that narrowing would the courts decide the nature of the speech to be allowed and applicable for that type of forum.

In *Perry*, a school district's teachers had duly elected one union to represent them. In an agreement with the school district, this union had sole access to the teachers' interoffice mail system, to the exclusion of a rival union. The Supreme Court decided that the rival union had no claim, even if it meant that only one union's point of view would be represented in the teachers' mailboxes. The Court also spelled out its reasoning by identifying, for the first time, three types of public fora: traditional, limited and non-public.

The process for analysis was explained as follows:

1. Does the First Amendment apply to the contested regulation or policy? In other words, in the public space under scrutiny, is there a constitutional right to public access to information and ideas?
2. If the answer to question 1 is yes, then is the public forum in question a traditional forum, a limited public forum or a non-public forum?
3. A level of review is then applied, appropriate to one of the three types of fora.

The distinction of the various public fora was then explained. A *traditional* public forum refers to "places which by long tradition or by government fiat have been devoted to assembly and debate . . . which have been immemorially held in trust for the use of the public, and, time out of mind, have been used for purposes of assembly, communicating thoughts between citizens, and discussing public questions" *(Perry* at 954–55, including quotations from *Hague).* Content-neutral "time, place, and manner" restrictions are permissible, but only under strict First Amendment scrutiny and to serve a compelling government interest. This type of restriction will be explained in more detail later, but essentially the Court recognized the need for policies to delimit the way in which the public space was used. For example, most city parks have closing hours, but while open, the city government should not place undue restrictions on the content of speech at that park—unless there are public safety concerns. The courts would scrutinize any such regulations very carefully. Common examples of traditional public fora include public sidewalks, streets and parks.

The second type, the *limited* or *designated* public forum, is a space that the government specifically designates as a public forum. As long as that forum is so designated, all speech regulation must be content neutral and held under the same strict scrutiny as in a traditional public forum. For example, once a state university is open to student organizations, all types of groups must be allowed on campus, as long as they do not threaten public safety or any other significant government interest. Libraries were placed in this category in 1992. This middle category of public forum is somewhat fuzzy at times, and many legal analysts view it as a way for conservative justices to limit free speech. For example, the judge in the first *Kreimer* case put libraries in the "traditional" category, while the appellate court changed that to "limited." A 1972 case about access to public school property, *Grayned* v. *City of Rockford* (408 U.S. 104), gives a helpful clarification using libraries as an example:

> The nature of the place, "the pattern of its normal activities, dictates the kinds of regulation of time, place, and manner that are reasonable." Although a silent vigil may not unduly interfere with a public library, making a speech in the reading room almost certainly would. That same speech should be perfectly appropriate in a park. The crucial question is whether the manner of expression is basically incompatible with the normal activity of a particular place at a particular time. Our cases make clear that in assessing the reasonableness of regulation,

> we must weigh heavily the fact that communication is involved; the regulation must be narrowly tailored to further the State's legitimate interest.

A third type is the *non-public* forum, where First Amendment protections are significantly restricted because of compelling government interest. An example would be the White House, where the privacy and safety of the president's family must be considered. The non-public forum designation is an interesting example of how the law adapts to the times. In an earlier period of United States history, the public could actually walk, unaccompanied, to the front door of the White House and enter! A non-public forum designation was arguably fashioned out of necessity. However, such distinguished scholars as Harry Kalven and Thomas Emerson have opposed undue limitations on the public forum. Kalven's classic 1965 essay on the public forum is viewed as an important precursor to the success of public civil rights protests.[2] Emerson views the non-public forum definition as a way for such conservative justices as William Rehnquist to suggest that no new types of public fora should be added to the traditional ones.[3] Interestingly, the Internet has forced the courts to rethink that assumption. Librarians need to be aware that this judicial trend to limit public fora is part of the current legal and political climate in which libraries operate; they can then work more effectively to ensure libraries' continued inclusion in this category. The profession may also decide to become actively involved in extending the public forum designation to shared computer networks and the National Information Infrastructure. Already many librarians are working to prevent this new electronic information environment from becoming non-public and elitist.[4]

"SHHHHH . . .!"

This most famous and joked-about library "policy" actually illustrates the Court's motivation for creating the "time, place, and manner" doctrine referred to in the preceding public forum discussion. This doctrine allows for certain public spaces to be regulated in order to maintain quiet, safety and other qualities required for that institution to carry out its mission. However, this type of restriction in a public forum must be content neutral, and the impact on speech cannot be overly repressive. For example, most libraries have at least one area—maybe the entire building—where the library users expect a reasonably quiet environment for reading or studying. It is permissible for a library to have a policy of no public speaking in such areas, as long as this policy applies to all library users in that area. Likewise, any rowdy patron in a designated quiet library space can be asked to quiet down, as long as *rowdy* is very narrowly (specifically) defined and applied to all such behavior and to all library patrons equitably. Perhaps the library decides to allow talking in one of its conference rooms. Once public speaking is allowed, the library cannot discriminate according to the content of the proposed speech. Similarly, a library can probably limit computer terminal use with a time schedule; however, the time must be allocated in a neutral manner, not according to the nature of the content or the user. All these assumptions, of course, should be clarified with the library legal counsel before proceeding, in order to comply with local restrictions or legal changes.

NOTES

1. I am indebted to the following sources for a general overview of the public forum doctrine: Donald A. Downs, "Public Forum Doctrine," in *The Oxford Companion to the Supreme Court of the United States*, ed. Kermit L. Hall (New York: Oxford University Pr., 1992), pp. 692–93; and the public forum analysis in Donald Gillmor et al., *Mass Communication Law: Cases and Comment*, 5th ed. (St. Paul: West, 1990), pp. 53–74.

2. Harry Kalven, "The Concept of the Public Forum," *Supreme Court Review* (1965): 1–32.

3. Thomas Emerson, "The Affirmative Side of the First Amendment," *Georgia Law Review* 15 (1981): 809. Also see Rick A. Swanson, "Regaining Lost Ground: Toward a Public Forum Doctrine under the Illinois Constitution," *Southern Illinois University Law Journal* 18 (1993–94): 453–80.

4. Nancy C. Kranich, *Staking a Claim in Cyberspace: Ensuring Public Places on the Info Highway* (Westfield, N.J.: Open Magazine Pamphlet Series, 1996).

CHAPTER 2

Kreimer v. *Morristown*: Tension between the Law and Library Policy

It was only in the 1990s, in *Kreimer* v. *Morristown*, that the limited public forum doctrine was specifically applied to libraries.[1] This case provides an interesting study of how the interaction of law, library policy, the media and other "policy players" affects the outcome of litigation.

Richard Kreimer was that so-called problem patron so many librarians encounter. He seemed to enjoy visiting the Joint Free Library of Morristown and Morris Township (hereafter the Morristown Public Library) for reading and reflection. According to the court records, however, Mr. Kreimer was homeless, so he often came to the Morristown Public Library unwashed. And his "reflection," according to patrons and library personnel, created an uncomfortable atmosphere because he stared at them for long periods of time. Sometimes he would also speak loudly to himself or others.

Until 1989, the library did not have written rules, though New Jersey state statute allowed the Board of Trustees to establish regulations. From 1986 to 1990, as a result of increased problem behavior on the part of some patrons, the library director held monthly staff meetings to discuss possible solutions. In 1987, the director decided to maintain written records on problem patron behavior. Entries suggested that Kreimer persisted in staring at librarians and followed at least one patron outside after the library closed. In May 1989, the board endorsed the drafting of written rules for library patron behavior. The rules included the following, which were especially scrutinized by the courts:

1. Patrons shall be engaged in normal activities associated with the use of a public library while in the building. Patrons not engaged in reading,

studying, or using library materials may be asked to leave the building. Loitering will not be tolerated.

5. Patrons shall respect the rights of other patrons and shall not annoy others through noisy or boisterous activities, by unnecessary staring, by following another person through the building, by playing walkmans or other audio equipment so that others can hear it, by singing or talking to onesself [sic] or by other behavior which may reasonably result in the disturbance of other persons.

9. Patron dress and personal hygiene shall conform to the standard of the community for public places. This shall include the repair or cleanliness of garments.

Any patron not abiding by these or other rules and regulations of the Library may be asked to leave the Library premises.

Based on the library's enforcement of these new rules, Kreimer was expelled several times. He sought recourse with the American Civil Liberties Union of New Jersey, which advised the library on July 5, 1989, that some of its regulations were unconstitutional: "Loitering" was too vague a term; "annoying" other patrons was not severe enough to warrant eviction; asking patrons' dress to comply with "community standards" was offensive; and allowing library officials to ban patrons from the library based on imprecise or nonexistent standards was too vague to pass constitutional muster.

Intense and frequent correspondence between the ACLU and the library ensued, resulting in the library officials reworking their written statement. The "loitering" language was dropped, and many of the offensive behaviors were more narrowly defined. The ACLU still had problems with the revised version, but the library decided to remain firm. On January 2, 1990, Richard Kreimer filed a complaint in the district court for a violation of his civil and First Amendment rights—and, later, his right to due process—by the Morristown Public Library's president, the chief of police and, eventually, numerous other library officers and staff.

There ensued a series of complex legal maneuvers not included in this abbreviated account. Briefly, in May 1991, Judge Lee Sarokin ruled, in the U.S. District Court case, that rules 1, 5 and 9 were null and void and he enjoined the library from enforcing them. The following summary is from the Freedom to Read Foundation (FTRF) of the American Library Association:

The U.S. District Court found that the library's Patron Policy "is not narrowly tailored to serve the stated significant government interest, nor does the policy

> leave open any alternative means of access to publicly provided reading materials" . . . that paragraphs 1 and 5 of the Patron Policy, with the exception of that portion pertaining to the playing of walkmans, are unconstitutionally overbroad . . . that paragraphs 1, 5, and 9 of the Patron Policy are unconstitutionally vague . . . that the Patron Policy violates the equal protection and due process clauses of the Fourteenth Amendment and the First Amendment guarantee of free assembly and association . . . and that the Patron Policy violates Article I of the New Jersey Constitution.[2]

In September 1991, the FTRF submitted this *amicus* brief, *on behalf of neither party*, for the appeal. This *amicus* brief, like much of the litigation, was misunderstood by many librarians to be support for Kreimer. In fact, the brief "respectfully submits that the principles set forth in this brief represent the proper framework for analysis of the issues before this Court. Correct application of these First Amendment principles—including both the right of access and libraries' circumscribed power to regulate in conformity with that right—is critically important if public libraries are to continue to hold open the doors of the marketplace of ideas for millions of Americans." The brief went on to urge the court to reflect the lower court's designation of publicly funded libraries as limited public fora. Even though the decision would be applicable only in the states of the Third Circuit—New Jersey, Pennsylvania, Delaware and the Virgin Islands—it could serve as an invaluable precedent for future litigation regarding libraries and intellectual freedom.

In the appeal to the United States Court of Appeals for the Third Circuit, the lower court's decision was reversed in part. Following the analysis described earlier, the court first decided that the case did, indeed, have First Amendment implications. The decision contains some very important affirmative language in this regard and does adopt, almost in full, the reasoning of the FTRF's brief.

Then the court determined that public libraries are *limited* public fora, not *traditional* as ruled at the district court level. Finally, the court moved on to the rules themselves—were they appropriate to a limited public forum? The appeals court reversed the district court by ruling the Patron Policy to be constitutional. This panel of judges believed that these particular rules were reasonable restrictions. They explained that the rules mainly focused on preventing behavior that disrupted the library's role as a limited public forum. Such rules, narrowly tailored to facilitate the library's service mission to the entire community—not just Kreimer—were judged reasonable by this court. Because most of the rules did not focus on content-related activity, the court rejected the assertion that Kreimer's First Amendment rights had been violated. This court also upheld what has been called the "smell rule." (However, librarians are advised to get an updated legal opinion, in view of more recent assertions that certain diseases cause an offensive body odor that cannot be controlled by the individual so afflicted and that the use of body deodorants differs among cultures.) The court was satisfied that as long as offenders would be readmitted to the library after correcting offending behaviors, no rights of access were being violated.

In short, the Third Circuit decided that library policies regarding patron conduct were appropriate in a limited public forum, as long as such "time, place, and manner" policies were content neutral and were applied equitably to all library users. Rules should be "narrowly tailored" to meet the government interest. In non-legalese, this means that library policy is more susceptible to litigation if the rules are too broad or vague. Accordingly, each rule should be clearly linked to carrying out the primary mission of the library—not targeted at particular individuals.

The library community's reaction to the Morristown case is a fascinating and complex chapter in itself. Throughout this litigation the library profession was divided; this division remains today. Even the most respected mainstream press confused the issue by reporting Kreimer's "victory" at the district court, and then his "defeat" on appeal. In addition, I believe that the conflict intensified because of incomplete understanding within the library profession about legal strategies and desired outcomes—one of the many reasons librarians should become more familiar with the connection between basic legal process and library operational policies. This is also a very important factor for handling the aftermath of any court case successfully—regardless of the decision—and maybe even avoiding litigation in the first place.

In 1992, the ALA Intellectual Freedom Committee (IFC) anticipated the ALA membership's desire for guidelines on writing policy that might avoid the costly experience of the Morristown Public Library. Accordingly, hearings were held at both the midwinter and summer meetings to discuss draft guidelines for writing such policies. The membership, however, wanted to vent anger about what some perceived as ALA's abandonment of the Morristown librarians and the lack of appreciation for the increasingly stressful environment in public libraries caused by threatening patron behavior. Finally, the IFC's policy, "Guidelines for the Development of Policies and Procedures regarding User Behavior and Library

Usage," was adopted and is included in appendix B. This is required reading for all librarians writing intellectual freedom policy to promote library users' positive right of access to information while, at the same time, supporting the library's mission with policies and procedures to ensure the safety of users and staff as well as protection of the library's resources.

Some important advice is contained in the first statement: "Libraries are advised to rely upon existing legislation and law enforcement mechanisms as the primary means of controlling behavior that involves public safety, criminal behavior, or other issues covered by existing local, state, or federal statutes. In many instances, this legal framework may be sufficient to provide the library with the necessary tools to maintain order." Throughout section IV, policy writers will be challenged to consider whether a policy for a particular problem is really necessary.

Another guideline is directly relevant to Internet use policy: "Policies and regulations . . . should not restrict access to the library by persons who merely inspire the anger or annoyance of others. Policies based upon appearance or behavior that is merely annoying or which merely generates negative subjective reactions from others, do not meet the necessary standard unless the behavior would interfere with access by an objectively reasonable person to library facilities and services."

A final note on the public relations dilemma of reporting that the designation of *limited* public forum is a victory! How can something that is "limited" be a positive thing? Despite its considerable experience and expertise with the issues, even the Freedom to Read Foundation could not prevent the mainstream press from misrepresenting the significance of the *Kreimer* decision to the library community and the general public. Library public relations officers must be sensitive to these problems when communicating with the press or writing promotional material.

NOTES

1. I am indebted to Anne Levinson Penway's legal analysis of this important library case in "Public Libraries as Limited Public Fora for Access to Information," in *Intellectual Freedom Manual,* 5th ed. (Chicago: ALA, 1996), pp. 328–34. The two *Kreimer* cases are: *Kreimer* v. *Bureau of Police for the Town of Morristown* (765 Suppl. 181 [D.N.J. 1991]) and (958 F.2d 1242 [1992]).

2. From the Brief Amicus Curiae of the Freedom to Read Foundation, submitted September 11, 1991, to the United States Court of Appeals for the Third Circuit, p. 4.

CHAPTER 3

What Can Be Learned from a Public Forum Analysis of Libraries?

The aforementioned "Guidelines for the Development of Policies and Procedures regarding User Behavior and Library Usage" emerged out of a costly and time-consuming case that tied up a public library for years and created controversy within the library profession. I will not play Monday morning quarterback here. Some litigation cannot—and should not—be avoided. Regarding ALA's costly and time-consuming efforts to overturn the Communications Decency Act, most librarians and closely allied information professionals and civil liberties activists will feel the important reverberations of that decision for decades to come. Regardless of the merits of the legal controversy at hand, it behooves the library profession to have a handle on the policy process from beginning to end. This handle includes an ongoing relationship with the library's legal counsel. In this way, there is a far better chance that the outcome will be compatible not only with the library profession's principled stance regarding ethics and intellectual freedom, but also with the individual library's ability to carry out its operational mission.

That's why *Kreimer* is so instructive. That case interweaves all the aspects of the intellectual freedom principles presented in this book: the law; library professional values; the complexities of policy writing for a limited public forum; public relations; and numerous other outcomes. And despite its divisiveness in some quarters, *Kreimer* did provide, for the first time, an affirmative statement about the right of access to information—with the public library as the designated forum for this activity. This places librarians in all publicly funded libraries in a privileged and influential position regarding the provision of access to information by the citizenry of the United States for the next century.

Along with this privileged position, however, come inevitable conflict and sticky legal and policy issues. The library profession does not have the luxury, nor would it be practical, to "wait until the dust settles." Had we waited until 1992 for the "limited public forum" designation, where would we be as a profession? Computer center professionals are in the same situation. They regularly receive threats of lawsuits for perceived campus network abuses that have no legal precedents or guidelines. Local policy can and should be written, but it often raises issues for which there are no easy answers. That is why writing good policy calls on more than knowledge of legal precedent; it challenges the profession's ethical commitment to intellectual freedom as well as our grasp of such intangibles as good communications skills.

If analyzed strictly from a public forum point of view, *Kreimer* v. *Morristown* describes public libraries as "limited" public fora. This means that libraries do have the option of restricting some forms of free speech that might detract from the library's mission. This presupposes that individual libraries have mission statements and policies to fit that mission. There are never any guarantees, but good-faith attempts to link regulations to positive outcomes—like enhanced library service—tend to be looked on more kindly by courts and the general public alike than seemingly arbitrary and disconnected rules. Any regulatory policies must be narrowly defined in terms of the "time, place, and manner" doctrine. The policies must be content and subject neutral, and must not abridge equal access to information by any individual, class or group.

Because the First Amendment covers only those actions taken by governmental entities, private libraries theoretically need not heed much of the advice given thus far. In reality, however, the American Association of University Professors (AAUP) seriously embraces principles of academic freedom on private and public higher education campuses. And most outstanding private schools would not dream of restricting scholarly access to constitutionally protected speech, because it would chill the work of professors and students in fulfilling the academic mission of the institution. However, it is particularly important for librarians to understand that in a private institution, they will probably need to rely more heavily on that academic mission, as well as on professional values and the *Library Bill of Rights* and its Interpretations, than on the First Amendment per se.

In private institutions with particularly strong doctrinal positions, a librarian is sometimes in the position of adding a book to the collection that is offensive to the majority of the faculty and students, but that was requested, for example, by a new, untenured faculty member who has very little clout. The librarian's strategy might be to anticipate such dilemmas, celebrate the library's mission and build coalitions with influential people on campus in order to weather potential collection development challenges.

Legal scholar Rodney Smolla has made the following important observation about the mission of private academic libraries:

> It is worth saying a word about *private* acts of censorship aimed at private-sector libraries, such as libraries at private universities. The decision by a private university to engage in censorship is not, of course, subject to the restraints of the First Amendment at all, because the Constitution places restrictions only on government. Borrowing on notions of academic, artistic, and scientific freedom, surely the nation's great private institutions of learning and culture ought to operate *as if* the First Amendment applied to them. The fabric of society's intellectual and cultural life is a tightly knit weave of private and public institutions. An open society committed to free expression as a transcendent value will be committed to principles of artistic and scholarly freedom in private universities, museums, theaters, and libraries as well as public institutions, encouraging the free flow of information among all of them. The life of the mind should not be cramped by the artificial distinctions of law.[1]

Kreimer contains many of the key legal terms, doctrines and processes with which librarians should be familiar in order to write and interpret policy and the law. Examples are: public forum; overbreadth; time, place and manner; and *amicus* briefs. *Kreimer* cites previous court decisions, thus embedding this case in precedent, as our common law tradition bids us to do. It demonstrates how decisions that had nothing to do with libraries are applied to libraries. Legal texts challenge the professional librarian to anticipate how certain language might apply to future information issues rising out of continued technological innovation.

Kreimer also shows how a court decision can be a "mixed bag." While the limited public forum designation and the right to receive information were affirmed, most of Morristown Public Library's revised rules, which some librarians—and Judge Sarokin—found to be too vague, were upheld. Some would argue that the Third Circuit Court's reversal was to the detriment of open access to information. Some librarians believe that regardless of the court's ruling on the patron policies, a different professional approach might lead to a better way of dealing with the Richard Kreimers. At any rate, the Third Circuit ruled that the library's rules were "reasonable 'manner' restrictions on patron conduct." But the Morristown case should challenge librarians to consider a variety of ways to deal with a so-called problem patron.

In formulating policy, law and professional values both come into play—usually in complex, fuzzy situations that make up the real world of library service. However, librarians should be reminded by such cases as *Kreimer* v. *Morristown* that the First Amendment does require that we balance rights and limits in the limited public forum, even if it means that professional values and patron interests will conflict.

Today, in efforts to cut costs and expand access to information, most libraries are committed to at least one consortial agreement. Library cooperative ventures might require them to collect in depth in assigned subject areas; to share the licensing costs of full-text databases; or to participate in an interlibrary loan network. In resource-sharing environments, vendor-mandated restrictions and a variety of local library policies may enter the picture. Librarians need to be aware of such potential conflicts and consult with legal counsel about successful resource-sharing ventures that also pass constitutional muster.

NOTE

1. Rodney A. Smolla, "Freedom of Speech for Libraries and Librarians," *Law Library Journal* 85 (1993): 78.

CHAPTER 4

The Public Forum in Various Types of Libraries and Consortia

The American Library Association is organized into divisions, representing various types and functions of libraries. The Association of College and Research Libraries (ACRL) represents the academic librarians' interests; the Public Library Association (PLA) represents public librarians; and so on. Each division has either an Intellectual Freedom Committee or a divisional intellectual freedom liaison to the ALA Intellectual Freedom Committee. The liaison relationship should be clearly defined in a written document for the chair or liaison of each division.

In many respects, however, the laws and policies regarding intellectual freedom cross the lines between the traditional types of libraries. Librarians themselves are pushing these boundaries. Cities, like San Jose, California, are beginning to look at ways for public libraries and universities to share one building or merge services. In some rural areas, the public and school libraries are one and the same. There are statewide consortia, such as MINITEX in Minnesota and Florida's extensive "kindergarten through nursing home" network, as well as such consortia as the Committee on Institutional Cooperation (CIC) for the Big Ten universities. In these consortia, a shared integrated library automation system is common, and assumptions about levels of patron privacy may emerge from negotiations with vendors. In such resource-sharing environments, it is increasingly common to cross state and county lines, patron age categories and boundaries among types of libraries. There are any number of unexplored, complex First Amendment issues as various types of libraries with somewhat different missions share resources with patrons of different ages, backgrounds and views. If each library must conform to a different set of collection development guidelines based on "local community standards," one can imagine the complexity of interlibrary loan. That is why the Illinois Library Association (ILA) lobbied so vigorously (and successfully thus far) against a proposed state law that would allow each county to write its own definition of obscenity. Interlibrary loan would have screeched to a grinding halt, as librarians pointed out so effectively to their legislators. This success story will be recounted in section III.

The good news about this increasing complexity is precisely what ILA discovered: The fewer barriers to access, the more easily librarians can provide cost-effective and excellent service. This resource-sharing environment may well provide a strong incentive to dissolve these borders, which are often difficult or impossible to enforce, especially on the Internet. Then librarians and other educators might shift from a focus on erecting barriers to a focus on user instruction and other ways to help patrons choose from, and reap the benefits of, the variety of information resources available.

ACADEMIC LIBRARIES

> The concept of academic freedom has a long history in this country. Developing out of the struggles for greater freedom in research, publication, and teaching . . . the basic precepts have been . . . embodied in formal statements, applied in concrete cases, and developed into a kind of common law by such organizations as the American Association of University Professors. . . . Although the tenets of academic freedom have never been incorporated fully into the first amendment, they have greatly influenced the courts in cases involving governmental intervention in the affairs of academic institutions.
>
> —Thomas Emerson[1]

One frequently hears the argument that the library profession's intellectual freedom initiatives are not as vital to academic libraries, since they are protected by academic freedom as espoused by such groups as the American Association of University Professors (AAUP). There is no doubt that the 1973 AAUP/ALA "Joint Statement on Faculty Status of College and University Librarians" extends the concept of academic freedom to librarians, and, in some cases, the AAUP has actually preceded ALA in articulating library-related policies.[2] However, library issues are increasingly complex and require policies written by librarians who understand intellectual freedom issues as they pertain specifically to libraries. There is no reason why these policies cannot continue to complement the AAUP academic freedom principles.

ACRL's recent addition of a divisional intellectual freedom committee attests to the realization that library intellectual freedom issues are now far more sophisticated and diverse than they were even five years ago. Academic librarians are especially important and welcomed in the library intellectual freedom arena. They are often in a position to conduct research, consult with colleagues on the library school faculty or engage with faculty in other disciplines regarding freedom of expression issues. And librarians in public and school libraries will attest to the assistance they have received through the years from their academic colleagues during difficult book removal challenges. The academic library can often provide book reviews and research-based support for use in public hearings or media relations. Academic librarians frequently act as expert witnesses as well.

Academic libraries are either "private" or "public" (there are some mixed cases) based on their predominant source of funding. And privately funded libraries are often extremely dedicated to First Amendment protection of speech; in some cases, they may have an advantage over their publicly funded counterparts. For example, although the renowned Kinsey Institute for Research in Sex, Gender, and Reproduction resides on the Indiana University campus, it is a private, not-for-profit corporation and is thus independent of the political problems such collections would encounter even in the most liberal state legislatures.

The public-private distinction is covered more thoroughly in chapter 3. For First Amendment purposes it is arguably as important as the more conventional public versus academic library split. Yet all academic libraries have much in common. Both public and private are serving a primary clientele usually limited by enrollment or faculty/administrator/student/staff status. Although this has broadened as a result of resource sharing, generally the full range of collections and services are available to the group most closely tied to the academic mission of the institution. Traditionally the courts have afforded libraries in institutions of higher learning a wider latitude regarding content, scope and subject matter of collections. This, however, may change as legislators become more sensitive to the facts that increasing numbers of minors are using campus libraries and that Internet access is a "hot button" with concerned parents.

While the academic library always supports the curriculum and research of its faculty and students as its primary mission, it also maintains some retrospective and current collections in areas not being taught or researched.

The same libraries may, by virtue of resource-sharing partnerships, be responsible for collecting at great depth, for the good of the partnership, in designated subject areas. At the same time, there must be a generally comprehensive collection, including electronic access, to meet a certain basic level of research needs at the local level. This is a daunting task, given the current uncertain economic climate regarding periodical subscription costs; equipment maintenance and replacement costs, and licensing fees associated with electronic access; the continuing explosion of information resources; and the cost to preserve and store these resources. The collections are usually weeded only to dispose of duplicate copies, not to get rid of outdated editions.[3]

When money for collections and access is tight, it is far more likely that intellectual freedom–related dilemmas will arise. It becomes easier to use "limited resources" as an excuse to avoid purchasing controversial materials. Similarly, too few public access terminals necessitates setting some type of limit on access. In a limited public forum these restrictions should be content neutral, but it is difficult for librarians to watch students playing computer games or reading their e-mail when others are waiting to access the full-text databases. Collecting a diversity of views is more difficult when there are limited funds to buy, store and preserve these materials.

Spending tax dollars on controversial information has been generally accepted by legislatures and courts in regard to academic libraries. In hard political and fiscal times, however, one can imagine legislators scrutinizing more carefully whether a library really needs a $10,000 journal subscription on an esoteric or controversial topic. And although academic libraries have always worked closely with campus faculty in developing the collections, the current economic climate has caused some faculties to demand greater participation in actual materials selection decisions. This potentially divisive and competitive environment threatens the library profession's commitment to take a comprehensive approach to collection decision making, to ensure diversity of views and subjects. A very detailed background relating intellectual freedom and collection development issues is found in section IV.

Another challenge for academic libraries is the often far-reaching and complex campus network, with remote access for students in dormitories and professors in offices, not to mention the general—sometimes anonymous—public access to terminals in the library. Privacy and access issues clash almost daily as library and computer center professionals try to write policies to assure both—often in a legal vacuum. Students are building Web sites with the illegal use of copyright-protected material. They may be sending harassing e-mail anonymously from a public access terminal in the library. And incidences of hacking into proprietary computer systems are on the rise. Increasingly, library transaction technology is capable of linking the patron to research behaviors. Most librarians are now familiar with the fact that state privacy laws protect patron circulation records. They remember the FBI Library Awareness Program beginning in the late 1980s, when agents asked academic librarians to identify foreign nationals and their database searching and research habits. But there are a number of new twists. If user services librarians are conducting online surveys on use of library resources, a participant should be made aware of any compromises to his or her privacy. Tenure committees have actually asked to see circulation records of their colleagues in order to gauge "scholarly progress." Professors have asked to see reserve circulation records to monitor student progress in a particular course.

Because of the severely limited resources of most campus computer centers, certain news groups or sites may be blocked. Depending on the scope of these restrictions, they can be viewed as efforts by computer center professionals to play a role in collection development in terms of limiting access to information and determining what information is "frivolous" and what is "serious."

To summarize: Take a high-tech environment with a diverse group of professionals approaching information management and ethics from a variety of perspectives. Add students and faculty, many of whom have the skill to hack the systems or otherwise abuse them. At the same time, these users may be woefully naive about limits to privacy on the campus network or the force of law regarding illegal use of copyrighted materials. Add an institution doing cutting-edge research and offering "push-the-envelope" content in the humanities and fine arts. Although computer systems administrators have more control in a private university environment, those in public universities share many of the same concerns as librarians in the public sector—though the First Amendment "limited public forum" implications do not yet extend to campus computer networks. The mix is producing some fascinating but problematic intellectual freedom issues. Access and privacy issues involving campus networks will probably be the biggest intellectual freedom challenge for academic librarians as we move into the next century.

Preservation presents another challenge, as librarians make difficult triage decisions on what content should be saved and what must be left to deteriorate because of lack of funds. Contrary to popular professional opinion, digital preservation will solve only part of this problem. This certain loss of diversity of information and views will have a tragic impact on the information legacy that libraries carry into the next century.

PUBLIC LIBRARIES

> Public libraries are also institutions that, in a democratic society, are designed not only for transmitting past culture but for developing autonomy and diversity. Here right-to-know factors are especially strong.
>
> —Thomas Emerson[4]

The American public library—which, in my view, is the bedrock of this nation's contribution to freedom of expression—shares virtually all the economic and political pressures just described for academic libraries. In addition, public libraries are especially vulnerable to the impact of social change, when lack of affordable day care forces latchkey children to use the library for that purpose, and when lack of affordable mental health services or housing forces at least some segments of the homeless population to use the library for shelter. And the public forum is arguably shrinking, as privately owned malls take over the role of the town square. Public libraries are one of the few spaces left, in some communities, that are truly "public."

As explained by Pungitore, public libraries usually receive their funding through tax dollars, whether real estate taxes, referenda, special funds created out of certain revenues or a combination.[5] This dependence on public funding means that most public libraries are indeed "limited public fora" in the eyes of the law. They are allowed to formulate written policies that follow the legal "time, place, and manner" restrictions, but all of this is much more difficult in reality than it appears in theory.

The Public Library Association has long been an active proponent of intellectual freedom initiatives on state and national levels. Therefore, one need only look at the *Library Bill of Rights* and its Interpretations to get a sense of the kinds of professional and ethical dilemmas public librarians face regularly. They are frequently the "lightning rod" for public outrage at the perceived decline of social civility accompanied by an explosion of offensive information. Public libraries, therefore, have been active in developing collection strategies for all formats and in advocating the diversity of content, as reflected in "Diversity in Collection Development." Their service mission to a wide constituency is evident in the language of "Economic Barriers to Information Access" and "Access to Library Resources and Services regardless of Gender or Sexual Orientation." And their commitment to free speech beyond reading is the reason for the interpretations on "Meeting Rooms" and "Exhibit Spaces and Bulletin Boards." These ALA policies are included in appendix C.

Perhaps the greatest challenge facing public libraries in the twenty-first century, however, relates to the profession's important commitment to access for minors in the face of a public backlash to protect minors from the perceived glut of offensive material that may cause children to become aggressive or sexually active at an early age. Although school librarians face similar issues and their role is evolving, their mission is often more limited because of the school system's specific curricular needs. And school librarians do not grapple with the mix of adult and youth use of the same "limited public forum." This mix has created the ongoing controversy about whether to filter publicly accessible Internet content for the sake of restricting information that may be legally "harmful to minors." Sometimes parents do not make the connection between demanding that librarians act *in loco parentis* in protecting their children and demanding that families retain control over what their children read. Often when librarians and parents analyze this together, they find common ground upon which to build a better relationship. At any rate, the ongoing controversy over filtering for minors in public libraries is covered in greater detail in chapter 21.

In terms of confidentiality and privacy, the same state laws apply to public and academic libraries alike. Public libraries are facing the same dilemmas as their academic colleagues regarding privacy versus access with networks and integrated library systems. In the face of the controversy over minors' use of the Internet, it is important that public librarians focus on access, not on barriers to young people's access. Adolescents especially need to feel a sense of privacy when they request certain information or check out certain books. A sensitivity to this need is one of the intangibles that can make or break the user-friendly atmosphere of a public library. The principle of privacy for minors is an extension of their First Amendment rights, which, except for the schools, have been affirmed by the Supreme Court (*In Re: Gault*, 387 U.S. 1 [1967]).

Informal discussions with public librarians have led me to conclude that those who will weather the storm with the most success and least emotional strain will depend heavily on excellent public relations and communications skills. Academic librarians are somewhat protected by legislators and a general public who are accustomed to granting greater latitude regarding collections in institutions of higher learning. But public librarians will need to continue to listen to individual citizens and special interest groups who are genuinely concerned about what they perceive as a decline of quality and alternative points of view in public libraries. As one very successful public library colleague confided: "You can't just shove the *Library Bill of Rights* in their face. You need to know the law, and patrons will respect you if you stand on principle, but it's also important that you listen actively. Ask yourself if you really have provided novels from Christian publishing houses, along with Stephen King, and materials for those parents who are home-schooling their children." And, as Gordon Conable has so well expressed,

> Thus, the contents of libraries may become targets for censors. . . . A public librarian cannot remain unconcerned but must understand the nature of censorship, the motives of censors, and what yielding to them means.
>
> Such attacks are often well intentioned; they are also frequently emotionally charged. They may represent the personal distress of an individual coming in contact with material that he or she is unprepared to deal with or finds frightening. Fear—often expressed as concern about harm that could be caused to children through exposure to certain books, films, videotapes, recordings, or ideas—motivates many complaints. Such a response is quite natural and human; parents are expected to protect their offspring. The concern may be real, but the requested response—the censorship of library materials—is an inappropriate means of dealing with perceived danger to children. Calm discussion will frequently provide the opportunity to reassure concerned parents, support the parents' role in guiding their own children's—and only their own children's—reading, and assist them in finding library materials that meet their own family needs.[6]

MULTITYPE LIBRARY CONSORTIA

How is a limited public forum created from a group of libraries of different types, some public and some private, sometimes in different states, with different clientele and missions? When these consortia share library materials, integrated library systems, reference services and the Internet, how are questions about controversial library materials decided when there are different state laws or different access policies? Interestingly, many of these questions remain unanswered or untested in the courts. Most of the library literature thus far focuses on the mechanics of running interlibrary loan, a shared library automation system and cooperative collection development. (A published legal guide for cooperative library ventures, with state-by-state analysis of the legal environment, would be welcomed by many librarians.) Further, many of the legal precedents on regulation of electronic media are based on media regulated by the Federal Communications Commission (FCC) and the concept of scarcity.[7] Those media—television and radio, for example—are legally subject to more content regulation because of their special status. Therefore, special legal advice must be sought for the Internet, because the Supreme Court did not judge it to be one of those "scarce" media.

Yet we can at least surmise from *Hamling* v. *United States* (418 U.S. 87 [1974]) that when speech is sent from one jurisdiction to another, the speaker is liable under the "local community standards" of the receiver's locale. Indeed in *United States* v. *Thomas* (74 F.3d 701 [6th Cir. 1996]), operators of an adult-oriented electronic bulletin board in California were convicted in Tennessee of violating the federal obscenity law, even though the Tennessee-based receiver had voluntarily signed up for the service and accessed the material by choice. Thus it appears that it is the responsibility of the sender, not the receiver, of information to know whether, under the receiver's jurisdiction, the speech being made accessible is constitutionally protected. Another important case should be mentioned here as well, though there are indications that parts of it may eventually be rejected. In *Sable Communications* v. *FCC* (492 U.S. 115 [1989]), the Supreme Court rejected the service provider's argument that it was in a double bind. It was required by federal obscenity statutes to follow "local community standards" in the community receiving the message. That meant the provider had to tailor its service to the least-tolerant community.

The Court further acknowledged that Sable might indeed incur some cost in hiring staff to determine standards in the communities of the callers. Just because the service is national, the justices conclude, does not mean that the provider can ignore the fact that "local community standards"—not any kind of national obscenity standards—apply to the way it operates its service. Librarians should contemplate the costly impact were this to be applicable to interlibrary loan.

If consortia are primarily funded with public monies, they probably fall under the category of "designated public fora." Multitype administrators should, however, consult with legal counsel to confirm this status. Then the question remains: Are the legal precedents for regulating electronic media applicable to multitype consortial transmissions of information?

The important implications for libraries are whether, for example, in an interlibrary loan situation a transmission of information must adhere to the least-tolerant community standard. Further, if a transmission is accidentally sent to a community that rejects this transmission as obscene, is the transmitter (perhaps a librarian) liable?

Numerous issues surround the confidentiality of user information on the shared automation system. Participating libraries need to make sure that their personnel understand that patron record access has legal implications. Some of the systems are designed by vendors with the school market in mind. In that case, there may be much more circulation information available than there would be for a system designed for public or academic libraries.

Most successful consortia depend on the hard work and determination of participants to work through problems outside the legal system. Staff training and update sessions should be mandatory. Activism is essential. Groups like the Illinois Library Association anticipated the problems that "local community standards" would cause for multitypes in that state and have, for the time being, convinced a majority of legislators to oppose an initiative to apply such standards to library resource sharing. Further, state library agencies often play an active role in helping develop and promote statewide access policies that are then far more likely to be accepted by legislators. Nonetheless, in compiling information for this book, I found a dearth of information on this very important legal topic.[8] Multitype administrators should anticipate potential problems and consult legal counsel for some preliminary advice on these matters. The potential intellectual freedom issues in multitype library systems need constant monitoring and further scrutiny and research by the library profession.

NOTES

1. Thomas Emerson, "The Affirmative Side of the First Amendment," *Georgia Law Review* 15 (1981): 841.

2. John Buschman, "A House Divided against Itself: ACRL Leadership, Academic Freedom, and Electronic Resources," *Progressive Librarian* 12/13 (1997): 7–17; http://www.libr.org/PL/html.

3. Although this book's scope does not encompass the very specific issues of the economics of library information, it does draw its assumptions from such important resources as *University Libraries and Scholarly Communication*, by Anthony M. Cummings et al. (ARL for The Andrew W. Mellon Foundation, 1992).

4. Emerson, "The Affirmative Side of the First Amendment," 842.

5. Verna Pungitore, *Innovation and the Library: The Adoption of New Ideas in Public Libraries* (Westport, Conn.: Greenwood Pr., 1995).

6. Gordon Conable, "Public Libraries and Intellectual Freedom," in *Intellectual Freedom Manual*, 5th ed. (Chicago: ALA, 1996), p. 261.

7. For a history of the contrast between the courts' treatment of print and broadcast media, it is useful to peruse "The Regulation of Electronic Media," in Donald Gillmor et al., *Mass Communication Law: Concepts and Cases*, 5th ed. (St. Paul: West, 1990), pp. 683–904.

8. Pungitore's *Innovation and the Library* includes the important role of state agencies throughout in an excellent analysis. An updated account with the impact of the Internet and the law would be welcome.

CHAPTER 5

The Public Forum Applied to Various Information Formats

Through the years the *Library Bill of Rights* and its Interpretations have been written with the assumption that access and content issues apply across the board to every information format or presentation—from videos to books, from rock music to exhibitions of photography.

But the big question, somewhat but not completely resolved last year, is: What is the Internet? Is it like a telephone? A post office? A book? The National Information Infrastructure, the network itself, and the vast public participation in America OnLine and such community-based services as PrairieNet in Champaign-Urbana (Illinois) have raised serious First Amendment issues. One supposes that Justice William Brennan would have reveled in the robust—indeed, Wild West—nature of the Internet, while for others it poses a truly ominous threat of exploitation by hackers, pedophiles and other predators. It has sparked a move to develop filtering mechanisms for the protection of children.

The question was at least partially addressed in 1997, when the Supreme Court overturned the Communications Decency Act, which declared that the Internet content was not subject to the stricter regulation of the broadcast media:

> Those factors [scarcity or invasive qualities of broadcast media] are not present in cyberspace. Neither before nor after the enactment of the CDA have the vast democratic fora of the Internet been subject to the type of government supervision and regulation that has attended the broadcast industry. Moreover, the Internet is not as "invasive" as radio or television. . . .

This dynamic, multifaceted category of communication includes not only traditional print and news services, but also audio, video, and still images, as well as interactive, real-time dialogue. Through the use of chat rooms, any person with a phone line can become a town crier with a voice that resonates farther than it could from any soapbox. Through the use of Web pages, mail exploders, and newsgroups, the same individual can become a pamphleteer.[1]

NOTE

1. *Reno et al.* v. *American Civil Liberties Union et al.*, 138 L.Ed 2d 874 1997.

CHAPTER 6

The Public Forum for a Diverse User Group

A major concern for public forum doctrine is that the forum in question be accessible on an equitable basis. The American Library Association acknowledged this in the 1939 *Library Bill of Rights*, which called for library meeting rooms to be available equitably to all community groups regardless of beliefs and affiliations. It goes without saying that federal law mandates that public facilities be open to all regardless of race or gender, in keeping with federal civil rights laws. The basic *Library Bill of Rights* document clearly states that "a person's right to use a library should not be denied or abridged because of origin, age, background, or views." (See appendix C.)

There is more than the law, however. It takes a committed, activist stance on the part of librarians to make the library welcoming to all. Exhibits can serve this purpose by advertising new books reflecting a diversity of views. Reference librarians should be particularly aware of their demeanor, since some people are reluctant to approach the desk. It also takes an effort to dig out the offerings of small presses and other groups who may not have the money for slick advertising mailings. Some extra effort may be needed to obtain materials from foreign countries lacking a publishing or marketing infrastructure. For newly emerging political issues, librarians will want to peruse pamphlet collections or extremely small presses. Helpful indexes are available for small press and alternative press material.

Such scholars as Jurgen Habermas and Noam Chomsky remind us that access to information and to the press can easily be relegated to the elite of any society. They also remind us of the key role of editors and other intermediaries of information. Their work serves as a constant reminder that as media conglomerates continue to merge, the danger of homogenized information increases. The alternative press and media thus become extremely important.[1]

NOTE

1. Jurgen Habermas, *The Structural Transformation of the Public Sphere: An Inquiry into a Category of Bourgeois Society*, trans. Thomas Burger (Cambridge, Mass.: MIT Pr., 1989); also *Manufacturing Consent: Noam Chomsky and the Media*, dir. Mark Achbar and Peter Wintonick, Zeitgeist Films, 1992, 2 videocassettes.

SECTION II

The Legal Foundation of Intellectual Freedom in a Public Forum

The library profession's position on intellectual freedom, and activities on behalf of same, derive from the U.S. political system of federalism, with legislative, executive and judicial decisions directly affecting library policy.

This section builds on the information in chapter 2 regarding the *Kreimer* v. *Morristown* case, which demonstrated the frequent tension among the domains of library policy, professional values and the law. Before writing policy it is important to understand basic legal concepts and specific applications of court decisions to libraries. Though there are no guarantees, this kind of analysis provides the foundation for library policy that is most likely to pass constitutional muster. However, this analysis does not substitute for legal advice. Given that the legal environment for intellectual freedom changes weekly, especially in regard to the Internet, it is imperative that someone in each library be responsible for monitoring the Office for Intellectual Freedom electronic list and other key sources for the most current information. Every library's legal counsel should determine how new laws and court decisions will affect that library.

As most readers know, a federalist system of government, like that of the United States, has three branches: legislative, executive and judicial. These three branches are duplicated at the national, state and local levels, and are creatures of constitutions. The U.S. Constitution specifies that any power not enumerated therein belongs to the states. Typically, the national government focuses on international relations and such nationwide organizations as the military and the post office. There is a constant tension about power distribution between federal and state governments, but generally the states deal with issues of public safety and "morality." Although states have their own constitutions, the Fourteenth Amendment to the U.S. Constitution prohibits the states from abridging citizens' rights. However, if a state constitution provides more rights to freedom of speech, for example, than does the U.S. Bill of Rights, then the state constitution takes precedence.

Although education and libraries are dealt with at all levels of government, local jurisdictions usually have the major say in running local schools and public libraries. As will be clarified later in this section, issues in which "local community standards" are thought to be a crucial factor receive more local input than do other issues. This, too, creates tensions as libraries develop resource-sharing plans that cross county and municipal boundaries, where different standards may apply.

Law is created at each level by elected legislators. These laws can be vetoed by the chief executive, who also provides leadership in setting priorities. And, of course, the judicial branch interprets the laws, sometimes overturning them or assisting legislatures in developing implementation guidelines.

Constitutional law will be a major focus of this section. It includes the U.S. Constitution, with subsequent Supreme Court interpretations regarding the structure, rights and functions of government. The first ten amendments comprise the Bill of Rights, which enumerates basic individual rights. When an individual sues because of a perceived violation of these rights, or if an individual or group sues because certain legislation appears to violate these rights, the case begins in a court of lower jurisdiction. Subsequent appeals could reach the Supreme Court, or court of last resort. According to most public policy analysts, constitutional law cases tend to support and protect the rights of minorities. This does not always mean racial minorities; it can also apply to a minority opinion or unpopular idea.

CHAPTER 7

The First Amendment

> Congress shall make no law respecting an establishment of religion, or prohibiting the free exercise thereof; or abridging the freedom of speech, or of the press; or the right of the people peaceably to assemble, and to petition the government for a redress of grievances.

The First Amendment to the Constitution, enacted in 1791, guarantees—but leaves open for interpretation—freedom of speech, the press, assembly and religion. Some of the most basic individual rights are enumerated in this celebrated sentence. It is still relatively unique, though similar guarantees are appearing in such documents as the new constitution for South Africa. Freedom of expression is the underpinning for the "robust" functioning of libraries, access to information and exchange of ideas.

As demonstrated in section I, the limited public forum concept evolved from the First Amendment. Publicly funded libraries would be totally different in mission, service and content were it not for the mandate of freedom of speech. Despite vigorous dispute among scholars regarding the original intent of the framers, and disagreement among other citizens about its scope and potential intrusion into deeply held personal values, this amendment has enjoyed a commendable level of consensus over the years. Even those citizens who are particularly offended by certain literature would often be more offended were the government to intervene and determine their reading habits.

Libraries, like other institutions for which the First Amendment is a foundation, have sought ways to apply this big picture statement to their daily operations. After the American Library Association integrated the

First Amendment into its professional values, it then adopted the *Library Bill of Rights* and subsequent Interpretations as needed.

In ALA deliberations, some librarians become particularly concerned when new Interpretations are added. They argue that the core document is sufficient. Such Interpretations are added only with great care, for the core document (which itself has been revised) does contain the key principles. However, as new services emerge and social conditions change, Interpretations are added as demanded by the membership. This process is in keeping with the philosophy of "legal realism." Developed and applied by such jurists as Oliver Wendell Holmes and Louis Brandeis and carried into present jurisprudence, this judicial theory assumes that the law itself is not oracular and unchanging, but a social construct that must adapt with the times. Legal scholars dispute this theory to this day, in terms of how much the U.S. Constitution should depart from what is envisioned as the original intent of the framers. But legal realism is certainly a helpful way to incorporate such new problems as the Internet, while still adhering to the basic constitutional principles of free speech.[1]

What are the key court cases, legislation and doctrines with which librarians should be familiar? The following paragraphs summarize those that I believe are critical for librarians to understand and apply in their policies.

LIMITS TO THE PUBLIC FORUM

As explained in section I, limits on a public forum can be established in keeping with that forum's mission. Hence, a library can have certain rules, as long as they are content neutral and do not discriminate against people by any means other than their conduct. For conduct to be restricted, the government entity must be able to show that such conduct is preventing the limited public forum from functioning or is threatening a larger interest, such as public safety. Although many are interested in designating a university computer network as a limited public forum, this has not yet happened in the courts.

TIME, PLACE AND MANNER RESTRICTIONS

The "time, place, and manner" doctrine holds that the government may balance freedom of speech against the need for maintaining societal order and other interests. However, these regulations must be content neutral, and they must not burden the free flow of ideas to any significant extent, especially if the speech has no alternative forum for being communicated. Based on this doctrine, libraries may set service hours and establish quiet reading areas discouraging talking, as long as the rules are not biased toward a specific point of view. Libraries may also establish patron conduct guidelines, as long as they are enforced equitably and only when the offending behavior is truly preventing the library from fulfilling its mission.

CONTENT NEUTRALITY

The concept of content neutrality is often misunderstood by librarians. A library can and does select materials; despite its rejection of some materials in favor of others, it can still be content neutral. The term is reflected in the approach of the "Diversity in Collection Development" interpretation:

> Collection development should reflect the philosophy inherent in Article II of the *Library Bill of Rights:* "Libraries should provide materials and information presenting all points of view on current and historical issues. Materials should not be proscribed or removed because of partisan or doctrinal disapproval." A balanced collection reflects a diversity of materials, not an equality of numbers. Collection development responsibilities include selecting materials in the languages in common use in the community which the library serves. Collection development and the selection of materials should be done according to professional standards and established selection and review procedures.

Applying this concept to reference service, a librarian can suggest resources that reviews and professional experience have identified as especially applicable for a particular query. But a librarian should not discourage a high school student, for example, from pursuing a particular topic because the librarian personally feels it is inappropriate for doctrinal reasons.

The current legislation about Internet filters may turn on content neutrality as a key factor; no filters are sophisticated enough to block content based on that legal concept. In the *Mainstream Loudoun* v. *the Loudoun County Library Board of Trustees* case to be described in a later section, a judge has analogized filtering *not* to collection development, but to removing integral articles from a set of encyclopedias:

> By purchasing Internet access, each Loudoun library has made all Internet publications instantly accessible to its patrons. Unlike an Interlibrary loan or outright book purchase, no appreciable expenditure of library time or resources is

> required to make a particular Internet publication available to a library patron. In contrast, a library must actually expend resources to restrict Internet access to a publication that is otherwise immediately available. In effect, by purchasing one such publication, the library has purchased them all. The Internet therefore more closely resembles plaintiffs' analogy of a collection of encyclopedias from which defendants have laboriously redacted portions deemed unfit for library patrons. As such, the Library Board's action is more appropriately characterized as a removal decision. We therefore conclude that the principles discussed in the *Pico* plurality are relevant and apply to the Library Board's decision to promulgate and enforce the Policy.[2]

This suggests, but is by no means conclusive, that filters will not be treated as materials selection tools in the courts.

OVERBREADTH OR VAGUENESS OF REGULATIONS

The courts will often strike down regulations as being overly broad or vague. For example, in a limited public forum, the courts have emphasized that regulations must be narrowly defined. This means that in terms of behavior, for example, people using a library must know what kind of behavior is expected of them. A prohibition against "loitering" is too vague, while a restriction against "playing a personal tape player loudly" is fairly clear. Broad terms like *offensive* or *indecent* cover some speech that is protected by the First Amendment and some that is not. The term *obscene*, on the other hand, is more precise because it has a commonly understood legal definition.

One of the biggest mistakes of library policies is their vagueness in defining unacceptable—or acceptable—behavior. The same is true in attempting to define types of Internet transactions. Some of this vagueness, of course, reflects the current legal environment. An attorney can assist with policy drafts so that libraries do not fall into the vagueness trap and have well-meaning policies backfire into a lawsuit.

THE MINORITY VIEW

> Some degree of abuse is inseparable from the proper use of everything, and in no instance is this more true than in that of the press. It has accordingly been decided . . . that it is better to leave a few of its noxious branches to their luxuri-

> ant growth, than, by pruning them away, to injure the vigour of those yielding the proper fruits.
>
> —James Madison, *Report on the Virginia Resolutions*

It is easy to forget that the point of the First Amendment is to protect what is sometimes a marginal view. Thus, some of the legally protected materials in any library are very likely to offend a large number of people. The key is to develop a diverse collection so that controversial views have a counterpoint. Although librarians will certainly want to respond to popular requests for adding certain materials, they should make an active effort to balance them with other views. In fact, a research library's value lies in the depth of collecting and in the very circumscribed weeding policies. Thus, the history of women's sexuality in such a collection will reflect some inaccurate and highly improbable theories. Incidentally, some of these "crackpot" theories were shunned, even by research libraries, out of fear of creating controversy or offending contemporary sensibilities about women's sexuality. As a result, these items are now hard to find and garner a high price on the rare book market. Most librarians would agree that if a particular author, title or theory is an integral part of a debate, some of this view should be represented, if just for the purposes of discussing the issue on a general level.

ACCURACY OF CONTENT

Litigation about the truth or falsity of speech today usually falls into the category of libel law, a very complex legal arena. Before 1964, however, it was never in the realm of constitutional law; it was a matter of an aggrieved individual suing a writer or publisher and proving that the writing was defamatory, targeted to that particular individual and widely available for people to read. If the publisher could prove that the written statements were true, then the publisher could be acquitted. But truth was the only defense. A newspaper's intent, its degree of negligence or the extent of injury to the plaintiff were irrelevant.[3]

Finally, in 1965, the opportunity arose for Justice William Brennan to link a libel suit to First Amendment issues and allow for some falsehood to be protected speech. A group of civil rights activists had placed a full-page editorial ad in the March 29, 1960, *New York Times.* The ad asserted that the nonviolent civil rights demonstrations were being met with terrorism by Alabama police and public officials, directed in particular against Dr. Martin Luther King. L. B. Sullivan, a Montgomery public official, brought a civil suit against the *Times* for injuries. The *New York Times* defense was cleverly stated; they begged the constitutional question, protesting that the doctrine of libel did not consider that there was no proof of injury, and assumed that the newspaper had acted with malice and intentional misrepresentation of facts. They added that this action was chilling to press freedom, which was clearly a constitutional issue.

In *Times* v. *Sullivan* (376 U.S. 254), the Supreme Court reiterated that "authoritative interpretations of the First Amendment guarantees have consistently refused to recognize an exception for any test of truth." The only possible exception, they state, extends into libel law, when "actual malice" is proven. In one of his most famous decisions, Brennan wrote for the Court:

> Thus we consider this case against the background of a profound national commitment to the principle that debate on public issues should be uninhibited, robust, and wide-open, and that it may well include vehement, caustic, and sometimes unpleasantly sharp attacks on government and public officials. . . . Erroneous statement is inevitable in free debate. . . . Just as factual error affords no warrant for repressing speech that would otherwise be free, the same is true of injury to official reputation.

Justices Douglas and Black went even farther in their attached concurring opinion:

> The Court goes on to hold that a State can subject such critics to damages if "actual malice" can be proved against them. "Malice," even as defined by the Court, is an elusive, abstract concept, hard to prove and hard to disprove. The requirement that malice be proved provides at best an evanescent protection for the right critically to discuss public affairs and certainly does not measure up to the sturdy safeguard embodied in the First Amendment. Unlike the Court, therefore, I vote to reverse exclusively on the ground that the *Times* and the individual defendants had an absolute, unconditional constitutional right to publish in the *Times* advertisement their criticisms of the Montgomery agencies and officials.

The *Library Bill of Rights* began its life with a "truth" qualification, which was revised over the years and fully deleted by the 1980s. One can only imagine the problems that could ensue were a librarian legally accountable for the "truth" of any reference response or recommendation for a particular book. But librarians cannot vouch for the accuracy of information in books, other than to select materials that have received favorable professional reviews. And the "Statement on Labeling" makes clear that labeling is a type of censorship because it imposes one person's attitude on another person's work. Librarians should be aware that labels could actually put them in jeopardy of being sued for breach of copyright. Further, "libraries do not advocate the ideas found in their collections. The presence of books and other resources in a library does not indicate endorsement of their contents by the library."

One of the key roles of a research library is to collect in depth, and that includes the evolution of a particular idea or topic through the ages. Retrospective collections reveal to contemporary scholars that academic fields and ideas evolve according to scientific research or trends. Imagine if this retrospective record were subjected to withdrawal of books that librarians were forced to review periodically for accuracy! It is important to have a collection development policy that carefully defines any type of weeding process. In a public library, for example, there might not be a need to collect back editions of *The Joy of Sex.* For a research library, however, a scholar in human sexuality would be interested in the fact that earlier editions did not include "safe sex" practices, but that in post-AIDS America they do.

One of the most painful areas is that of Holocaust denial literature. Librarians are urged to read "Controversial Materials in the Jewish Library," a panel discussion at the June 1986 meeting of the Association of Jewish Libraries.[4] Some lobbied the Library of Congress to create a special subject heading subdivision, "—Denial Literature," so patrons could distinguish between "pseudo-history" and traditional historical documentation. Some place denial literature in closed stacks or limit its access to adults. Some, of course, refuse to collect it. Chapter 21 contains an interesting account of how the Skidmore College student newspaper dealt with the Holocaust denial issue. The various points of view regarding this genre could be applied to other types of collections as well.

"FIGHTING WORDS"

This well-known legal concept began with *Chaplinsky* v. *New Hampshire* (315 U.S. 568 [1942]), in which Chaplinsky, a Jehovah's Witness, was distributing pamphlets and attracted a hostile crowd. When city law officers intervened, Chaplinsky verbally denounced them, calling them "Fascists" and other derogatory descriptions. He was convicted for violating a state law against such derogatory and profane speech in public, and the Supreme Court upheld that conviction. The High Court's reasoning was that there are two tiers to the First Amendment—*protected* and *unprotected* speech. The latter category includes speech that incites violent action—what one justice called "fighting words": "The English language has a number of words and expressions which by general consent are 'fighting words' when said without a disarming smile. . . . Such words, as ordinary men know, are likely to cause a fight."

If the government believes that certain speech could incite violence, it can restrain such speech. Related to this is "speech plus," which describes speech integrally related to action. An example would be picketing or marching in a demonstration. Colleges and universities used the "speech plus" and "fighting words" concepts to justify the "hate speech" policies that many campuses adopted in the early 1990s. These codes prohibited such "speech plus" as marching on campus with signs that could provoke violent reaction. Most of these were eventually overturned in the courts because they were overly vague and too broadly encompassing of different types of speech.[5] In fact, the "fighting words" concept is diminishing in importance in the courts, and several attempts to apply it have been unsuccessful, including cases in which verbal challenges to police officers have been upheld as protected speech. Librarians are unlikely to run into this concept except in a case of a program in a meeting room. However, it is important to understand that in a limited public forum, some restrictions apply to speech that might incite overreaction.

OBSCENITY

> It is a fair summary of history to say that the safeguards of liberty have frequently been forged in controversies involving not very nice people.
>
> —Justice Felix Frankfurter, *U.S.* v. *Rabinowitz* (1950)

Speech that is legally defined as *obscene* is unprotected speech. A problem arises because the word is used frequently to describe legal speech; further, such vague words as *indecent* and *offensive* are used and have no standard legal definition. *Pornography* is more specific; it describes materials depicting erotic or sexually explicit behavior, some of which may constitutionally be protected. *Obscene,* in short, is the legal term used to draw the line between protected and unprotected speech.

Librarians must be aware that legal action regarding obscenity occurs in a number of arenas in the U.S. federalist system. Nationally there is a federal obscenity statute. Congress frequently attempts to amend it or to sponsor legislation with implications for obscenity law, such as the recently overturned Communications Decency Act (CDA) and the currently pending Senator John McCain legislation, "The Children's Internet Protection Act" (S.97). The Supreme Court interprets or overturns obscenity legislation and has tried to develop standardized ways to define and "process" contested materials. The Court has also made clear that the actual determination of what is obscene will not be a national standard but will be left to local community standards.

On the state level, most states have obscenity statutes and "harmful to minors" statutes. It is fair to say that all levels of government and library professional groups support the courts' decisions that child pornography is unprotected speech. ALA has been consistent in this position, except in cases in which an overbroad statute would include materials that are constitutionally protected for children and adults. This is an extremely important message to clarify to the general public and even to some fellow librarians, who mistakenly believe that the profession's anticensorship attempts are going to harm children.

On the local level, some communities have attempted to pass city ordinances banning pornography or other types of offensive material. There will be more on this topic in chapter 16.

At all levels there are probably special exceptions or interpretations of the law regarding children.

Librarians must be extremely knowledgeable, and consult with their legal counsel, on how the obscenity laws on all levels of government apply in their local situation.

Until the mid-1900s, there seemed to be enough societal consensus about the nature of obscenity that the issue did not reach the Supreme Court. The official censors were the Customs Bureau from 1842 to 1865, and then the post office. There was in place a statutory definition from the 1876 version of the Comstock Act. Under this law a book could be held obscene on the basis of isolated passages having a corrupting effect on defenseless readers. This was called the Hicklin Test, which survived several constitutional challenges in the early 1900s. In 1929, relying on this test, a New York City court declared Radclyffe Hall's lesbian-themed novel *The Well of Loneliness* obscene (*People* v. *Friede*, 233 N.Y.S. 565). A year later, Theodore Dreiser's *An American Tragedy* was so banned in Boston.

Finally, in 1933, in *U.S.* v. *One Book Called "Ulysses"* (5 F.Suppl. 182 [D.N.Y. 1933]), Judge John M. Woolsey replaced Hicklin with a test involving the impact of the entire book on the average reader. This landmark case continues to have an impact on standards for determining obscenity. It is also the basis for most library policy for book challenges—that the offending passages should be looked at in the context of the entire book. In addition to these cases, there was considerable activity in Congress to remove the post office from its role as unofficial censor. This was finally achieved in 1970, when the Supreme Court upheld the Pandering Advertisement Act of 1968, which permitted individuals to determine for themselves what was considered to be obscene.

During the 1950s, the number of cases increased, and Justice William Brennan began his career-long attempt to find a definition of obscenity and a way to determine the extent to which it would be protected by the First Amendment. In *Roth* v. *United States* (354 U.S. 476 [1957]), Brennan declared that obscenity is constitutionally unprotected and is defined as being "utterly without redeeming social importance." Speech is obscene if to the "average person, applying contemporary community standards, the dominant theme of the material taken as a whole appeals to prurient interest." Some of the words used to describe *prurient* were: "lustful thoughts," "itching," "longing" and "lascivious desire." The legal concept of obscenity was further refined in a series of cases, including *Jacobellis* v. *State of Ohio* (378 U.S. 184 [1964]), when Justice Potter Stewart wrote in a concurring opinion that though he couldn't define obscenity, "I know it when I see it."

In the 1960s, Justice Brennan began to work on a standard formula to be applied to contested material. The formula in *Miller* v. *State of California* (413 U.S.15 [1973]) is still applied. Chief Justice Warren Burger wrote:

> The basic guidelines for the trier of fact must be: (a) whether "the average person, applying contemporary community standards" would find that the work, taken as a whole, appeals to the prurient interest, (b) whether the work depicts or describes, in a patently offensive way, sexual conduct specifically defined by the applicable state law, and (c) whether the work, taken as a whole, lacks serious literary, artistic, political, or scientific value.

The above cases are important legal precedents for librarians. *Roth* upheld the constitutionality of the federal obscenity statute and declared that obscenity was unprotected by the First Amendment. But Brennan distinguished obscenity from other types of sexual expression that would and should be protected. However, when he later wrote about his frustrating attempts to define obscenity, Brennan regretted the precedent begun in *Roth*. Who was the "average person," and what were "community standards"? Nevertheless, this language is in keeping with the tradition, upheld in several cases during this period, that such standards would be determined on the local level. A state legislature can pass obscenity legislation, but it is required to leave the definition as applied to a particular work to an "average juror" in a court of law.

The courts have frequently and consistently ruled that some materials may be designated obscene for minors, but not for adults. In *Ginsburg* v. *State of New York* (390 U.S. 624 [1968]), the concept of "variable obscenity" definitions for adults and juveniles is established. Even the most staunch libertarians like William Brennan believed that the state had a claim to regulate in the interest of protecting children, as evidenced in his opinions in *Paris Adult Theatre I et al.* v. *Slaton* (413 U.S. 49 [1973]) and *New York* v. *Ferber* (458 U.S. 747). In the latter case, the Supreme Court placed child pornography in a special category outside the guidelines for adult obscenity. Child pornography became unprotected speech, at least where precise state statutes were in place:

> The prevention of sexual exploitation and abuse of children constitutes a government objective of surpassing importance. The legislative findings accompanying passage of the New York laws reflect this concern. . . . We shall not second-guess this legislative judgment. [There follows an extensive and very important discussion about child pornography.]

To summarize, the current legal environment for obscenity challenges the librarian to be familiar with the current federal obscenity statute; with federal Supreme Court decisions, especially the *Miller* three-prong test and the recent overturning of the CDA; with state laws regarding obscenity and "harmful to children" statutes; and with local ordinances, if any. Further, the Hatch Amendment of 1995–96 has amended child pornography statutes. Previously, child pornography was visual material that depicted real children engaging in sexual or lewd acts. Verbal or written material could be "obscene" under federal law, but not "child pornography." The Hatch Amendment makes computer-generated images of children "child pornography" as well. This has created constitutional problems because speech that is not action is presumptively protected by the First Amendment, while conduct (which is what the child pornography statutes were about) was unprotected. This has now created a problem in that content, not just action, has been criminalized.

THE TIN DRUM CASE

An Oklahoma City case is included here as an example of how government agencies, libraries, special interest groups and others combine when a controversy over obscenity occurs. The following is a summary presented at a recent Freedom to Read Foundation meeting by Jenner & Block, counsel on behalf of the Foundation. It is included here in full, in the hope that this case will be carefully studied by practicing librarians.

Video Software Dealers Association, Inc. *v.* City of Oklahoma City

In June 1997, the Oklahoma City police department received a copy of the movie *Tin Drum*, which was borrowed from the Metropolitan Library of Oklahoma City by a citizen. The movie is an adaptation of a novel with the same title written by Gunther [sic] Grass. The movie was released in 1979 and won both the Academy Award for best foreign film as well as the Cannes Film Festival best picture award.

The police allegedly took the film to a judge to inquire whether several scenes constituted obscenity under Oklahoma state law. The library was not informed that this judicial review was taking place and had no opportunity to participate in these proceedings. After viewing several scenes out of the movie, the judge concluded in an advisory opinion that the movie constituted "obscenity" as that term is defined under Oklahoma law. The library then was informed that the police considered the movie obscene and that there would be prosecutions if the library secured another copy of the film.

Police officers then proceeded to various video stores and confiscated any films in the stores while demanding the names of all renters of the film who still were in possession of the movie. After securing the names of the renters, police officers headed to their homes and confiscated the film from the people who had rented it from the video stores.

Meanwhile, in July 1997, the Tulsa County District Attorney issued a press release stating that he believed that the movie did *not* constitute obscenity under Oklahoma law.

The ACLU filed a complaint on behalf of Michael Canfield, an ACLU employee whose video was seized by police from his home. [This was apparently a total coincidence!] The Complaint alleged violations of Mr. Canfield's due process rights as well as his First Amendment rights. The Complaint argued that the tape was unlawfully seized by police officers and that police officers violated federal law (the Video Privacy Protection Act) by asking video store employees for the names of renters.

The Video Software Dealers Association ("VSDA") also filed suit alleging violation of the First and Fifth Amendments of the United States Constitution. The VSDA suit alleged that the videos were unlawfully seized and that the officers violated the Video Privacy Protection Act by securing the names of renters from video store clerks. The District Attorney for Oklahoma City filed his own complaint against the Metropolitan Library System of Oklahoma City and Blockbuster Video seeking a declaration from the court that the movie *Tin Drum* constitutes child pornography under Oklahoma law.

On December 24, 1997, the district court held that the government officials had unconstitutionally removed the film from public access (from the public library, video stores and private individuals) without a prior adversarial hearing. The court did not reach the issue of whether the film violated Oklahoma obscenity law. The court did, however, enjoin law enforcement officials from retaining all copies of the film during the pendency of the proceeding.

On October 20, 1998, the District Court for the Western District of Oklahoma held that the movie *Tin Drum* did not constitute child pornography or obscenity as those terms were defined by Oklahoma law. The district court based its decision on the fact that the statute provided an exception for "bona fide works of art not appealing to prurient interest." The District Attorney did not appeal that order.

On December 18, 1998, the district court issued a ruling in the case brought by the Video Software Dealers Association. As an initial matter, the district court held that it need not address the claim that the Oklahoma statute's definitions of obscenity and child pornography were overbroad. The district court held that it need not resolve this issue because by applying the "bona fide works of art" exception it could interpret the statute in a manner that "precludes penalizing constitutionally protected material while allowing prosecutions of child pornography." (Slip Opinion at 3.)

The district court also held that: (1) the police removal of the film without an adversarial proceeding constituted an unlawful prior restraint; and (2) the police actions of obtaining identifying customer information from Blockbuster regarding movie rentals of *Tin Drum* without a prior search warrant, grand jury subpoena or court order violated the Video Privacy Protection Act.[6]

NOTES

1. For a good summary of the concept, see Laura Kalman, *Legal Realism at Yale, 1927–1960* (Chapel Hill: University of North Carolina Pr., 1986).

2. *Mainstream Loudoun* v. *the Loudoun County Board of Trustees*, District Court Order, April 7, 1998, Slip Opinion at 23.

3. I am indebted to Robert S. Peck's historical perspectives on "truth as a defense" in his beautifully written *The Bill of Rights and the Politics of Interpretation* (St. Paul: West, 1992).

4. "Controversial Materials in the Jewish Library," *Judaica Librarianship* 3 (1986–87): 49–57.

5. For current information on hate speech policy on campus, see two new books: Timothy C. Shiell, *Campus Hate Speech on Trial* (Lawrence: University Press of Kansas, 1998); and Nicholas Wolfson, *Hate Speech, Sex Speech, Free Speech* (London: Praeger, 1997).

6. From Memorandum from Jenner & Block, "Midwinter Meeting Project Update," to Freedom to Read Foundation, Board of Trustees, January 1999, pp. 5–8.

CHAPTER 8

The Fourteenth Amendment: Due Process and Equal Protection

> No State shall make or enforce any law which shall abridge the privileges or immunities of citizens of the United States; nor shall any State deprive any person of life, liberty, or property, without due process of law; nor deny to any person within its jurisdiction the equal protection of the laws.
>
> —U.S. Constitution, Amendment XIV

The Fourteenth Amendment applies to libraries in at least two important ways: the concept of due process and the concept of equal protection. The doctrine of equal protection is an extension of federal rights to apply to the states as well. It is a prime example of the expansion of meaning of constitutional law. Originally this amendment was intended to ease the reentry of the South into the Union by guaranteeing citizenship to the Confederacy, among other guarantees. It was interpreted very narrowly in the beginning. In the twentieth century it has been used to protect not only economic interests but also other liberties. The equal protection clause is used to guarantee minorities, such as African Americans, all protections of the laws. This, of course, applies not only to schools but also to publicly funded libraries or any libraries receiving funding from the federal government. It has also been extended to non-U.S. citizens. Thus libraries are open to all, in keeping with civil rights laws. It also means that states cannot pass laws or adopt constitutional rights that are less strict than federal laws.

Due process refers to a person's right to a fair procedure when arrested or deprived of liberty or property. For example, if a university deprives a student of computer privileges because of alleged abuse, the student should have recourse to appeal. This usually occurs within the student affairs administrative policies and procedures and includes an opportunity for a hearing, not a full trial.

CHAPTER 9

The Right to Give and Receive Information

The right to give and receive information is auxiliary to the original constitutional rights. The *Kreimer* v. *Morristown* case contains a comprehensive analysis of this right (958 F.2d at 1250–55). The right to receive information and ideas was also affirmed by Justice William Brennan in *Board of Education* v. *Pico* (457 U.S. 853 [1982]).

The right to give information is a corollary. As law professor Rodney Smolla reasons, "The right to receive inures in the right to send, for without both a listener and a speaker, freedom of expression is as empty as the sound of one hand clapping."[1] This means that the library profession should take seriously its role in the process of giving access to information.

NOTE

1. Rodney A. Smolla, "Freedom of Speech for Libraries and Librarians," *Law Library Journal* 85 (1993): 77.

CHAPTER 10

The Right to Privacy

> The common law secures to each individual the right of determining, ordinarily, to what extent his thoughts, sentiments, and emotions shall be communicated to others. Under our system of government, he can never be compelled to express them (except when upon the witness stand); and even if he has chosen to give them expression, he generally retains the power to fix the limits of the publicity which shall be given them. The existence of this right does not depend on the particular method of expression adopted . . . neither does the existence of the right depend upon the nature or value of the thought or emotion, nor upon the excellence of the means of expression.
>
> —Samuel D. Warren and Louis D. Brandeis[1]

The "right to privacy" is not one amendment or law, but a series of legal interpretations that continues to develop. For librarians, the "right to privacy" has become an important counterpoint to the "right to access" in terms of writing policy.[2]

Legal scholar Thomas Emerson's description is probably the most relevant way for librarians to view privacy in terms of the public forum: "a sphere of space that has not been dedicated to public use or control."[3] Thus library service must constantly maintain the balance between the service of providing access and the right of the patron to keep that transaction as private as possible, between the patron and the librarian only.

Privacy was described as a constitutional issue protecting individuals and information sought by individuals in *Griswold* v. *Connecticut* (381 U.S. 479 [1965]). This important opinion, written by Justice William O. Douglas, concerned a Connecticut state law prohibiting the use (not manufacture or sale) of contraceptives or the provision of medical information to a woman about using contraception. Under that law Mrs. Griswold, executive director of the Planned Parenthood League, was prosecuted by the state and convicted.

The Supreme Court not only reversed her conviction, on the basis that it violated her and her patients' rights to privacy, but also declared the law unconstitutional. To search bedrooms for evidence of contraception would be extraordinary government invasion of privacy, in the Court's opinion. Justice Douglas cited what he saw as the applicable constitutional amendments:

> Specific guarantees in the Bill of Rights have penumbras, formed by emanations from those guarantees that give them life and substance. *Various guarantees create zones of privacy.* The right of association contained in the penumbra of the First Amendment is one. . . . The Third Amendment in its prohibition against the quartering of soldiers "in any house" in time of peace without the consent of the owner is another facet of that privacy. The Fourth Amendment explicitly affirms the "right of the people to be secure in their persons, houses, papers, and effects, against unreasonable searches and seizures." The Fifth Amendment in its Self Incrimination Clause enables the citizen to create a zone of privacy which government may not force him to surrender to his detriment. The Ninth Amendment provides: "The enumeration in the Constitution, of certain rights, shall not be construed to deny or disparage others retained by the people." . . . We have had many controversies over these penumbral rights of "privacy and repose." . . . These cases bear witness that the right of privacy which presses for recognition here is a legitimate one.[4]

To bolster and clarify this highly controversial judicial theory and to acknowledge the importance of computer privacy, Congress passed the Privacy Act of 1974 (5 U.S.C. #552[a]), as summarized in the Office for Intellectual Freedom's modular education program for confidentiality:

1. There must be no personal data record-keeping systems whose very existence is secret;
2. There must be a way for an individual to find out what information is in his or her file and how the information is being used;
3. There must be a way for an individual to correct information in his or her records;

4. Any organization creating, maintaining, using or disseminating records of personally identifiable information must assure the reliability of the data for its intended use and must take precautions to prevent misuse; and
5. There must be a way for an individual to prevent personal information obtained for one purpose from being used for another purpose without consent.

In 1988, the law was amended to add further protections for individuals. However, this legislation has some inadequacies, so most states have added the "right to privacy" to their statutory laws. In addition, most states have specific laws covering the confidentiality of library records. Over the years many of these laws have been enhanced to protect patrons even further.[5]

In libraries, several issues relate to privacy and they grow with the computer networks and electronic resources that prompt so much of the recent legal activity regarding privacy. These issues include the following and will be discussed as policy issues in chapter 23: confidentiality of records from an integrated library system, including circulation and user survey data; confidentiality of records from a shared computer network, including e-mail and Internet queries; and the legality of posting public notices regarding suspected book thieves and others suspected of criminal activity.

NOTES

1. "The Right to Privacy," *Harvard Law Review* 4 (1890): 198–99.

2. I here acknowledge the excellent background provided by Anne Levinson Penway's legal analyses in the Intellectual Freedom Modular Education series, *Confidentiality in Libraries: An Intellectual Freedom Modular Education Program* (Chicago: ALA, 1993).

3. Thomas Emerson, *The System of Freedom of Expression* (New York: Random House, 1970).

4. *Griswold* v. *Connecticut*, 381 U.S. 479 (1965) at 484–85.

5. *Confidentiality in Libraries*, Module III, "Libraries and the Law," p. 5.

CHAPTER 11

The Legal Environment and Issues Affecting Internet Access

The single most significant intellectual freedom issue today is the aftermath of the Supreme Court's overturning of the Communications Decency Act in June 1997. The act was overturned thanks to a coalition of plaintiffs, including the ACLU and ALA. Following is the summary by Jenner & Block, the law firm of Bruce Ennis, who argued the case for the plaintiffs at the Supreme Court:

> On June 26, 1997, the United States Supreme Court issued a sweeping reaffirmation of core First Amendment principles and held that communications over the Internet deserve the highest level of constitutional protection. The Court's decision affirmed the injunction entered in June 1996 against portions of the Communications Decency Act ("CDA") by a three-judge court in Philadelphia in the consolidated case of *American Library Association v. U.S. Department of Justice* and *Reno v. American Civil Liberties Union.* Bruce Ennis of Jenner & Block argued the case in the Supreme Court on behalf of the American Library Association and the other plaintiffs.
>
> The Court's most fundamental holding is that communications on the Internet deserve the same level of constitutional protection as books, magazines, newspapers, and speakers on a street corner soapbox. The Court found that the Internet "constitutes a vast platform from which to address and hear from a world-wide audience of millions of readers, viewers, researchers, and buyers," and that "any person with a phone line can become a town crier with a voice that resonates farther than it could from any soapbox."
>
> The Court's legal analysis emphasizes that the Communications Decency Act, if allowed to stand, would "reduce[] the adult population [on the Internet]

> to reading only what is fit for children." The Court specifically acknowledged that the CDA would have harmed the ability of libraries and nonprofit institutions to provide content to their patrons. The Court rejected the attempt to regulate and restrict the Internet, and instead the Court embraced the idea that the Internet would flourish in the *absence* of governmental interference.
>
> For libraries, the most critical holding of the Supreme Court is that libraries that make content available on the Internet can continue to do so with the same constitutional protections that apply to the books on libraries' shelves. A library's posting on the Internet of literature, or research, or popular culture, or even a card catalog is constitutionally protected, even if some of the material is controversial or might be considered by some to be offensive.
>
> The Court's conclusion that "the vast democratic fora of the Internet" merit full constitutional protection will also serve to protect libraries that provide their patrons with access to the Internet. The Court recognized the importance of enabling individuals to speak to the entire world, and to receive speech from the entire world. The library can provide that opportunity to many who would not otherwise have it, and the Supreme Court's decision will go a long way to protecting that access.[1]

It is understatement to say that legislation and litigation surrounding the relationship of library service to the Internet is evolving. Librarians simply must commit themselves, for the next few years at least, to checking with their legal counsel and with the American Library Association regularly to monitor the situation. It is hoped that during this time librarians will use their professional expertise to become activists in this arena, so that the significant gains made by libraries in the Supreme Court's CDA decision will not be lost or diverted.

The most significant issue currently is whether libraries will choose, or be forced, to filter Internet access on their library terminals. Filters are software that can be placed on a network or a terminal to block content. They can be purchased by parents or by a library system. Currently filtering is being applied mostly to protect children, but there are also efforts to use it to prevent employees from accessing non-work-related materials in the workplace. Though filter technology is evolving, there are various types and results, depending on the product chosen:

> Blocking/filtering software is a mechanism used to:
>
> restrict access to Internet content, based on an internal database of the product, or;
>
> restrict access to Internet content through a database maintained external to the product itself, or;

restrict access to Internet content to certain ratings assigned to those sites by a third party, or;
restrict access to Internet content by scanning content, based on a keyword, phrase or text string, or;
restrict access to Internet content based on the source of the information.[2]

The possibility of filters was an integral part of the argument when the Supreme Court debated the Communications Decency Act. The Supreme Court was unwilling to censor speech in the interest of child protection if such censorship also abridged the speech of adults. Ennis reminded the Court that "there is a broad range of technologies and software programs that enable parents either completely to block all access to the Internet, if the parents are really concerned, or, more selectively, to screen and filter access to the Internet if they want to allow their children to have access to certain parts of the Internet but not to others."[3]

The final Supreme Court decision concludes: "The District Court found that 'currently available *user-based* software suggests that a reasonably effective method by which *parents* can prevent their children from accessing material which the *parents* believe is inappropriate will soon be widely available.'"[4]

As a result of this decision, many librarians feel "damned if they do, damned if they don't." A publicly funded library, according to the CDA decision, cannot restrict Internet access for adults to constitutionally protected speech. Filters are certainly allowable in the "private sphere"—a home or private library—but not in a public forum if it chills adult speech. The dilemma for a library: If a filter is mounted on a library terminal, it can filter out most (but not guaranteed all) speech illegal for minors, but it will also filter out speech that is constitutionally protected for adults. To further complicate matters, there is legal precedent for older adolescents to be distinguished from younger children regarding access to library content (*American Booksellers* v. *Web* [919 F.2d 1493]). And, as we know from *Pico*, minors have successfully sued for their right of access to information.

In this confusion, many librarians and library boards have decided to take the safe route and mount filters at least in children's areas. At this date, I know of no academic public library that has filtered content, and the trend at the state library association level appears to be toward adopting resolutions opposing filtering.

Currently the most visible litigation is the previously cited Loudoun County, Virginia, case, in which a group of concerned citizens successfully sued the library's board when they installed filters on public terminals. This case is summarized later in this book and is required reading for all librarians being pressured to filter access to the Internet.

The Children's Internet Protection Act, S.97, is making its way through congressional hearings at the time of this writing. This bill would require schools and libraries subscribing to the e-rate program to install blocking software on terminals accessed by children. Librarians are urged to follow this bill carefully.

How to operate in this legal vacuum? Section IV will offer some suggestions.

NOTES

1. Bruce Ennis, attorney for the plaintiffs, *Reno* v. *ACLU*, summary of case, presented at American Library Association, Summer 1997 Annual Conference, copy from Freedom to Read Foundation files.

2. *Statement on Library Use of Filtering Software*, American Library Association/Intellectual Freedom Committee, July 1, 1997, here in appendix H.

3. Bruce Ennis, attorney for the plaintiffs, in oral arguments before the Supreme Court, March 19, 1997, *Reno* v. *ACLU*, p. 22.

4. *Reno* v. *ACLU* (138 L.Ed. 2d 874), p. 901.

CHAPTER 12

International Law

International law regarding freedom of expression presents a vast array of diverse constitutions, laws and other documents. As will be seen in chapter 15, the new international body called the Committee on Freedom of Access to Information and Freedom of Expression (FAIFE) uses Article 19 of the Universal Declaration of Human Rights as its guide (see appendix D):

> Everyone has the right to freedom of opinion and expression; this right includes freedom to hold opinions without interference and to seek, receive and impart information and ideas through any media regardless of frontiers.

In March 1999, FAIFE issued its own "Statement on Libraries and Intellectual Freedom" (see appendix D).

CHAPTER 13

Documents with the Force of Law

Other documents, some with the force of law, differ from library to library. These could range from state charters that establish public libraries, to university statutes, to bylaws for multitype library consortia. At the University of Illinois, for example, the legislature created the university by state statute, and it is funded by annual appropriations of state funds. The Board of Trustees is given the power to run the university and to set regulations and statutes. These statutes are not laws, but, rather, establish the structure of the university. In addition, many subgroups participate in the development of policy in close consultation with the office of the University Legal Counsel and the campus leadership, including the Council of Deans. When drafting the campus computer use policy, for example, the committee included, among others, representatives from the School of Law, the Library, the Faculty Senate and the Computing and Communications Services Office (CCSO). Their work was checked by the University Legal Counsel at critical junctures. The Office of the Provost and others attempt to ensure that policies do not conflict with or duplicate each other and are consonant with the academic governance structure that includes faculty and student members.

CHAPTER 14

Other Laws

Civil rights laws, the ADA (Americans with Disabilities Act) and many other regulations pertain to the limited public forum. Thus, buildings must be handicapped accessible, and all programs, spaces and materials must be open to all, regardless of race, gender or other categories recognized in civil rights legislation. Librarians must understand that these important laws play a key role in assuring equitable access and upholding intellectual freedom principles.

SECTION III

The Policy Players and Process for Library Public Forum Issues

Section II surveyed the legal environment in which the public forum is debated, crafted, interpreted and altered. This is achieved in the United States through the federal system, which includes legislation and litigation on the national, state and local levels. Librarians need to know the historical context of the current legislation, so that they can communicate effectively with their legal counsel and legislators and craft effective policies for regulating publicly funded libraries.

In addition to the legal environment there is the broader policy arena of which the government is an important—but only one—part. There are also professional organizations, such as the American Library Association, with professional ethics statements and policy documents, including the *Library Bill of Rights* and its Interpretations. There are also those special interest groups that take positions on intellectual freedom–related issues. These groups are invaluable for forming coalitions for political action, as witnessed by the CDA decision.

This section will deal with the process by which these players and their concerns become public issues. Several theories about how this process works generally in the United States will be presented, followed by a chapter on how the process works specifically for public and academic libraries.

CHAPTER 15

Professional Library Associations

PROFESSIONAL ETHICS

> Education for professional ethics is a preparation for life in a complex and pressure-filled world in which the pressures will be particularly to conform, to compromise, to get along, to avoid "rocking the boat."
>
> —Herbert S. White[1]

The concept of "professionalism" is continuously debated and analyzed by sociologists—and certainly by librarians in reference to their own field. The focus of this book is not to take a position on this issue, but to illuminate the professional model the United States library profession emulates. This model includes a national organization that arguably predominates over all others in terms of its credibility and authority among other professions and policymakers. And this national organization has adopted a code of ethics, called by some sociologists a "documentary approach" to professionalism. This model, like many others, allows for a diverse membership, which possesses personal and professional ethics that may sometimes conflict. A profession built on written ethical principles has advantages and disadvantages.

In *The System of Professions: An Essay on the Division of Expert Labor*, Andrew Abbott uses three professions to illustrate his theories about the meaning of professionalism: lawyers, psychiatrists—and information professionals, including librarians. The book underscores the concept that professionalism goes beyond a code of ethics, though it does not necessarily exclude such a code. Abbott emphasizes the importance of professional identity as a way to define what one does at work; to establish what "jurisdiction" a certain professional holds in the world of work; and to stake a claim in the midst of "competition." Also, a profession must hold "a knowledge system governed by abstractions," which help that profession "redefine its problems and tasks, defend them from interlopers, and seize new problems." Abbott maintains that the library profession's traditional jurisdiction is facing competition from the computer professions. Because entry to the information profession has always been relatively "permeable," traditional librarianship is likely to end up sharing its jurisdiction with other types of information professionals, and that dynamic holds the potential for conflict.[2]

Using Abbott's theory as a jumping-off point, I believe that now, more than ever, the library profession needs to understand the legacy of its "documentary structure" and how it affects what librarians do. Newcomers to the information profession (computer programmers, for example) may have differing sets of values, codified or not, and it is important for librarians to understand how the traditional value of intellectual freedom has affected this country's library service. This value has also placed the library profession in a unique and generally positive relationship with the legal profession, the courts, policymakers and the general public. That should not be taken lightly.

THE AMERICAN LIBRARY ASSOCIATION

The American Library Association is the largest professional library group in the United States and arguably the most influential on behalf of librarians in publicly funded libraries. Two of its largest divisions, in fact, are the Public Library Association (PLA) and the Association of College and Research Libraries (ACRL). It maintains an office in Washington, D.C., for optimal impact on Congress.

Its membership has also adopted a "Code of Ethics," included as appendix E. Although all eight principles of the code are related to intellectual freedom, the second specifically states: "We uphold the principles of intellectual freedom and resist all efforts to censor library resources." Further, the introduction states, "In a political system grounded in an informed citizenry, we are members of a profession explicitly committed to intellectual freedom and the freedom of access to information." Finally, the code acknowledges that values are inevitably going to conflict in a "changing information environment." Other ALA groups, such as ACRL's

Rare Book and Manuscripts Section (RBMS), have amplified and supplemented that code—for example, with the "Standards for Ethical Conduct for Rare Book, Manuscript, and Special Collections Librarians" (1994). As Lindsey and Prentice conclude, "The code of ethics of a professional association is a direct expression of its service orientation and its feelings of responsibility to its clientele."[3]

It is important in a volatile environment to have a set of values as a foundation, even if that foundation is buffeted—even altered—by the changing nature of librarianship. Recent debates in the medical profession over cloning, for example, have arguably been enriched by the restraining influence of traditional medical ethics conflicting with the acknowledged need to incorporate the impact of new medical technologies.

In an important article in *American Libraries,* ALA President Ann Symons and university librarian Carla Stoffle write about clashing values: "Many patrons and staff members complain that we now have a sexually harassing environment. Many of us are asked to patrol and curtail Internet use. We don't know how to do this within our values system. Our strong support for one value—intellectual freedom—is in conflict with our value of responding to community desires and the social value of creating safe and welcoming library environments. We need help both in dealing with this conflict and with explaining our values to what has always been a very supportive public."[4]

This dilemma and its variants should continue to be a major topic of discussion both within and outside the profession. Many believe that the general public respects a profession that acts like a profession. In that sense, the commitment to intellectual freedom, while not always supported as wholeheartedly by the general public as within the library profession, does garner librarians the designation as "experts" concerning that important issue. This has been proven again and again by the admiration afforded the library profession by nonlibrarians who associate the profession with the expertise to uphold freedom of expression principles in the United States. And with that comes a certain amount of respect, albeit it grudging at times.

Further, librarians' knowledge of the historical context of intellectual freedom tells us that a public forum does not always feel intellectually "safe and welcoming." While it is certainly true that library users must be assured of an environment free of such criminal offenses as violent and harassing behavior, they should also understand that a diversity of ideas sometimes creates intellectual discomfort. Those who were college students in the 1960s may remember that the campus was sometimes a disruptive environment in terms of the clash of ideas. While this was certainly unsettling at times, some remember it as an experience that exposed them, for the first time, to a diversity of views and helped them learn to analyze political events critically.

Some librarians have questioned the profession's dedication to intellectual freedom, perhaps to the detriment of other compelling issues. The American Library Association and other library organizations in the United States offer ample opportunities for dialogue about the myriad of priorities the profession must juggle. There have been, and will continue to be, intense and important debates about these issues. There is a mechanism and a process, through the ALA Council and committee structure, for shaping the association's policy for the future. However, it must be stated that ALA's support of intellectual freedom has garnered admiration from other professions, such as journalism, with some of the same interests, and, on the international level, ALA's intellectual freedom organization is being used as a model for current efforts to establish an office within the International Federation of Library Associations and Institutions (IFLA).

Law professor Rodney Smolla offers one example of how librarians' professionalism is an essential element in the process of selecting materials for the library. He reasons that if librarians do not select materials for the library, those materials will be selected by the legislature. If there is no professional judgment, then government interference is more likely. He notes that in the *Pico* case, the Supreme Court chastised the school board for removing books contrary to established policy, which included professional judgment of each challenge to library acquisitions. Smolla advises librarians to take their role as professionals seriously:

> My suggestion that courts should begin to recognize a "professionalism principle" is designed to create what might be thought of as "insulation material" between the legislature and free expression, helping to combat disguised censorship. There is always reason to be highly suspicious of interference by elective bodies in the details of content-based regulation of speech concerning governmental programs. More often than not, the real motivation will not be neutral, but will be aimed at skewing the general marketplace through the leverage of government funding. The professionalism principle recognizes this commonsense judgment of experience and instructs courts to scrutinize with heightened skepticism any attempt by the legislature to bypass the routine channels of professional discretion.[5]

The Office for Intellectual Freedom

The Office for Intellectual Freedom (OIF) is headquartered in the Chicago ALA office and serves as an important liaison with the ALA membership. The Intellectual Freedom Committee (IFC) is appointed by the ALA president to formulate intellectual freedom policy. The grassroots arm of ALA's intellectual freedom organization is the Intellectual Freedom Round Table, which focuses on state- and local-level problems encountered by librarians in the trenches. Further, each division of ALA has an intellectual freedom committee or liaison to the IFC.

The evolution of what are now the Office for Intellectual Freedom and the Intellectual Freedom Committee is a history yet to be written at a depth to afford them the status they deserve within the system of the library profession. Although there will always be controversy about the OIF's mission and priority within the association's structure, here we examine its history, evolution and activity as they relate to writing good library policies.

The American Library Association began its intellectual freedom policy in a reactive manner—with the Executive Board's responses to censorship complaints brought by the membership or other interested individuals or groups.[6] One early complaint concerned a 1929 federal tariff proposal that would prohibit importation of materials "advocating or urging treason, insurrection, or forcible resistance to any law of the U.S. . . . or any obscene book, paper, etc." The Executive Board opposed this tariff because, among other things, it was "a reflection upon the intelligence of the American people by implying that they are so stupid and untrustworthy that they cannot read about revolutions without immediately becoming traitors and revolutionaries themselves; and because the question of social policy is withdrawn from the ordinary courts and placed in the hands of officials primarily chosen for their special qualifications in dealing with the administrative details of tariff laws."[7]

In those early days there was little consistency in the association's support of intellectual freedom; for example, the Executive Board decided to take no action regarding the book burnings in Nazi Germany. Its first protest against a ban of a specific publication was in 1933–34, when the WPA's Civilian Conservation Corps (CCC) banned *You and Machines* because officials thought the pamphlet was too nihilistic about the governmental structures of the time. The ALA president and executive secretary wrote a letter of protest to President Franklin Roosevelt. The Executive Board then established a committee to write a more formal letter for

Council approval. That letter specifically requested that federal education officials get more involved in the selection of reading matter for the CCC camps. It is of interest that in those two early cases, the ALA's argument centered around concerns that inappropriate officials were making selection decisions and that such decisions should be made in the courts or by educators. Also, both cases concerned matters of a broader nature, matters outside libraries. Thus ALA's commitment to intellectual freedom has always reached beyond libraries to broader social implications of threats to intellectual freedom. In fact, the 1980 version of the *Library Bill of Rights* recognizes that censorship from any source eventually affects libraries.

In 1939, the association protested the widespread banning of John Steinbeck's *The Grapes of Wrath.* At this point, ALA was sufficiently mobilized in the fight against censorship that the *Library's Bill of Rights* could be adopted. It was a spare document lacking some of the sophistication of today's, but it stated three core beliefs: that books should be chosen for library purchase because of "value and interest to the people of the community," and in no case should the selection be influenced by the political or religious views of the writers; that all sides of an issue should be represented; and that library meeting rooms should be available "on equal terms to all groups in the community regardless of their beliefs or affiliations." These core beliefs are an early reflection of the public forum doctrine: unbiased selection, balanced collections and open meeting rooms. The meeting rooms language has remained substantially the same and is certainly a confirmation of the profession's vision of the library as a public forum.

In 1940, the ALA Council established the Committee on Intellectual Freedom to Safeguard the Rights of Library Users to Freedom of Inquiry, now known as the Intellectual Freedom Committee. Since then, its role has been to "recommend such steps as may be necessary to safeguard the rights of library users in accordance with the Bill of Rights and the *Library's Bill of Rights*, as adopted by Council."[8]

The organization's approach to the importance of "truthfulness" with regard to censorship evolved over the years. In 1944, the *Library's Bill of Rights* was revised to include opposition to censorship. Article I said that books "believed to be factually correct" should not be banned or removed from the shelves. In 1948, this was changed to "books . . . of sound factual authority." A phrase of this type was included until 1967, when the phrase "factually correct" was deleted. This evolution reflects the courts' rulings, which eventually in *Times* v. *Sullivan* reiterated that perceived factual errors are still protected speech. This also shows that policy—just like the law—does change with the times.

Academic librarians should note that the latest major revision of the *Library Bill of Rights* occurred partly in response to requests that the document specifically include the sometimes unique censorship problems of academic libraries as well as the more common public and school library challenges.

The Freedom to Read statement began evolving in 1953 and was most recently updated in 1991. It is the ALA's affirmative statement of the *Library Bill of Rights* and has been jointly sponsored by a number of national organizations concerned about the rise of censorship. It is found in appendix F.

The Office for Intellectual Freedom has long understood that public understanding about intellectual freedom is vital to successful policy supporting freedom of expression in libraries. Banned Books Week, special training sessions, an active publications program, a censorship database, an office to offer solace and expertise to librarians under pressure from censors—all these continue to be helpful public relations tools within and outside the profession.

The Freedom to Read *Foundation*

The Freedom to Read Foundation was incorporated by the American Library Association in 1969 as a separate organization to serve as ALA's legal defense arm for intellectual freedom issues. Membership is open to anyone. The Foundation's Board of Trustees confers regularly regarding legislation and litigation affecting intellectual freedom in libraries. The board decides whether to support particular cases coming to its attention. It also decides the best means of support—money for a defense fund, an *amicus curiae* brief or correspondence with the parties involved are but three examples. The board retains the legal counsel of First Amendment specialists. The Freedom to Read Foundation played a vital role in helping ALA coordinate and monitor the successful challenge to the Communications Decency Act.

Many other ALA groups also play crucial roles in defending and advocating for intellectual freedom. They include the Legislative Committee and GODORT (the Government Documents Round Table), which is extremely active in promoting open and low-cost access to government information for all.

STATE LIBRARY ASSOCIATIONS

Almost all state-level library organizations have an intellectual freedom committee or officer. These committees monitor state legislation likely to affect intellectual freedom, assist librarians in their state with real-world censorship experiences and often publish intellectual freedom manuals with pertinent state- and local-level legal information.

The Illinois Library Association's Success Story

The Illinois Library Association (ILA) is notable for its successful work to defeat legislation that threatened the free flow of information in resource-sharing arrangements. This case is provided here in detail to demonstrate how much intellectual freedom interest and expertise are needed at the state level, and how the ILA succeeded in handling and continues to monitor an extremely volatile situation. An excellent presentation of the entire incident can be found in the article "Further Obscenity Legislation Fails" by ILA Executive Director Robert Doyle.[9]

In March 1995, the Neighborhood Protection Act was introduced in the Illinois House of Representatives. The bill was a proposed amendment to the state's obscenity legislation, which defines obscenity and child pornography and is similar to state laws described earlier. The new bill proposed changing the obscenity standard from a statewide to an individual county standard. Prosecutors would thus turn to what could be 102 different counties' definitions of obscenity. The legislators' argument was an oft-used "downstate" versus Chicago complaint—in this case, that the city's standard for obscenity was too lenient. When librarians proposed an amendment to the bill exempting libraries, it was rejected by the bill's sponsors. This sent a clear signal to the library community that the legislature intended for them to be covered by this action. Special interest groups supporting this legislation were well organized and well funded, and included the Illinois Christian Coalition and the National Law Center for Children and Families.

The Illinois Library Association recognized immediately that this proposed bill would negatively affect practical library operations. Interlibrary loan, consortial arrangements and other services would be jeopardized. Sharing of electronic information would be yet another problem, as would the sharing of on-site collections in libraries serving more than one county. ILA therefore mobilized a coalition of dozens of special interest groups, including the American Civil Liberties Union, the American Booksellers Foundation for Free Expression and the Motion Picture Association of America. Coalition members conducted a letter-writing campaign to legislators. Fact sheets were prepared and updated on the ILA Web site. Certificates of appreciation were issued to supportive legislators. ILA and other expert witnesses testified at legislative hearings.

What arguments were used against such emotionally charged and well-meaning legislation? First, librarians pointed out the legal precedent—that Illinois and sixteen other states (almost all of them large and many bordering Illinois) apply a statewide standard in obscenity cases. Only two states have a county standard. Second, they reminded legislators that Illinois libraries lead the nation in resource sharing, which means a savings to taxpayers. The first challenge to the proposed new law would effectively begin to dismantle that system.

Finally, librarians pointed out why the bill was bad public policy in general. First, it would create a fragmented set of rulings. It assumed that county lines were the most significant public opinion boundary. These jurisdictions would conflict with school district boundaries, which would almost certainly create a problem sooner or later. The bill was bad for such businesses as cable television, bookselling and video rental. Finally, librarians reminded legislators that most people resented further government intrusion into their private lives, particularly when it applied to their reading habits.

The legislation was narrowly defeated. Again, in early 1999, similar county-based obscenity standards legislation was reintroduced in the Illinois legislature and narrowly defeated. It is hoped that ILA's groundwork will serve well in continuing this struggle. The association has provided several educational opportunities for librarians; it is expanding the coalition; it is training supporters to work with the media and to learn how to express concerns "to defeat censorship, but not reject our fellow citizens."

Librarians should study the Illinois experience carefully not only to identify what made the initial success possible, but also to note ILA's ongoing strategies for maximizing support, based on a realistic assessment of what the future may hold.

INTERNATIONAL EFFORTS ON BEHALF OF INTELLECTUAL FREEDOM

The International Federation of Library Associations and Institutions (IFLA) is leading the world's library community in its first effort to organize a freedom of expression and access initiative. The August 1998 annual meeting in Amsterdam welcomed the first official meetings and open hearings for FAIFE (Committee on Freedom of Access to Information and Freedom of Expression). At the 1997 meeting the Danish government offered to establish an office in Copenhagen to help IFLA focus on handling censorship cases, capitalizing on the capabilities of Internet and other technology to increase and democratize access to information around the world.

FAIFE deliberated on how the new office should prioritize the multitude of urgent tasks, as government repression prevents many populations from receiving, and librarians from providing, even the most basic library service. The group reviewed its scope and strategic and working plans. They will follow Article 19 of the United Nations Universal Declaration of Human Rights (see appendix D):

> Everyone has the right to freedom of opinion and expression; this right includes freedom to hold opinions without interference and to seek, receive, and impart information and ideas through any media regardless of frontiers.

Appendix D also includes the March 1999 FAIFE policy on freedom of expression.

Interestingly, one of the points on the office's work plan is to "carefully study methods and accomplishments of the American Library Association and its Office for Intellectual Freedom." The United States library association's commitment to intellectual freedom is just as culturally bound as that of any other country and yet most of the world's librarians acknowledge the ALA's strong leadership in this area and want to model it for their specific situation.

The international censorship situation is sensitive and complex, and there is a troubling number of censorship incidents, many of them deadly. These are documented systematically by Amnesty International, the Article 19 organization, and the publication *Index on Censorship.* Yet until 1998, no group focused on library censorship. At the 1998 IFLA meeting in Amsterdam, librarians from all continents reported troubling incidents at the open meeting or in formal papers. Topics included the difficult task of ensuring the right to information in developing countries, and the lasting impact of Soviet censorship on the current arts scene in that part of the world.

It is a well-worn and cliché-ridden statement, but it does appear that American librarians often take intellectual freedom for granted, while librarians and other information professionals in some countries are losing their jobs and sometimes their lives because of government repression. As one librarian exclaimed at an open meeting after describing the passivity to the repression of information in his country, likely out of fear of reprisal, "Defending freedom of expression is what makes us professionals and not clerks."

NOTES

1. Herbert S. White, "Teaching Professional Ethics to Students of Library and Information Science," in *Ethics and the Librarian*, ed. F. W. Lancaster (Urbana: University of Illinois Graduate School of Library and Information Science, 1989).

2. Andrew Abbott, *The System of Professions: An Essay on the Division of Expert Labor* (Chicago: University of Chicago Pr., 1988). The importance of a code of ethics is covered in Michael F. Winter, *The Culture and Control of Expertise* (New York: Greenwood Pr., 1988). A feminist view of library professionalism is found in Roma M. Harris, *Librarianship: The Erosion of a Woman's Profession* (Norwood, N.J.: Ablex, 1992).

3. Jonathan A. Lindsey and Ann E. Prentice, *Professional Ethics and Librarians* (Phoenix: Oryx Pr., 1985), p. 3.

4. Ann K. Symons and Carla J. Stoffle, "When Values Conflict," *American Libraries* (May 1998): 56–58. See also Lindsey and Prentice, *Professional Ethics and Librarians.*

5. Rodney A. Smolla, "Freedom of Speech for Libraries and Librarians," *Law Library Journal* 85 (1993): 75.

6. From an undated and unnamed document from the Office for Intellectual Freedom.

7. American Library Association, "Minutes of Executive Board Meetings," mimeo, 5:11 (January 1, 1930).

8. "Cincinnati Proceedings—Council," *ALA Bulletin* 34:P-37 (August 1940).

9. *Illinois Library Association Reporter* (June 1997): 1, 8–9, 11–12.

CHAPTER 16

Special Interest Groups

Librarians have always been coalition builders. This is partly because the profession's work is often community-based with strong links to other educational institutions and common concerns with civil liberties groups, journalists, publishers and others whose livelihood and professional missions depend upon intellectual freedom. This sometimes means that, as with all coalitions, the library profession must work with groups whose business may conflict with libraries in some respects. This is certainly true with bookstores, for example. Some argue that the mega-chains are taking away library clientele by encouraging browsing and allowing food and espresso. However, when the chips are down, librarians would be among the first to support any bookseller who was visited by special interest group members who entered the store and tore up books they did not like.

Following is a list of some of the groups who have been helpful allies in defending and promoting intellectual freedom. There is also a list of some of the groups who have actively worked against libraries' intellectual freedom concerns. This list is by no means complete. It is offered not only to identify some significant special interest groups in the policy process, but also to emphasize to librarians the importance of forming coalitions with special interest groups to achieve intellectual freedom objectives. For an excellent explanation of the role of pressure and special interest groups, with a focus on those groups opposing intellectual freedom and their tactics, see Carol Nielsen's chapter, "Pressure Groups: Politics, Religion, and Censorship in Libraries," in the *Intellectual Freedom Manual.*[1] Nielsen makes the important point that the trend in the United States from a vision of diversity as a "melting pot" to one of a "salad bowl" has alarmed many groups who believe that the United States' strength derives from certain commonalities in language, values—and reading material. Although many of these groups come from the newer fundamentalist Christian religious groups, in opposition to the more liberal "mainstream" denominations, this is not the entire picture. As will be seen in the account of Catharine MacKinnon in this chapter, feminists and other groups have also supported censorship. Another book essential to understanding the current ideological divisions in the United States as they affect support of and opposition to public libraries and other cultural institutions is James Davison Hunter's *Culture Wars: The Struggle to Define America* (New York: Basic Books, 1991).

The attempt to censor diversity is in direct contrast to trends in colleges and universities and in society as a whole. The United States is increasingly diverse in religion, languages and ethnicity, and many groups now celebrate their unique identity rather than try to blend in. Libraries reflect these differences as patrons demand new types of literature. Therefore, some of the conflict among diverse opinions about the nature of libraries is inevitable. The key is to include library materials reflecting many points of view and, at the same time, to try to find common ground among these demands. For example, libraries have always been family oriented, and the statement by ALA President Symons, "Libraries: An American Value," reflects this eloquently. Reading can be not only a solitary but also a communal activity, with discussions, storytelling and other means for creating a cohesive but diverse community.

FREQUENT SUPPORTERS OF INTELLECTUAL FREEDOM ISSUES

The following list is a good place to begin. Web sites will often be hotlinked to related sites.

American Civil Liberties Union (ACLU)

http://www.aclu.org
125 Broad Street, 18th Fl.
New York, NY 10004-2400

The ACLU is the organization that some people love to hate. This mainstream civil liberties group has a long tradition in the United States and deals with all types of civil liberties issues. This 75,000-member organization is "devoted exclusively to protecting the basic civil liberties of all Americans, and extending them to groups that have traditionally been denied them." The ACLU was a co-plaintiff in the CDA suit along with the American Library Association and others.

The ACLU Web site is ideal for historical perspective because the organization is seventy-seven years old. The organization has transcripts of the court cases it has been involved in, plus the Top 77 cases, one for each year of the ACLU's existence.

Association of American Publishers (AAP)

http://www.publishers.org
1718 Connecticut Avenue NW, 7th Fl.
Washington, DC 20009
202-232-3335

The AAP is the national trade association of the U.S. book publishing industry. Its Freedom to Read Committee collaborates with ALA on many activities, including court cases, congressional testimony and public programs.

Electronic Frontier Foundation (EFF)

http://www.eff.org
1550 Bryant Street, Suite 725
San Francisco, CA 94103-4832
415-436-9333

The EFF was founded in 1990 "to ensure that the principles embodied in the U.S. Constitution and Bill of Rights (and the UN Universal Declaration of Human Rights) are protected as new communications technologies emerge." The foundation sponsors court cases in which a user's online civil liberties have been violated, filing *amicus* briefs and the like. It produces position papers on topics of concern that can be used in court and in other arenas where expertise is needed. Its Web site includes information important to activists and legislators, offering not only the latest legislative updates, but also position papers that can be used in speaking to groups or writing books like this one!

Electronic Privacy Information Center (EPIC)

http://www.epic.org
666 Pennsylvania Avenue SE, Suite 301
Washington, DC 20003
202-544-9240

EPIC's Web site is valuable for its current news briefs, its "bookstore" bibliography of civil liberties books and its transcripts of Supreme Court cases. It has an "A to Z of Privacy, from Airline Passenger Profiling and Caller ID to Social Security Numbers and Wiretapping." EPIC is a project of the Fund for Constitutional Government.

Feminists for Free Expression

http://www.well.com/user/freedom
2525 Times Square Station
New York, NY 10108
212-702-6292

This diverse group of feminists ranges from psychiatrists to creative artists. They believe that "there is no feminist code about which words and images are dangerous or sexist." They believe that freedom of expression is the key to women's rights, thereby taking a view directly opposing Catharine MacKinnon. Their Web presence is especially informative, and there is much information to counter the MacKinnon view, including research challenging the opinion that pornography causes violence toward women.

Free Expression Clearinghouse (FEC)

http://www.freeexpression.org

The Free Expression Clearinghouse is a national coalition of free expression groups, and its membership directory is an invaluable source of information. Groups include the ALA, the Media Coalition, the American Association of University Professors, several religious groups who oppose the fundamentalist approach, Rock the Vote, and the Thomas Jefferson Center for the Protection of Free Expression.

FEC's homepage includes all the latest censorship news as well. This is by far one of the most valuable Internet sites to check on a regular basis.

The Interfaith Alliance

http://www.tialliance.org
1012 4th Street NW, Suite 700
Washington, DC 20005
202-639-6370

The Interfaith Alliance is a national organization "built by people of faith from all religions and denominations who believe the radical religious right is not the majority voice of the spiritual community in America."

This group opposes current attempts to alter the First Amendment. This is a good source of information to counter the religious groups listed in the following section.

FREQUENT CHALLENGERS TO INTELLECTUAL FREEDOM ISSUES

This discussion begins not with "the usual suspects," but with an account of the work of feminist law professor Catharine MacKinnon. Many librarians and members of the general public assume that censorship comes from the far right of the U.S. political spectrum or from fundamentalist religious groups. Although those types of groups will be listed later, it is important to emphasize that censorship comes from all quarters. It often begins with a political issue or movement with passionate followers who believe that repression of certain information will help their point of view prevail.

Catharine A. MacKinnon and Feminist Mobilization against Pornography

Catharine A. MacKinnon is a professor of law at the University of Michigan. For some decades she has been an activist and a theorist on issues of women and pornography. She is important to mention here in some detail because her work gave many librarians pause—at least in the heyday of the antiporn movement—regarding their commitment to the First Amendment. Also, especially in public and academic settings, librarians are likely to find many users, including influential faculty, who accept MacKinnon's theories and try to influence library collection development accordingly.

Although I do not accept MacKinnon's theories or actions, much of the press opposition to her has been dismissive but not substantive and a correction is needed. Librarians, especially in academe, are quite likely to hear arguments like MacKinnon's about violating not only women's rights, but also the rights of other groups. The argument needs to be examined very carefully and thoughtfully. It is also important to note that much of the speech MacKinnon was attacking was constitutionally protected. It was not legally obscene.

In the late 1970s, MacKinnon, like many feminists, was discouraged by the defeat of the Equal Rights Amendment (ERA) and the slow movement toward women's rights in the United States. Some women at this time began to focus on violence toward women, particularly rape, and the legal system's abysmal record regarding prosecutions and punishment of offenders. Some, like writer Andrea Dworkin and MacKinnon, took it a step farther by asserting that pornography ignited and sustained violence toward women. In 1979, Dworkin published *Pornography: Men Possessing Women* as the battle cry for the antipornography movement.

In those early days, Catharine MacKinnon's legal theories were not as fully formed as they are today. In the early 1980s, she and Dworkin focused on pornography as a violation of women's civil rights—it not only promoted violence, but also prolonged sexual inequality in society. While the First Amendment focuses on individual rights to free speech in constitutional law, MacKinnon defined pornography not as speech, but as action—a violation of the civil rights of women as a group. Her argument: Because the abstract "speech" of a porn movie requires a woman to suffer degradation while she performs in the film, the movie becomes a vehicle for violent action. Just as Oliver Wendell Holmes stated that shouting "fire" in a crowded theater was not protected speech, MacKinnon declared that speech that required hostile action toward women should not be protected, either:

> For those of you who think pornography is only an idea, consider the possibility that obscenity law got one thing right. Pornography is more actlike than thoughtlike. The fact that pornography, in a feminist view, furthers the idea of the sexual inferiority of women, which is a political idea, doesn't make the pornography itself into a political idea. One can express the idea a practice embodies. That does not make that practice into an idea. Segregation expresses the idea of the inferiority of one group to another on the basis of race. That does not make segregation an idea. A sign that says "Whites Only" is only words. Is it therefore protected by the First Amendment? Is it not an act, a practice, of segregation because what it means is inseparable from what it does? *Law* is only words.[2]

As a result, MacKinnon and Dworkin began drafting antipornography ordinances to be adopted by various cities. They began in 1984 with Minneapolis. The proposed ordinance would have authorized the city of Minneapolis to suppress any book, magazine, film or recording that expressed "the sexually explicit subordination of women." MacKinnon explains:

> At the request of the city of Minneapolis, Andrea Dworkin and I conceived and designed a local human rights ordinance in accordance with our approach to the pornography issue. We define pornography as a practice of sex discrimination, a violation of women's civil rights. . . . Its point is to hold those who profit from and benefit from that injury accountable to those who are injured. It

> means that women's injury—our damage, our pain, our enforced inferiority—should outweigh their pleasure and their profits.[3]

The definition of pornography was very broad and covered protected as well as unprotected speech. Opponents pointed out that such works as romance novels with the infamous but not illegal "bodice-ripper" cover illustrations would need to be banned under MacKinnon's definition, not to mention *The Taming of the Shrew* and *The Arabian Nights*, which theoretically could fall under this broad definition. Nonetheless, the Minneapolis City Council approved the ordinance in 1984, only to have Mayor Donald Fraser veto it, citing its threat to First Amendment rights.

Next MacKinnon tried Indianapolis, where the mayor was supportive of her efforts. (Ironically, the city councilwoman who led the effort to pass the ordinance had also been instrumental in the defeat of the ERA in Indiana.) Federal District Court Judge Sara Evans Barker heard the case and overturned the Indianapolis ordinance. Basically Evans weighed the harm caused by pornography against the threat to the First Amendment and decided for the latter (*American Booksellers Association, Inc., et al.* v. *William H. Hudnut III, et al.* [771 F.2d 323, 7th Cir. 1985]).

Although the issue of pornography and women currently is not as prominent in First Amendment or feminist discourse as it was in the 1980s, MacKinnon did write another book, *Only Words*, in 1993, the title referring ironically to her continued anger that pornography is considered to be just that by the courts. And there are still many activist groups. The issue of pornography or any other kind of literature directed against an oppressed group understandably challenges librarians, many of whom are women and feminists and, at the same time, intellectual freedom advocates. For some, this was the first time in their professional careers that they were forced to deal with this philosophical "split." (In the same vein and around the same time, *Huckleberry Finn* was denounced by the NAACP, and, although to date there is no announced plan to mount a campaign, it is precisely the MacKinnon argument that could be used for banning that particular title.)

What are some of the arguments against MacKinnon's approach? One argument provides common ground for conservatives and liberals alike—that this approach creates legislation that chills speech protected by the First Amendment. For example, the city ordinances' language talked about speech that expressed the subjugation of women. This could include a universe of information and could be especially threatening to research libraries' retrospective holdings, which are frequently at odds with contemporary political thought.

Why not extend the law against child pornography to women, MacKinnon asks. Treating women legally as children is fraught with repercussions that would not advance their equality with male adults.

And what about the argument that pornography is "speech-action" or "fighting words"? Almost all speech could be construed as such. It would require that all creative art be investigated, and perhaps restrained, if it was found to exploit models, actors, stunt artists and even extras. What about stunt artists who die while making movies? The traditional political structure in the United States supports ways to reform such abuses, rather than applying "prior restraint" to the creative work itself. If women are being kept in slavery, for example, or physically abused, there should be a movement to raise public awareness through the legal system, not suppress that knowledge. Similarly, libraries should be sure to have information covering all aspects of such controversies and, perhaps, even sponsor discussions of such material. And, certainly, pornographers and organized criminals should be prosecuted for criminal activity. Librarians should be mindful that for minority groups, equity of access should be an integral and clearly stated part of the mission. Every effort should be made to support equity of access for all sides of an issue, within the limited public forum.

What about the argument that speech causes action once it is published? This argument has been used against numerous publications, including an article on how to make an atomic bomb. There are any number of research reports from all perspectives on the question of whether literature can cause action. One interesting approach is Thelma McCormack's "Making Sense of Research on Pornography," in which she explains how social-scientific studies are constructed and how to interpret the results. McCormack concludes:

> There is no systematic evidence that people copy what they see or read about in pornography. . . . It is possible to say that a cultural milieu in which women are perceived as sex objects contributes to the devaluation of women. Goals such as greater participation in public life, equal pay for work of equal value, day care, etc., are that much more difficult to achieve without the strong positive images that establish credibility.[4]

Other groups, such as the Feminists for Free Expression, report all research in this area and present evidence that pornography does not cause violence against women.

Scholar Henry Louis Gates Jr. presented another interesting perspective in a book review in *The Nation:*

> The real challenge, for feminists and free-speech sentimentalists alike, is *not* to defend obscenity on the ground of innocuousness. Such a defense is perfectly tenable, and it remains important to rebut overstated claims to the contrary. "Girls lean back everywhere," argued Jane Heap, editor of *The Little Review*, when she was prosecuted in 1920 for publishing a salacious episode of James Joyce's *Ulysses*, "and no one is corrupted." . . .
>
> And yet, and yet . . . the capacity to "deprave and corrupt," quaint as it sounds, must be taken seriously. Because I want to believe that culture *matters*, I cannot refuse to contemplate that texts have effects as well as causes. The (pro-porn) literary critic Anne McClintock deals with this issue head-on when she remarks: "I am as unconvinced by the argument that porn inhabits a remote, frenzied land safely beyond the green door of the mind as I am by the argument that porn is practice for rape." Surely a civil liberties agenda that depended on the neutrality or inertness of any of our expressive practices would be devoid of content.[5]

These points of view are, it seems to me, the strongest possible mandate for librarians *not* to censor, but to provide broad access to a diversity of opinion, and to open the public forum to exhibitions and programming of same.

Concerned Women for America

http://www.cwfa.org
1015 15th Street NW
Washington, DC 20005
202-488-7000

Beverly LaHaye founded Concerned Women for America "to protect the interests of American families and provide a voice for women throughout the U.S. who believe in Judeo-Christian values." This organization supports women in seeking membership on library and school boards in order to promote its agenda, which includes opposition to any library material that might reflect the decline of moral values. The group's tactic is to place these women as "stealth candidates," which means that when running for office or appointment, they hide their real motive until they are elected or appointed.

The Eagle Forum

http://www.eagleforum.org
P.O. Box 618
Alton, IL 62002
618-462-5415

Founded by Phyllis Schlafly, the Eagle Forum, according to its homepage, "stands for the fundamental right of parents to guide the education of their own children." The organization has pressured the public schools to use "back to basics" curricula and opposes "profane and immoral fiction or videos, New Age practices, anti-Biblical materials, or 'Politically Correct' liberal attitudes."

Focus on the Family

http://www.family.org
Focus on the Family
Colorado Springs, CO 80995
719-531-3328

In 1997, Dr. James Dobson, who holds a Ph.D. in child development, formed Focus on the Family. Dobson believes that the United States needs home-based family values. A Christian organization opposing the "humanistic notions of today's theorists," Focus on the Family draws on "the wisdom of the Bible and Judeo-Christian ethic." The group publishes books, magazines and videos that are often used by local pressure groups to challenge books in public libraries. Their Web site is very informative and does give a good idea of their philosophy.

NOTES

1. Carol Nielsen, "Pressure Groups: Politics, Religion, and Censorship in Libraries," in *Intellectual Freedom Manual*, 5th ed. (Chicago: ALA, 1996), pp. 244–54.

2. Catharine MacKinnon, *Feminism Unmodified* (Cambridge: Harvard University Pr., 1987), pp. 193–94.

3. Ibid., p. 175.

4. Thelma McCormack, "Making Sense of Research on Pornography," in Appendix I, *Women Against Censorship*, ed. Varda Burstyn (Vancouver: Douglas & McIntyre, 1985), p. 198.

5. Henry Louis Gates Jr., "To 'Deprave and Corrupt,'" *The Nation* (June 29, 1992): 903.

CHAPTER 17

Public Policy: An Overview

It takes more than a knowledge of the law and professional ethics to write and implement successful library policy for promoting intellectual freedom. General public policy theory offers a broad context, a historical perspective and practical considerations that could ultimately determine the success or failure of library policy.

Public policy analysis, like any scholarly field, is approached and explained in diverse ways. This general introduction includes the role of legislation, special interest groups (including ALA) and the courts. One way to analyze public policy is to look at the various "policy players," such as those listed in chapter 16. Another is to look at the policy process. Yet another is to look at a particular issue, like intellectual freedom, and determine how the players and process fit in. Chapters 17, 18 and 19 will approach public policy formulation and analysis in all three ways.

THE PLAYERS

The authors of *Politics and Public Policy* describe six "policy domains."[1] First is the "Boardroom," which encompasses corporate concerns. For libraries, this includes publishers and integrated system vendors, and Internet providers, among others. A clear profit motive exists, yet such groups as the Association of American Publishers have enduring ties to ALA's intellectual freedom efforts. The past decade's expansion into licensing for full-text databases, plus the rise in journal subscription prices, has caused tension between librarians and publishers. It has also led to more use of fee-based services for libraries to recover costs. There are software companies interested in producing filtering options for beleaguered public librarians. Other companies, such as Microsoft and America OnLine, have often supported legislation and other lobbying efforts on behalf of intellectual freedom. Textbook publishers have always been sensitive to such groups as the Eagle Forum. This sensitivity has been a concern for ALA for decades, as the publishers bow to such special interest groups, especially in populous states like Texas, and change content accordingly. On the other hand, the American Booksellers Association and similar groups ardently support intellectual freedom.

As media giants like Time-Warner continue to gain market share, libraries grow increasingly concerned about lack of diversity of ideas. As government information becomes privatized, similar concerns arise. In the United States, the private sector has been an important partner for libraries since the beginning. Yet librarians must be alert to the fact that sometimes coalition partners' interests may diverge, and the partnership may not last or may force coalitions with groups more closely allied to librarians' professional values.

"Bureaucratic Politics" is the second domain in the Van Horn book. This category includes administrative agencies, such as the Internal Revenue Service (IRS) or the Interstate Commerce Commission (ICC). Any regulatory rules or statutes have the force of law and affect libraries.

The third domain, "Cloakroom Politics," should be studied closely as it describes the workings of legislative bodies. Legislators not only make law, they also debate ideas. Van Horn, Baumer and Gormley believe that in many ways, the debating function is the most important role for legislators in American society. While research shows that certain issues stay at the top of the agenda for any given year, it is fascinating to see how concerns about the Internet hit Congress and the general public relatively quickly. This issue thus was forced to move forward very quickly, leaving many loose ends. There is likely to be a shakedown period lasting well into the twenty-first century as the technology continues to develop and access to information shrinks or expands according to the policy formulations.

"Chief Executive Politics," the fourth domain, is important in the sense that leaders like Al Gore made the National Information Infrastructure (NII) an important policy issue. The Clinton White House was the first to use the Internet in a big way. The ALA Washington Office monitors legislation and makes sure that the Office for Intellectual Freedom is aware of any pending legislation or executive branch initiatives that affect libraries.

The fifth domain, "Courtroom Politics," is critical for intellectual freedom issues, as has been amply demonstrated in previous chapters. Judges make law as much as legislators do. In fact, some laws cannot be implemented without court order or interpretation. The most important areas of constitutional law for librarians to monitor concern speech and privacy. The U.S. Supreme Court and state supreme courts are the usual deliberating bodies for constitutional issues. On an ideologically divided court such as Rehnquist's, centrists like David Souter provide crucial "swing votes" because the judge writing the decision wants to minimize dissent, which indicates fragmentation.

The Supreme Court looks to the Constitution for guidance and precedent. "Freedom of speech" is not defined and interpretations have changed over the years. Many Americans believe that the Supreme Court is above the political fray; nothing could be farther from the truth. A recent trend in legislatures is to abdicate responsibility for lawmaking by relying on the courts to make the decision. This has led courts to play a more prominent role in legislation.

Interest groups like the American Library Association have considerable experience in filing suits or *amicus* briefs and know how to use the courts. The current Supreme Court is not afraid to overturn the legislative branch, but it is certainly not as activist regarding the First Amendment as some previous courts.

Court decisions inevitably need further interpretation or raise further confusion in their implementation. This was certainly true with *Brown* v. *Board of Education* in desegregating the public schools, and it is true in the aftermath of the Communications Decency Act. Filtering is the best example. The courts' decisions do not always fit library interests specifically. A good example is the *Pico* case, which gave the intellectual freedom initiative only part of what it had hoped for. This is why ALA and state library organizations, experienced in negotiating, compromising and prioritizing, are essential players in this mix of policy domains.

Finally, "Living Room Politics" includes the opinion of those people Bill Clinton calls "Joe Six-Packs"—ordinary citizens. Public opinion is important, but increasingly diverse. Most average citizens are inconsistent from issue to issue. The religious right has become a particularly important interest group in shaping public opinion. The press and television are very important in this process, too. Increasingly, Americans are having their opinions shaped by the media before they have had time to learn all the issues. Therefore, the public is becoming more vulnerable to "spin" and a digestion of the information before having the opportunity to critically analyze the raw data. Libraries are very important in this environment, because they have that raw material and are committed to making accessible a diversity of points of view.

THE PROCESS

In their 1996 text, *The Policy Puzzle*, Donald Wells and Chris Hamilton take a somewhat different, though not contradictory, approach to policy analysis by talking more about process and specific issues, such as health care and education, than about the actual domains.[2] They also talk about historical context for public policy. This approach helps illuminate the political environment that led to the Communications Decency Act. The authors document and explain the country's swing to the right on social issues and the emphasis on family values. Understanding this trend is helpful for creating good public relations surrounding new and potentially controversial policies. For example, ALA President Ann Symons sought common ground with this concerned public with her emphasis on "Libraries: An American Value."

THE ISSUES

In the United States, a conservative reaction to government intervention and to cultural trends began in the 1960s and moved into full swing by the 1970s. A religious fundamentalism, not tied to institutional religion, grew among all faiths, not just Christianity. Although the initial reaction for intellectual freedom advocates might be discouragement—based on past experience with these groups—it is important to remember that the public library is one of America's time-honored traditions. We can also remember that privacy, individual liberties and freedom from government intervention are hallmarks of intellectual freedom policy as well as traditional conservative values. Thus it is very important to understand national trends and where common ground might be found with the various special interests. Strong conservative libertarians can be some of libraries' best allies. So can grassroots parents' groups that are concerned about children's issues. Although Tipper Gore's crusade against recordings was misfocused, in the minds of most intellectual freedom activists, her concern for children can be drawn upon for other issues.

As we consider library policy in particular, it is important to revisit this material and apply it to the dynamics of library intellectual freedom policy. It helps in choosing the proper strategy, forming the most effective coalitions and using the right language to reach our audience, because a policy isn't just a set of rules. It is a reflection of the library profession's beliefs and mission.

It is precisely this richness and complexity of American policy culture that libraries both serve and depend on. There are many alliances and strategies possible in such a diverse environment, if one listens and is not afraid to be creative.

NOTES

1. Carl E. Van Horn, Donald C. Baumer, and William T. Gormley Jr., *Politics and Public Policy*, 2d ed. (Washington, D.C.: Congressional Quarterly Pr., 1992).

2. Donald T. Wells and Chris R. Hamilton, *The Policy Puzzle: Finding Solutions in the Diverse American System* (Upper Saddle River, N.J.: Prentice-Hall, 1996).

CHAPTER 18

The Policy Process in Public Libraries and Academic Institutions

> Because of the nature of the issues and because they're not going to get resolved quickly by the Supreme Court in a direct appeal, they're going to come up through a lot of states and percolate for years. We're going to lose a lot of those battles along the way. There's going to be a lot of litigation, a lot of ferment, a lot of misunderstanding, a lot of problems, . . . and it's not going to be easy. On the other hand, this case we just won wasn't easy either. So let's just keep up the fight.
>
> —Bruce Ennis, attorney for the ACLU, ALA and other plaintiffs, following the Supreme Court's overturning of the Communications Decency Act

Mr. Ennis's words are a suitable introduction to a discussion of writing and implementing policy for publicly funded libraries. He understands that even as dramatic a decision as overturning the CDA does not resolve the future for librarians, who will win some and lose some in the quest to define access in the Internet age. *The key to effective policy is to develop a library mission and to pursue that mission according to the law, professional ethics and the unique community being served.* Along the way there will be setbacks; one learns from those and continues to move forward. This is especially the case with First Amendment issues dealing with the Internet and other new technology, where a public understanding must grow along with the law.

It is my hope that the preceding chapters have demonstrated the ways in which policy is a combination of players and processes. The librarian must consider all the areas discussed previously in this guidebook: legal, professional, political and ethical responses. In addition to principles, there are practical matters. If one pays attention to these, many of which are political in nature, one is less likely to run into trouble with implementation or with public relations. While it is essential that library policies follow the law, and while it is certainly desirable for policies to reflect professional ethics and ALA policy, the practicalities include understanding the process by which policy is made. This knowledge makes successful implementation more likely. Many of these considerations involve common sense; many have to do with knowing your library's particular political situation by understanding the culture of the community that it serves. For academic librarians, this means understanding the dynamics of policy formulation in academe; for public librarians, it means understanding the interaction of such players as the municipal executive, the library's governing board and special interest groups. Librarians must understand how decisions are made by the governmental body that oversees their policies.

CHAPTER 19

The FBI Library Awareness Program: A Case Study of Values Conflict and Ambiguity in the Policy Process

It is important to understand the ALA's confrontation with the FBI if you are ever in doubt that "it can't happen here." This was the most challenging period in the history of ALA's intellectual freedom activity. It was front-page news in the *New York Times* and *The Nation*. It involved seventeen academic libraries, though some were never specifically verified as part of the Bureau's acknowledged Library Awareness Program. In this program, FBI agents would approach public service desks, ask attendants (often students) about library use by "suspicious looking foreigners" and sometimes ask to see library circulation records.

In October 1987, the Intellectual Freedom Committee (IFC) and the Office for Intellectual Freedom (OIF) issued press releases and sent letters to U.S. academic and research librarians and to the Senate and House committees with oversight for the FBI. In December, then FBI director William Sessions confirmed the existence of the Library Awareness Program but refused to say whether it was limited to the New York City area.

The first few months of 1988 were spent in closed briefings between the FBI and the National Commission on Libraries and Information Science (NCLIS), with the Office for Intellectual Freedom attempting through Freedom of Information Act (FOIA) requests to obtain transcripts and other details about the program. Persistent requests to meet with the FBI were ignored, though the library community did meet with various Senate and House members.

When ALA finally met with the FBI in 1989, they reviewed library professional and legal mandates. The FBI continued to suggest that librarians were often used as "dupes" by foreign operatives.

Finally, in fall 1989, an FOIA request by ALA produced a list of 266 people, all of whom had objected to the Library Awareness Program and were subjects of a Bureau "index check." Through 1990, ALA and various involved members wrote to President George Bush and to William Sessions and submitted FOIA requests for personal information. The FBI, meanwhile, was in litigation with the National Security Archive over the same issue. Eventually the Bureau turned over documentation, much of which was blackened to be illegible. To date, the FBI has never publicly announced the cessation of the Library Awareness Program.

Specific ALA policy emerged from this harrowing experience. Already available was the "Policy on Confidentiality of Library Records" (appendix J). During the FBI matter, procedures were revised, including instructions on how to deal with requests from officials (see page 153). Finally, two other statements were added: "Policy concerning Confidentiality of Personally Identifiable Information about Library Users" (appendix J) and "Policy on Governmental Intimidation" (see *Intellectual Freedom Manual).* The latter was not motivated by the FBI incident, but is certainly applicable.

Local policy should be developed from ALA's positions. First, staff members, including all student or part-time workers, must learn what to do when a law enforcement official comes to a service desk for information. This kind of situation, even if the officials are very courteous, tends to intimidate, so one must be prepared and know the law. A short procedure is all that is necessary. The state's confidentiality policy should be readily available. When in doubt, the desk attendant should consult with the library director or designee.

The library should reaffirm the policies regarding confidentiality of library records and of personally identifiable information about users collected by any means, including user surveys. Even a subpoena should be referred to the library director, who may consult with an attorney and attempt to quash it. In recent years there have been several reported requests from such government agencies as the IRS to go on "fishing expeditions" with patron records.

To support this policy, patron records no longer of use should be destroyed in whatever format.

Rare book and special collections libraries often keep circulation records for a longer time as a security measure, should an item appear to have been mutilated or be missing altogether. It is far better for all concerned to check the book or manuscript before the patron leaves and then destroy the record. Special collections libraries also tend to receive a great deal of researcher correspondence or maintain on-site researcher sign-in sheets. These should never be shared with other researchers, some of whom may be curious to know what colleagues are working on. A librarian should reveal that information only if both researchers give express permission for the librarian to act as a go-between.

An interesting example from my own experience involved both sides of a court case, the federal government and a Native American tribe, using the same boxes of archival material as evidence. One side had flagged those papers for which it ordered photocopies. It was extremely important to remove those flags before the next patron used the box in order to protect the privacy of the first group. In this case, had the flags not been removed, the prosecution's case could have been revealed.

SECTION IV

Putting It All Together: How to Write and Implement Policy

Previous sections of this book have surveyed the legal, professional and public policy environments, all of which must be brought to bear in writing and implementing intellectual freedom policy. Successful policy is more than careful wordsmithing and well-researched content. Section III reviewed the policy process most U.S. academic and public libraries follow for intellectual freedom issues. This includes consulting with key players, planning public relations and monitoring the policy's impact—all within the context of the library's mission. And one ignores at peril the informal advice based on colleagues' real-world experience.

Section IV begins with general considerations—both formal and informal—for writing intellectual freedom policy. Next comes practical advice for writing and implementing policies for three types of intellectual freedom issues: content; access; and privacy, including representative employee and patron privacy issues. Obviously some areas—library services for children, for example—have aspects of all three issues. Such areas will be covered comprehensively in one of the three chapters. Each content, access and privacy issue will be analyzed as follows:

1. Definition and brief history;
2. Current legal and professional status;
3. Public policy considerations: domains, special interests, public opinion and others;
4. Potential common ground to unite diverse interests and form consensus;
5. Supporting documents and concepts;

6. Implementation plan, including public relations and ways to monitor the policy's impact.

Once again I acknowledge the inspiration and practical ideas obtained from the Office for Intellectual Freedom's *Modular Education Program: Confidentiality in Libraries.*

CHAPTER 20

Writing and Implementing Good Policy

Discussion in earlier chapters provides useful theoretical background for writing and implementing good policy. Now, as we begin the actual writing, we must ask: Why have written procedures at all?

The *Intellectual Freedom Manual* offers many reasons, based on general management theory and practical library experience:

1. They show everyone that the library is running a businesslike operation.
2. They inform everyone about the library's intent, goals, and aspirations.
3. They give credence to library actions; people respect what is in writing, even though they may not agree with everything in the library's procedures manual.
4. They are impersonal; they make whimsical administration difficult.
5. They give the public a means to evaluate library performance; publicly pronounced policy statements prove that the library is willing to be held accountable for its decisions.
6. They contribute to the library's efficiency; many routine decisions can be incorporated into written procedures.
7. They help disarm potential censors; unfounded accusations seldom prevail when the library's operations are based on clear-cut and timely written procedures that reflect thorough research, sound judgment, and careful planning.[1]

PREPARATION

Certain preparations are essential before sitting down to write a policy. First, you should ask yourself if policy is the best way to handle the issue at hand. Is a less formal approach—a newsletter notice, for example—or a more formal approach—a statute, for example—a better route? Or does an existing federal law cover the issue so that a policy statement only adds redundancy and confusion?

Many librarians complain that the profession already has too much written intellectual freedom policy and wonder why the *Library Bill of Rights* needs interpretations. It is true that any time one adds specifications to general policy statements, one runs the risk of being too specific. For instance, a well-meaning library policy might include a "laundry list" of minority groups for whom equitable library access is reaffirmed. What happens if a group is inadvertently omitted? Further, some librarians argue that civil rights laws already make it clear that discrimination against protected groups is prohibited in libraries or any other public forum.

Historical perspective assists in answering these important questions. The U.S. Constitution did not have a Bill of Rights until 1789 (appendix A) precisely because many of the framers thought it unnecessary. They believed that the Constitution itself offered sufficient protection from government intervention into citizens' lives. But the Bill of Rights was added when Thomas Jefferson, James Madison and others began to see the need for a legal check on federal power. Later amendments address specific social concerns and changes in the nation's values; note in particular the Twenty-First Amendment's repeal of Amendment Eighteen's national prohibition of alcohol. And the rights of all U.S. citizens to vote—regardless of race or gender—justified Amendments Fifteen and Nineteen. In all cases the amendments were tied to political considerations of the time; they were not written in an ideological vacuum.

Though not a legal document, the *Library Bill of Rights* applies many of the values of the U.S. Constitution's first ten amendments to specific situations in libraries. But librarians, citizens and Boards of Trustees have asked for even more clarification or interpretation of these broad statements. For example, how does the *Library Bill of Rights* apply to children? To people with AIDS? As new formats, such as video, joined the traditional book in library holdings, librarians formulated interpretations conveying the belief that the *Library Bill of Rights* applied to all formats. Based on experience with library users and on the general public perception of library materials, the profession felt the need to clarify that the First Amendment applies to videos, too.

Therefore, while the American Library Association tries to limit changes to the core *Library Bill of Rights* document, there have been and will continue to be situations calling for formal interpretations or other types of policy documents. In some cases, a Council resolution will be more appropriate. Or no action at all. These interpretations and other documents are included in the appendixes to this book, and readers are urged to check the ALA Web site for the most current information. Policy formulation at a local library level should be subjected to the same careful scrutiny.

A first step in policy formulation should be to engage colleagues and interested parties in a discourse. This could be done at a faculty or Board of Trustees meeting, over lunch or in whatever forum allows for the issues to be presented in a thoughtful, comprehensive manner. Sometimes it is better to begin informally. In some cases, you will want to approach key players privately. Understandably, some people do not like to be confronted with a controversial proposal for the first time in a formal group setting. As it progresses, the discussion will raise awareness of the problem and will help you identify people to help write this policy. It will also make you aware of potential resistance or of areas requiring negotiation among interested parties.

Be sure to bring library professional values to the table. Generally, it is better not to begin with a formal written statement, such as the *Library Bill of Rights*, but to keep these values in mind during a general discussion. Sometimes, however, it is essential that these formal statements be presented at the very beginning and constitute the foundation for the discussion. Remember that people generally respect a profession with written ethics—and professionals committed to upholding them.

STRATEGY, STYLE AND SUBSTANCE

Under each of the three topics in section IV—content, access and privacy—librarians will find lists of documents and key policy concepts to include. In general, all policies should have *strategy*, *style* and *substance*. First, policies should be written strategically—that is, with an understanding of their audience and reception. Strategic policy entails a careful linking of the policy to the library's mission, rather than presenting it simply as an idealistic document with no perceived connection to reality.

In fact, intellectual freedom is such an integral part of a library's practical mission of providing information and access that libraries often forget to incorporate these principles into the policy process. The following computer access policy draft is a good example of incorporating intellectual freedom principles: "In order to promote access to a vast, up-to-date universe of information, Our Town Public Library is proud to provide two public terminals with Internet access at no additional charge to users. Because we are anticipating a huge demand, we are beginning with a policy limiting use to 30 minutes per patron. We will monitor the demand and revise this policy if necessary. If this service is popular, we will consider adding more terminals." This policy clearly communicates attempts at fairness and equity of access to the user community. It also communicates strategically to funding officials that any request for more terminals will be based on a careful assessment of user demand. Also, the drafters have wisely tied policy content to the positive features of the Internet.

The second element of well-written policies, *style*, involves such basic considerations as using the active voice. If a statement reads, "You will be asked to give up the terminal after 30 minutes," the question remains: Asked by whom? A much clearer statement would read, "The reference librarian will monitor the time and ask you to give up the terminal after 30 minutes." Style also includes tone and conveying the correct meaning. Consider the difference between "No talking allowed!" and "This room is for quiet study; conversation welcome in Lounge B."

Finally, *substance* implies an organized presentation with relevant points covered and documented if necessary. You might anticipate the library user's reaction and potential questions when outlining your policy. Examples include: How do these public access terminals relate to the library's mission? How do I get access? What will happen if there is a long line? Will I get kicked off if I am reading e-mail? Who will enforce terminal use and how? What will happen to me if I don't follow the rules? Doesn't this rule violate my rights? How does the library plan to alleviate these long lines? and Is there something I, the patron, can do to help the library make its case to the appropriate officials for getting more terminals?

All policies should be written with an awareness of the balance between being general and being specific. See section II for legal definitions of *vagueness* and *overbreadth*, and keep in mind the "laundry list" syndrome mentioned in the beginning of this chapter. When possible, back up your policy by citing law, ALA policy or other authoritative support. Section IV will offer numerous practical and specific suggestions for the substance of your policy.

Before widely distributing the draft, run it past your legal counsel. Based on suggestions in the *Modular Education Program*, here are some questions to ask of the draft:

1. Is the policy related to intellectual freedom principles? To the library's mission?
2. Has such language as "including, but not limited to" been checked with legal counsel, to protect yourself in case of unforeseen developments or circumstances?
3. To whom does this policy apply? Is it stated in a way that is nondiscriminatory in terms of the law?
4. If any procedures are involved, are they presented clearly? Who is responsible for implementation? For training others? Did you clarify who is to talk with the press or with such other outside contacts as the police?
5. What is the procedure for adoption or reconsideration of this policy?
6. If specific incidents are involved, did you emphasize reporting them to the Office for Intellectual Freedom? To the appropriate local authorities? To the press? To the public?
7. Does the policy conform to supporting documents? These should include local policy documents in your library and on your campus.[2]

Writing the policy is the easy part. Implementation and review are far more difficult. You must obtain agreement and support from key people. Librarians are responsible for identifying these people, who might include influential members of governing boards or campus offices and committees. It most certainly involves your library colleagues who will be responsible for enforcing these policies. The network of special interest organizations is important, too. You should know your local press and officials, including law enforcement. Just as you wish to be included when the campus writes network use policy, you will want to include key people in drafting your policies on various topics. Inclusion of key players is an invaluable consideration for gaining consensus and commitment to enforcing the policy. You may wish to avoid using "outsiders" from national organizations if you can get local people to support your policy. This precaution might avoid resentment or distrust. Sometimes this is impossible and the outside expertise brings necessary political pressure or moral support. You must judge this on a case-by-case basis.

Once you have achieved reasonable consensus in the library, talk with the president, the board, or other appropriate people and urge them to help publicize the policy in a positive manner. The local paper may do an article, for example, on the library's Internet policy. Don't forget the student senate, the graduate student association, the faculty senate or the friends of the library. Don't make the mistake of assuming that all smart people will naturally agree with your policy. For example, your campus probably has at least one renowned feminist scholar who agrees with Catharine MacKinnon's assessment of the First Amendment. This could create an opportunity for a spirited debate or it could be the downfall of your policy, and much depends on your approach to implementation.

Intellectual freedom policies should be part of freshman library orientation and presentations on library use. The Jake Baker case, for example, has proven to invoke lively discussions and provide an opportunity to present the library's views on intellectual freedom (see chapter 23). Academic librarians have found that intellectual freedom is an issue that readily engages faculty in other disciplines, for example, political science, philosophy, law and women's studies. Librarians should take advantage of the rich intellectual and interdisciplinary content in this area of librarianship.

Finally, don't forget to schedule a periodic policy review in your tickler file. The law pertaining to intellectual freedom is changing constantly, so you must check authoritative sources regularly to see if the changes affect your policies. For controversial policies, you should anticipate public desire for discussion and schedule appropriate opportunities accordingly.

In spite of your best efforts at writing and communicating, conflict is sometimes inevitable and you should anticipate fallout. It is unwise, for example, to implement a controversial policy or dramatic change in library service when key library administrators are going to be on vacation. This does not mean that you need to write or act defensively. It does mean that you should garner support just in case. You should gather documents and overprepare for presenting your policy stance. Intellectual freedom issues cut to people's core values. It is useful to remember this and to prepare yourself to use your skills in listening actively and controlling anger. Numerous short courses are available through community education or professional library organizations for sharpening these kinds of communications skills. Judith Powell's *Peoplework: Communications Dynamics for Librarians* (Chicago: ALA, 1979) is an excellent handbook.

More recent literature on general interpersonal communications is available as well. The practical advice given here may also help.

INFORMAL CONSIDERATIONS

The preliminary outline of this book assumed a predominantly formal approach to intellectual freedom policy. Then I began consulting with countless librarians and officials who offered success stories based on what they called, again and again, "plain common sense." It became clear that a section devoted to informal observation and experiences was a necessary complement to the formal policy-writing guidelines.

The following advice is in no particular order. I wish to emphasize that these commonsense ideas do not substitute for written policy. Informal arrangements can often lead to abuse or inequitable treatment of individuals. However, written policy alone is insufficient. The librarian needs to know how to publicize and implement policies so that they gain wide acceptance not only by the public but also by the staff who will be implementing them. Successful implementation requires communications skills sometimes best described as "informal," though many librarians will tell you that these skills are actually based on sound management and communications theory and can be practiced and learned. At any rate, here are some of the most frequently offered observations:

1. Those librarians who successfully weathered challenges did so by being firm in their principles yet willing to listen actively. They tried to work with opponents by seeking common ground to defuse the conflict. This process might lead to the realization, for example, that a library has not provided diverse sources of information based on its user community's demands, and that the addition of some key titles or resources could solve this problem.

2. Ask yourself if you need a policy at all. Sometimes isolated incidents are best solved on the spot. In the case of a parent's distress over a book in the children's room, a sympathetic ear is often more effective than a formal policy or procedure. Some librarians have found that thirty minutes of active listening saved them countless weeks of costly litigation.

Sometimes a policy is unnecessary because it is already covered by a law and should be handled by a law enforcement agency. If an antismut group enters a library and begins tearing up books they find offensive, they are likely destroying legally defined public property and a librarian should feel free to call the police. Librarians need not even address the content issue in a situation like this; it is a violation in most communities to tear up library books, regardless of content.

3. If a policy cannot be enforced, it's useless. A good example is the often futile attempt to enforce "no food or drink" policies. If librarians, as is frequently the case, are uncomfortable in confronting each and every offender, then the policy is unenforceable. It does not mean that there should be no policy about food or beverages in the library. It does mean that there needs to be a commitment and an ability to enforce—from staff as well as library users. Student workers, guards, librarians and others must understand why such a policy exists and be willing to enforce it consistently and equitably. Cooperation from key student governing bodies and other key players is a must.

4. If your community decides to have a forum to debate the pros and cons of the Internet for kids, be sure that the library not only is represented at the forum, but also helps shape the agenda. There is a big difference between a forum titled "The Perils of the Internet for Your Kids" and one titled "What Parents Need to Know to Help Their Kids Get the Most out of the Internet." Such fora should present all perspectives. Organizers need to be prepared not only to address parents' very real concerns about obscenity, but also to present information about the child-friendly sites.

5. If you are interviewed by the press, try to shape the questions. For example, if a reporter sticks a microphone in your face and asks you why the library buys "smut," you should turn that accusation into an affirmative reply: "Let me tell you about all the good things the library buys." Practice not being defensive.

6. Given the diversity of protected speech in the United States today, it is inevitable that some patrons will be offended by some content in your library. When values clash, offer choices: A different type of novel. A terminal in a different location. For example, if a patron is offended by his or her neighbor's screen display on an adjacent terminal, you might consider directing the offended patron to another terminal, rather than confronting the user who may well be accessing constitutionally protected speech. Privacy screens are another alternative.

The same applies for staff who are often offended when they boot up public service terminals in the morning, only to confront obscene screen displays deliberately set by patrons the night before. Ask your systems staff to set the terminals to a default screen.

Sometimes the best policy is short: "Some patrons may find materials in this library that offends them." Or, you could add a statement inviting users to consult with a librarian to find alternative information sources. Then you must follow through. For example, if a public library patron is invited to suggest alternatives and requests "more religious novels," the library should be prepared to buy some titles, even if some librarians find them objectionable.

7. Being prepared is the best defense against panic during a challenge. Know basic legal definitions and procedures. If a parent complains about an objectionable book his or her child checked out, you will listen much more actively if you have anticipated this type of encounter. If the circulation desk clerk has a folder of legal documents and policies, coupled with a written procedure and good communications skills, he or she is in a far better position when the sheriff pays a surprise visit to remove a book from the library shelves. Some state library association intellectual freedom committees have prepared manuals with applicable laws. When such material is presented in an attractive, authoritative format, the potential censor will at least get the message that this policy is important to the library and that the librarians are well informed.

8. You must obtain staff support for library policies. This includes fellow librarians, who may be unaware of the intellectual freedom implications of certain actions. For example, library staff must understand why they can't tell one patron what another patron has checked out—even if they are neighbors or colleagues. The same applies to the situation in which a senior faculty member tries to bully a freshman work-study student into revealing circulation records. In anticipation of this type of pressure, many academic libraries do not give full system access to student workers. At the very least, all desk personnel must be fully informed about state confidentiality laws and local procedure for challenges to those laws.

9. Never assume that your legal counsel is familiar with specific library court cases or the specific application of laws to libraries. You must be prepared to show him or her the same documents folder you show the local sheriff. The attorney will know the basic legal principles, but not always how they have been applied to libraries. You must be prepared to advocate the intellectual freedom position if the attorney is tempted to take the easy way out of a potential conflict. Many librarians have found themselves poorly served by their attorneys because neither party was knowledgeable about library legal issues. An informed librarian—in conjunction with an attorney who will apply information provided by the librarian—will produce a far better result.

10. Advertise your policies through fora, brochures, your library Web page or other means. Do not be afraid to confront a diversity of opinion in your presentation of the policy, but do offer thoughtful rationale for your stance.

11. Anticipate problems; avoid writing last-minute policies to address a particular crisis.

12. Add regularly to your library's collections on the subject of the Internet and the glories and perils of electronic information. It is a rich literature, covering technical, political and intellectual issues. Be sure to have everything from *Silicon Snake Oil* to *The Virtual Community*.[3] There is certainly a diverse set of views! These holdings will assist your library in formulating policy and anticipating the user community's concerns.

13. When formulating policy for patron misconduct, focus on specific behaviors and how they impact library service. Targeting one person or incident can lead to twisting the law to fit a case, or to writing a narrow policy to fit one person's behavior. Then, if that narrow rule doesn't work with other patrons, the tendency is to add yet another narrow rule. Soon you have a "laundry list." A shrewd patron who is determined to challenge rules will find a loophole. Don't use a policy just to judge or avenge a problem patron.

14. Never assume that your academic colleagues—including your colleagues in the library—are sympathetic or knowledgeable about intellectual freedom issues. Most academic librarians do not focus on these issues, and many library schools cover this topic only to the extent required for accreditation.

In the past, academic librarians may have had reason to view intellectual freedom as a low-priority concern. This can no longer be the case. All the major intellectual freedom issues of the past decade are arguably more applicable to academic libraries than to any other type of library. Issues surrounding the Internet and computer networks would be reason enough, but there are also issues about fee-based services, collections of controversial materials and hate speech. There are ample avenues for academic librarians to get involved at the national, state and local levels. Academic librarians can provide critical support for their colleagues in other types of libraries. A small public library may need book reviews from journals in the local college library. Or an academic librarian may be able to give a supportive interview to the local television news or write a letter to the editor of the local paper. Other good sources of academic expertise are scholars in the fields of journalism, library science and law. Fine arts students and scholars or their works are often targets of censorship, so they are usually very sensitive to these issues as well.

15. Emphasize "rights" first, then "responsibilities." When an issue over computer network use arises, it is often framed by network administrators or other policymakers as "irresponsible use." The rights of the individual user are often ignored. Librarians are professionally obligated to consider the rights of the user, even in situations in which the user is perceived to have abused his or her privileges.

16. Remember that Internet content, in most cases, is legally treated the same as book content. Form your analogies and policies accordingly. For example, if a student is sitting at a crowded library table and is perusing Robert Mapplethorpe books of photographs—offensive to many but probably constitutionally protected speech—would you, the librarian, ask that patron to close the book because the images are bothering the student across the table? If a student at a crowded bank of terminals is accessing Mapplethorpe photos on a Web site and displaying them on the screen, would you ask that patron to close the screen because the images are bothering the user at a neighboring workstation? These types of analogies can be useful when writing Internet policy regarding access, content and privacy. In most cases, your policies should be the same regardless of the format of the information. If your collecting policy includes Mapplethorpe books, then it should probably include Mapplethorpe on the Web.

17. Don't implement your computer center's policy until you study it carefully in conjunction with ALA's intellectual freedom principles.

18. Don't be afraid to say that a particular policy is in flux and is subject to change.

19. Last, but certainly not least, use the legal system only after you have tried less formal means. An example can be drawn from those campuses that decided not to draft hate speech codes. Many of them decided to try a different route—making the campus aware of civility issues through freshman orientation, classroom interaction, role playing or specific reading assignments to help raise student and faculty sensitivity to respect for diversity. Any conflict can be played out in many different ways. Hateful graffiti is one way; a debate in class is another. Preventive measures against abuse of computer networks should begin during student and faculty orientation, in which all network users are warned not to copy software or other copyright-protected material, such as music. At

the same time, network users should be made aware of "netiquette," through required reading on that topic.

NOTES

1. "Before the Censor Comes: Essential Preparations," in *Intellectual Freedom Manual*, 5th ed. (Chicago: ALA, 1996), pp. 197–98.

2. Adapted from *Confidentiality in Libraries: An Intellectual Freedom Modular Education Program*, Module I (Chicago: ALA, 1993), p. 21.

3. The discourse is well represented by such books as Clifford Stoll, *Silicon Snake Oil: Second Thoughts along the Information Highway* (New York: Doubleday, 1995); and Howard Rheingold, *The Virtual Community: Homesteading on the Electronic Frontier* (Reading, Mass.: Addison-Wesley, 1993).

CHAPTER 21

Intellectual Freedom Policies for Information Content

In Cervantes' *Don Quijote*, the barber, the priest, the niece, and the housekeeper argue about which of the mad knight's library books to burn and which to keep.

> "Now this one is something of a mystery, because, according to what I've heard, this was the first of the chivalric stories ever printed in Spain, and all those that came after have had their beginning and very origin in the doctrines of such an evil sect, there's absolutely no reason for not throwing it into the fire—we've got to do it."
>
> "No, sir," said the barber, "because I've also heard it said this is the very best book of chivalry ever composed, and so, because it's a unique specimen of the art, it ought to be pardoned."
>
> "Which is true," said the priest, "and for that reason let's grant it its life, at least for now. Let's have a look at the one standing next to it."[1]

In this age of information overload, librarians are faced with a similar dilemma: what to include in and exclude from the collection—and why. This chapter discusses the development of library policy for content—regardless of format or means of presentation—within the limited public forum. This content could be presented in an exhibit, spoken in a library meeting room, displayed on a computer screen or conveyed to a patron in the course of a reference interview. It could be material owned by the library, borrowed through interlibrary loan or received through a document delivery service. In fact, as more content is shared among public and academic libraries through resource-sharing consortia, the collection policy differences among libraries will blur and be more difficult to control. This situation, combined with economic constraints, is causing many libraries to rethink the traditional concept of collection development.

The most frequently encountered controversies over content involve one or a combination of the following concerns: sexually explicit content; speech that is perceived to be inappropriate or perhaps illegal for minors; speech of questionable scholarship or accuracy; or the special problems surrounding electronic speech.

Writing intellectual freedom policy for this set of content issues should be viewed as an opportunity to expand—not contract—the universe of content available to library users. The Internet and resource-sharing consortia continue to generate the potential for expanded access to information. Instead of creating barriers to restrict or circumscribe that information, librarians should be designing user instruction programs on how to apply critical thinking skills to assess information and to discover the diversity of ideas on the Internet.

It's not that simple, of course. Librarians and users alike complain increasingly about what David Shenk calls "datasmog" in his book of the same name.[2] Though the Supreme Court and other legal experts have stated that Internet content is comparable to other formats, like books, this powerful information source is nonetheless disturbing to many people. Much Internet content is unedited and unverified. The electronic medium is overstimulating for some. Unquestionably, the Internet pushes the envelope; this is exhilarating to some and frightening to others. Internet communication can be viewed as an unprecedented opportunity for the "publishing" of a diversity of opinion, or as an enabling technology for an information glut. A situation like this begs not for censorship, but for an educated society with analytical skills to assess accuracy, relevance and scholarly credibility of information.

The library profession is uniquely qualified to provide leadership in this arena. At the same time, librarians must address many complex questions:

1. How much should I allow my professional assessment of various information resources to affect a reference interview? A lot of Internet resources are junk; shouldn't I alert the library researcher?
2. Instead of buying controversial titles, why not avoid potential conflict by using interlibrary loan to obtain such titles?
3. Given our impossibly tight materials budget, how can I justify buying Professor X's requested list? His field is a controversial, faddish area of questionable scholarly import.

4. How can I live with myself as a feminist if I buy books that condone the subjugation of women?
5. Isn't protecting future generations of children from violence and obscenity a higher ethical good than defending the First Amendment?

If librarians have mixed feelings about these content-related issues, imagine the diversity of opinion among legislators and taxpayers! These constituencies may well feel that they should have more say about a library's content—especially in terms of what the library purchases as permanent holdings. This is likely to be a far more common issue in public libraries than in academe, where legislators and the courts have traditionally assumed the necessity for broader latitude in content. However, higher education has also been under fiscal scrutiny, especially in those units viewed as "money pits"—the library and the computer center. Both provide service with few tangible or measurable outcomes, though statistical analyses are increasingly mandated for such academic service units.

Although a public library is more likely to receive complaints about offensive content in terms of sexually explicit novels or current controversial topics, such as abortion or witchcraft, academic libraries may need to defend content that is sometimes demeaning to certain ethnic or gender groups. This can be a problem in research libraries, since retrospective holdings inevitably contain outdated theories and "evidence" that has been superseded by new research. Academic libraries are always expected to provide balanced views on important scholarly debates. Consider the publication of *Time on the Cross*, which posed a view of slavery so controversial that it was actually covered by the mainstream press.[3]

Although public libraries are more likely to respond to patron demand for current materials and topics, an academic research library must collect retrospectively as well. Given current fiscal restraints and the changing economics of information, all types of libraries are feeling the pressure to be more discerning of each purchase request or subscription renewal. At the same time that they are feeling pressure locally, libraries are probably taking on increased obligations within consortial partnerships to share database licensing costs or to collect in-depth within specifically assigned subject areas.

GENERAL CONSIDERATIONS

The fifth edition of the ALA *Intellectual Freedom Manual* has an excellent chapter, "Development of a Materials Selection Policy," that begins: "The primary purpose of a materials selection or collection development policy is to promote the development of a collection based on institutional goals and user needs. A secondary purpose is defending the principles of intellectual freedom" (see appendix G). Written collection development (selection) policies are an absolute necessity for all types of libraries. Though their approach and strategy will differ widely depending on the particular library's mission, all collecting policies convey to the user community a recognition of fiscal constraints and of the library profession's expertise in making informed choices about collections.

Because there is already a wealth of library literature about collection development and management, this book will not review the entire area. Rather, it will focus on those aspects of a collection development policy that pertain to intellectual freedom.

The first aspect is strategic. A collection development policy, ideally written well before a fiscal or traditional censorship crisis arises, will not be driven by an immediate problem and will thus be far more likely to reflect a big-picture perspective directed at the library's mission. Whether a challenge comes from a faculty senate library committee or from a group of concerned citizens, the presence of a current, comprehensive, written collection development policy that is linked to institutional mission and that is periodically reviewed helps instill user confidence. The librarians taking on the admittedly time-consuming process will gain confidence from the expertise and research that go into such written statements. This background work, it is hoped, will prevent last-minute scrambles for help in crisis situations. Written policy can also reassure special interest groups or campus administrators that the library makes its selections in a businesslike and ethical, and not a frivolous, manner.

The second aspect involves one of the most important components of a selection policy that supports intellectual freedom—the concept of content neutrality in a limited public forum, as explained in sections I and II. The *Intellectual Freedom Manual* suggests this simple statement for collection development policies: "The library serves a traditional role as a public forum for access to the full range of recorded information within the marketplace of ideas. Collection development shall be content neutral so that the library represents significant viewpoints on subjects of interest and does not favor any particular viewpoint."[4]

This statement helps clarify some librarians' misunderstanding of ALA's intellectual freedom position regarding collection development. It does not mean that libraries cannot make choices about purchasing materials and access; physical and fiscal limitations mandate such decision making. It does mean that on any given subject, a diversity of views should be available to the library user. For example, the controversial issue of abortion is likely to be included in most public and academic library collections because of high user interest as well as long-term historical significance. This topic can be represented not only by opinions for and against abortion, but also by viewpoints from diverse fields—religion, medical ethics and feminism, for example. When a library cannot afford or, based on its mission, does not choose to collect this topic in-depth, it should ensure access to at least minimal coverage with diversity of views. Bibliographies, finding aids and access to consortial holdings can supplement user access, but should not be used as a strategy to avoid purchasing controversial materials. Librarians frequently tell stories about interlibrary loan pressure on the single consortial copy owned by the one library courageous enough to buy the controversial book!

Selectors should base purchasing decisions on professional reviews and curricular or user demand, not on their personal biases. Most private academic libraries follow this policy, too—if not because of First Amendment mandates, then because of support for institutional mission and student-faculty demand.

THE PROCESS FOR MAKING COLLECTION AND ACCESS DECISIONS

The process of materials or access selection should be clearly described in the written collection policy. This might include sources for reviews, consortial assignments with accompanying documentation mandating that assignment, user requests and curricular priorities as expressed by the academic institution.

Academic librarians often forget to include with their collecting policy the forms or campus procedural guidelines for adding or dropping curricular areas. Too frequently, faculty curriculum advisory committees, in their zeal to shepherd the requests for new courses through the process, overlook library implications and are angered later when the library cannot support a particular area of study with new journals, monographs and reference materials.

A written procedure should be included for user complaints about particular selection decisions along with a procedure for reviewing and responding to such challenges. Librarians are urged to report *any* First Amendment–related challenges to the ALA Office for Intellectual Freedom.

There should be a written procedure for maintaining collections. This often includes a procedure for permanent withdrawal ("weeding") of library material, which must never be mistaken for a means to remove controversial items from the shelves. "De-selection" criteria must be thoughtfully discussed and carefully implemented, or a public relations disaster could result. The same applies to preservation and conservation decisions. When difficult choices must be made in the face of extremely limited funds for preservation, who performs triage on the titles needing repair, and by what criteria?

In addition to locally applicable documents, the following ALA materials should be cited or included: *The Freedom to Read* statement (appendix F), the *Library Bill of Rights* (appendix C) and at the very least the following Interpretations: "Access to Electronic Information, Services, and Networks"; "Challenged Materials"; "Diversity in Collection Development"; "Evaluating Library Collections"; and "Expurgation of Library Materials" (all in appendix C). If applicable, all statements relating to collections and access for minors should be included as well.

Librarians are advised to pay particular attention to the "Q & A" supplement to the Interpretation on "Access to Electronic Information, Services, and Networks," which includes the following explanation:

> Selection begins with the institution's mission and objectives. The librarian performs an initial selection from available resources, and then the user makes a choice from that collection. Many electronic resources, such as CDs, are acquired for the library's collection in this traditional manner. Collections consist of fixed discrete items.
>
> When libraries provide Internet access, they provide a means for people to use the wealth of information stored on computers throughout the world, whose ever-changing contents are created, maintained and made available beyond the library. The library also provides a means for the individual user to choose for him- or herself the resources accessed and to interact electronically with other computer users throughout the world.[5]

Increasingly, librarians will find it more difficult to define an institution's "collection" in the traditional manner. This is an important consideration for the overall policy as well as for the potential issues it raises for those legislators and other policy players who expect libraries to have more control over content than may be possible in the "access not ownership" environment.

If one reviews the major components of a collection development policy that will best support intellectual freedom, it is clear that such a policy serves other admirable purposes as well. Carefully outlining selection criteria, for example, is an important first step toward curriculum evaluation and prioritizing as well as assuring collection diversity. Written preservation policy decisions could lead to more preservation funding if the triage data are collected and used strategically to prove need. And, such a policy communicates to trustees or faculty that the library is making decisions in a planned fashion. This can only instill overall confidence in the library operation and help the library gain support in intellectual freedom–related or other challenges to its collection content or fiscal decisions.

SEXUALLY EXPLICIT CONTENT

One of the primary complaints librarians hear from legislators and the general public concerns sexually explicit content, including multimedia materials and the Internet. Implicit in Supreme Court Justice Potter Stewart's famous declaration, "I know it when I see it," is the fact that the perception of indecent or offensive literature differs among cultures in significant ways. This is particularly true within the diverse United States population. That is why the Supreme Court, aside from trying to establish a definition of "obscenity" in *Miller* (see chapter 7) has consistently relegated to the states any enactment of obscenity legislation. Further, as explained in section II, the courts have specified that even a state's determination of what is obscene is often left to the "local community standards" of jurors to apply to the particular title or work under litigation.

Thus there is no concrete, nationwide definition of obscenity. For librarians, of course, this can pose real problems for interlibrary loan among communities and states, where standards vary. A further problem relates to differentiating obscenity from "harmful to minors" statutes and determining potential liability for librarians, though some state statutes specifically exempt such institutions as libraries and museums.

The legal environment for obscenity legislation and litigation is detailed in section II. Essential distinctions in terminology (for example, *obscenity* versus *pornography* versus *indecent literature*) as well as principles and precedents are included. Such background will be helpful as librarians develop policy and work with legal counsel who, to the surprise of some librarians, are often relatively unaware of how the First Amendment applies to specific library issues. It is also helpful to know which words describing sexually explicit material have a legal definition and which are emotionally charged but have no meaning in the courts.

It is crucial that librarians monitor current legislative and judicial efforts to filter Internet content with the purpose of protecting minors from offensive material. Because this particular legal environment is volatile, librarians are urged to consult ALA's Office for Intellectual Freedom for the latest developments on how to interpret and apply current laws—or the lack thereof—to specific locales.

The U.S. Supreme Court overturned the Communications Decency Act while ALA was holding its 1997 annual summer conference. In many instances, ALA committees simply continued their agendas without interruption, since the final decision so closely matched the ACLU/ALA arguments before the Court. Those arguments will be covered in chapter 22. Most important was the much-hoped-for determination that the Internet is to be treated, in the eyes of the law, as a platform for content—content with the same level of constitutional protection as books and other formats. Further, the Internet is not to be treated like radio or other communications media regulated by the Federal Communications Commission (FCC). This decision, of course, may be revisited as technology changes. The industry predicts that the general public will soon use one monitor for everything from e-mail to full text to television programs. The most concise yet comprehensive overview of the technology is actually found not in the Supreme Court's final decision, but in that of the United States District Court for the Eastern District of Pennsylvania (929 F.Suppl. 824 [1996]), to which the final decision defers in many of the sections describing Internet technology. Policies regarding Internet content should be written with this evolving technology in mind.

The American Library Association, its ACLU co-plaintiff, state associations and other interest groups generally supportive of freedom of expression on the Internet are continuing their commitment to oppose any efforts to abridge First Amendment rights on the Internet. Opposition groups are continuing their fight to force the filtering of public access terminals, especially those available to children. Much energy, in fact, is now being focused toward the filtering option, and librarians should become aware of what that technology can and cannot achieve regarding the abridging of content.[6] Appendix H provides the ALA stand on policies regarding Internet filters.

In obscenity litigation, both sides utilize social scientific research, and updated or new conceptual data are always welcome. There is always a need to analyze the link between reading, viewing or listening, and action. Does movie content that debases women lead viewers to commit violent actions toward women? Do children's books with hilarious but dangerous pranks cause "copy-cat" actions? Further, how does one interpret and analyze data in this field? Research is needed in the new area of analyzing the effectiveness of software filters for content. Can filters, for example, distinguish between legally protected and unprotected speech?

"Common ground" issues are especially helpful tools for reaching consensus on some of the difficult issues surrounding materials perceived to be obscene. Librarians, probably more than any other group, know the dark side of the Internet and other materials, because they use the Internet so often and browse reviews and bookstore shelves as well as their own library holdings. They can certainly sympathize with other parents who are concerned about the kinds of information that their children might find, especially on the Internet. ALA has never opposed child pornography legislation unless such laws include, in their overbreadth, speech that is protected under the First Amendment. When communicating with the general public about this sensitive issue, a clear distinction should be made between legislation against child pornography and "harmful to minors" legislation, the latter of which does sometimes cover speech that might be constitutionally protected.

In most cases, however, librarians will encounter challenges to speech that are protected by the First Amendment—offensive to many, but nonetheless protected. The CDA decision leaves a legal ambiguity. The Court suggests that the filtering of content for minors be left to parental discretion; yet, without filters on public access library terminals, minors could theoretically search and retrieve legally obscene material (though the Supreme Court decision states that it is difficult to find such material). Librarians must remain alert to the treatment of this legal dilemma in the courts and decide on appropriate library policies for the interim.

Don't Ban—Balance!

The library profession's intellectual freedom principles mirror the courts' distinctions regarding obscenity. In other words, ALA distinguishes obscenity, which is unprotected by the First Amendment, from materials that may be perceived as "pornographic," "indecent" or "offensive" to some, but may be constitutionally protected. The library profession's approach to material that is legal but offensive to some has been *not* to establish barriers against it, but to balance that type of speech with other types of information and views. This policy is actually based on the theory of "more speech," first promulgated by Justice Louis Brandeis. The philosophy underlying intellectual freedom has always been to expand the universe of information potentially available to users. Then the diversity of information will be put to the test in the "marketplace of ideas," a judicial theory first set forth by Oliver Wendell Holmes in 1919.[7] Library users who want assistance in navigating this growing mass of information can turn to professional librarians for help. Here is the opportunity to institute a high-quality user instruction program empowering users to apply their own critical skills in evaluating information resources.

Of course, parents are free to filter Internet resources on their home computers. And librarians can recommend, but not prescribe, appropriate Internet sites in the same way they might recommend a book that has received favorable reviews. This kind of outreach on the part of librarians underscores another American Library Association principle—that parents, not librarians, should determine the reading and study habits of young children. Librarians should not use personal doctrinal biases to exclude library materials from purchase or use. This refusal to act *in loco parentis*, when presented in those terms, often resonates with parents.

Other common ground, especially on a college campus or in a public library with a particularly diverse clientele, can be found in understanding that the concept "offensive" varies immensely from culture to culture. Linking that respect for diversity to the library's diverse collections may be part of a successful strategy in working with campus or community decision makers.

Crafting a Policy regarding Sexually Explicit Materials

In crafting policy for sexually explicit materials, the first question should be whether a specific policy is necessary at all. If the library has a collection development policy offering a process for user complaint, and if the policy integrates legal requirements with professional values, that is the most important defense against any challenge of any content. The unanswered question, of course, concerns the Internet and the legality of filtering. In this rapidly changing environment, it seems reasonable to state in the collection development policy or Internet access policy that "some users might find material that is offensive to them." That is most likely the case with speech in any public forum. The library could also add a statement assuring users that a librarian would be happy to assist a dissatisfied patron in locating alternative resources. A good-faith attempt to address obscenity concerns in a written Internet policy, even if that policy may evolve with upcoming court decisions, could be helpful. The danger in this situation, however, is the tendency to be overly cautious and inadvertently censor constitutionally protected speech.

In any case, the absence of a specific policy regarding obscenity does not excuse a librarian from being thoroughly grounded in the relevant state and local laws. Obscenity policy or not, the following information should be kept in a "just in case" folder. (There is an underlying assumption that a written collection development policy is already in place.)

1. The federal obscenity standard (as of this writing, it is in *Miller*).
2. The federal obscenity statute.
3. The state obscenity statute, if any.
4. The state "harmful to minors" statute, if any.
5. The state "child pornography" statute, if any.
6. Any applicable local ordinances.
7. For all of the above, an assessment from legal counsel regarding the extent to which libraries, librarians or the college or university are liable to or exempt from lawsuits involving First Amendment issues. Often the phrase "knowingly provide" is used to exempt librarians who unwittingly give a patron constitutionally unprotected information.
8. Any library enactment legislation, bylaws or statutes with the force of law.
9. For academic libraries, any campus policies pertaining to free speech on campus. Talk with legal counsel to make sure that these campus policies are consistent with those of the library. This is particularly important in regard to hate speech and campus network use policies.
10. A local environmental scan of special interest group positions on censorship of controversial content. This should also include any local newspaper coverage, including small presses, on all sides of the issue. Librarians should have a network of supporters to call upon in time of crisis. They should always include a telephone call or an e-mail to the Office for Intellectual Freedom, not only to receive moral support, but to report the incident for the OIF's

nationwide database. It is hoped this kind of groundwork will have been laid long before a crisis arises!

11. Any statements by network systems administrators regarding their policies on offensive material on the Internet and the type of disciplinary action taken in suspected cases of abuse.
12. Any consortial agreements or commitments that mandate collecting in certain areas for the common good of the partnership. This should be appended to the collection development policy.
13. Any pending legislation or court cases that the library is monitoring, with periodic updates entered into the folder.
14. In the case of a private institution, the applicability of local and state obscenity statutes.
15. All applicable ALA policy and *Library Bill of Rights* material.
16. Citations or copies of professional reviews from respected journals in the particular field for any acquisitions that have a controversial history.
17. Procedures for all staff to follow in case law enforcement officials attempt to confiscate material, access patron records, present a court order or arrest a patron. This should include procedures for apprehending (or not) a library user who is suspected of book theft and appears in the library.
18. A clear ruling from the library attorney about when, if at all, the display of offensive material crosses the line of constitutionally protected speech and becomes harassment of a patron or library employee.

Because so much of the above discussion applies not only to sexually explicit material, the library may in the end decide to integrate that type into the overall collecting policy. Regardless, it is important to raise staff awareness about the problem of library materials deemed offensive to some. This could be done in a formal presentation or through role-playing sessions, followed by discussion. A comment frequently made during the interviews for this book was that some library job seekers assume that libraries are sheltered environments. They are often shocked and unhappy to discover the extent to which speech of all kinds is not only protected but promoted. It is important in job interviews to tell candidates about the nature of the limited public forum in regard to free speech.

It is also important to respond to any potential threats to the library's collecting policy. If, for example, a well-meaning local couple begins a campaign against indecent literature, letters to the editor, using very affirmative statements about library service, might be in order. If the campus women's studies program presents a debate or campus forum on the impact of pornography on women's rights, a librarian reflecting the intellectual freedom perspective should be part of the mix.

CHILDREN IN THE LIMITED PUBLIC FORUM: LIBRARY CONTENT, ACCESS AND PRIVACY CONCERNS

Surely the most emotionally charged and legally complex dilemma in today's intellectual freedom arena relates to minors and free speech. Despite the multitude of sensationalist newspapers in the supermarket checkout line, and despite the often surprising magazine content found in pediatricians' waiting rooms, libraries have become the lightning rod for society's concerns that its youth will be harmed by exposure to uncensored information. Academic librarians are facing this phenomenon increasingly as freshmen get younger and younger. It must be underscored again that this book and ALA policy focus on constitutionally protected speech. Child pornography statutes exist in almost all states, and ALA has never opposed these statutes. The issue is whether to extend legislation dealing with sexually explicit materials to speech that currently is legally protected and sometimes accessible to minors. A further dilemma is how to provide unfettered access to adults, as mandated by the CDA decision, and still protect children from speech that may be legally obscene for them under state statute.

As explained in section II, it has long been established legally that minors have a right to receive information (see especially *Tinker* v. *Des Moines Independent School District*, 393 U.S. 503 [1969]). In fact, minors have sued for these rights (see *Pico* v. *Board of Education*, 638 F.2d 404 [2d Cir. 1980]). Both *Pico* and *Tinker*, interestingly, are school cases, in which courts have often ruled that, in contrast with university or public librarians, K–12 administrators have more control of information content and student conduct because of the primacy of the curriculum. Even so, some cases have argued that older minors (adolescents) should be considered adults for purposes of the right to receive information.

Traditionally, public libraries have dealt with access to minors by segregating collections and services. This arrangement has major advantages in terms of space design, furnishings and reference service geared to young people's information needs. ALA's youth divisions have never opposed this segregation, as long as children and adults were free to move among all parts of the library, regardless of content of various collections. Adolescents are frequently on the cusp of library collections and services and need to avail themselves of both youth and adult materials.

Academic libraries have rarely attempted to divide or offer different levels of services because the vast majority of their users have been adults. This is changing for two reasons. Many academic libraries, including private ones, are serving increasing numbers of high school students (and even younger) as public and school libraries cut staff, services and collections. Advanced Placement (AP) courses, better public access terminals and increasingly rigorous high school curricula send these students to community college and university libraries for specialized journals and reference works and services. Summer institutes for gifted and talented youth often hold regular sessions in the host university's library.

Although admittedly the Internet and the accompanying filtering controversy have muddied the waters, some librarians and members of the general public do not appreciate the legal and professional policy support young people should be afforded when using library services and collections. These rights of library access for minors are based on constitutional rights, on ALA policy and on *Library Bill of Rights* Interpretations, some of which have been on the books for decades. Some of these are cited in section II, and most are format neutral. The American Library Association and its youth divisions have, since the late 1960s, supported policies granting minors equitable access to quality library service and materials. These same youth advocates are in the forefront of protecting the rights of minors in regard to Internet access.

It must also be emphasized that ALA policies are the result not only of extensive research but also of librarians' professional expertise and experience working with children and young adults to meet their information and recreational needs. An account of this ongoing commitment to children's services on the part of ALA is summarized in the "Free Access to Libraries for Minors" chapter in the *Intellectual Freedom Manual.*

Content Policy for Minors

For content-based issues related to minors, an absolute foundation is a written collection policy. General guidelines are found in chapter 20, "Writing and Implementing Good Policy"; additional suggestions are found in the

"General Considerations" and "Sexually Explicit Content" sections of this chapter. For youth collections, the policy should explain the materials selection process for children and young adults, and it is imperative to collect and have at hand those reviews (in professional and library sources) that informed the library's choices. This precaution doesn't immunize a library from challenges to certain titles, but it does help garner support and credibility should a case arise. Do not fall into the trap of guaranteeing that certain subject headings or areas—"nudity," for example—won't be found in the library's children's collections. Contemporary art and biology books alone make that an impossible assurance. Further, even the courts have stated that it is unconstitutional to prohibit such broad categories of content.

The library's complaint-response process should be applicable to children's materials. Several librarians interviewed for this book suggested that when talking with distraught parents, it is important to discuss the offending book as a whole so that the context is considered. Also, some libraries hold reading groups for parents, children and librarians to review together potentially controversial material and to raise awareness of what children are reading. This is a particularly successful way to introduce a book that the librarian believes, based on the community profile, might pose problems.

In addition to a collection development policy, the library should have the following material in that "just in case" folder (which includes a written collection development policy!):

1. All federal, state and local laws and court decisions applying to children in libraries. See the general list in the "Crafting a Policy regarding Sexually Explicit Materials" section of this chapter. Include any "child pornography," "harmful to minors" and "obscenity" statutes.
2. The latest professional advice, updated regularly, from ALA regarding minors and the Internet. Filtering legislation and litigation are prime concerns.
3. Any supporting documents or research from such professional organizations as the National Council of Teachers of English and other groups focused on children's reading. Documentation should include book reviews supporting the library's selection decisions for children's materials.
4. Any research offprints showing the impact of reading—or viewing media—on children. Don't limit the material to the "copycat"

theme. Also collect information showing, for example, that children's grades improve as a result of recreational reading.

5. ALA policies pertaining to children's collections, access and privacy, including: "Access for Children and Young People to Videotapes and Other Nonprint Formats"; "Free Access to Libraries for Minors"; and Article V of the *Library Bill of Rights:* "A person's right to use a library should not be denied or abridged because of origin, age, background, or views."

Filtering Internet Content

> Spending time online with your child is one of the best ways to learn and to teach responsibility, good conduct and values that are important to you. The best way to ensure your child's safety on the Internet is to be there.[8]

It is clear from court transcripts and from general public reaction that the software filter issue is a children's issue. Filtering software technology and the related legal climate are both evolving. Librarians considering filters—or being pressured to consider filters—should contact the Office for Intellectual Freedom for advice. Librarians should be aware that there is legal precedent for minors suing for the alleged loss of their First Amendment rights. Most important is that in some of the cases previously cited, older adolescents have been distinguished from younger minors and treated more like adults.

Even in this highly emotional arena there is common ground, especially regarding *in loco parentis.* Most American parents, in this age of widely diverse parenting values and styles, do not want a librarian or any other extension of government to determine their children's learning. The rise of alternative schools and the home-schooling movement is witness to this trend. It is for this reason that the well-meaning values clarification movement in public schools has been treated with such cautious support by all types of special interest groups. Children's librarians have long resisted any suggestion of a role *in loco parentis.* As the "Free Access to Libraries for Minors" Interpretation states:

> The mission, goals, and objectives of libaries do not authorize librarians or governing bodies to assume, abrogate, or overrule the rights and responsibilities of parents or legal guardians. Librarians and governing bodies should maintain that parents—and only parents—have the right and the responsibility to restrict the access of their children—and only their children—to library resources. Parents or legal guardians who do not want their children to have access to certain

library services, materials, or facilities, should so advise their children. Librarians and governing bodies cannot assume the role of parents or the functions of parental authority in the private relationship between parent and child.[9]

The Supreme Court related parental rights to Internet filters in its CDA decision, which clearly states that filters are tools for use in the home. The legal status of filters in publicly funded libraries is uncertain; librarians are urged to contact ALA's Office for Intellectual Freedom for updated information.

The recent decision in the *Mainstream Loudoun* case suggests that the courts are going to strike down the use of filters on library terminals except, perhaps, when a library offers both filtered and unfiltered access. Following is a partial summary of the latest *Loudoun* decision as presented to the Freedom to Read Foundation Board by their counsel, Jenner & Block:

On November 23, 1998, the district court held that the Loudoun County Public Library filtering policy was unconstitutional. As part of its ruling, the district court concluded that the Loudoun County Public Library was a limited public forum for the purpose of the expressive activities provided by the library, including the receipt and communication of information through the Internet.[10] The district court thus held that because the Loudoun policy placed restrictions on receipt and communication in a limited public forum based on content of that information, it could only be upheld if it was necessary to serve a compelling state interest and was narrowly drawn to achieve that interest.[11]

Applying that test, the district court held that the Loudoun County library had asserted two compelling interests: minimizing access to illegal pornography and avoidance of a sexually hostile environment.[12] In order to support its argument that the policy was necessary to prevent creation of a hostile work environment, the defendant library board relied on the fact that (1) one patron in a different Virginia public library system had complained that a boy was viewing what she believed to be pornography (thereafter remedied by the use of privacy screens); and (2) that there were three isolated incidents of harassment in Los Angeles, Florida and Austin, Texas. The district court held that these incidents were insufficient to support the claim that the policy was necessary.

The district court also held that even if the library board could demonstrate that the policy were reasonably necessary to further their compelling interests, the library board could achieve that interest with less-restrictive means, such as: (1) privacy screens; (2) library staff monitoring of Internet use, which the district court found to be a method used to enforce other library policies; (3) filtering software installed on some Internet terminals with minors limited to

> using those terminals; and (4) filtering software installed on all terminals and turned off when adults use the terminals.[13] The district court cautioned: "While we find that all of these alternatives are less restrictive than the policy, we do not find that any of them would necessarily be constitutional if implemented."[14]

Although it is not clear if there will be further appeals, this case should be required reading for any library being pressured to install filters on its terminals. The *Loudoun* decision not only declares that filtered terminals are unconstitutional, but also implies that even lesser solutions (such as installing filters to be turned off for adult use of terminals) might be unconstitutional, too.

Several state library associations have issued policies regarding filtering, and most reflect the liberal stance of the *Loudoun* decision. Librarians are urged to consult the OIF Web site for the most current information regarding filtering software on library terminals.

Access Policy for Minors

ALA's previously cited access policies apply across the board for minors. Exceptions occur when states have declared that certain materials legal for adults are "harmful to minors." Librarians need to be aware of these distinctions as applicable in their locale. Otherwise, ALA has always advocated that although a separate children's room is acceptable, minors who wish to access adult materials should be able to do so. Parents, not librarians, will be responsible for what their children read. Any restrictions on children's library access should be determined by parents, not librarians. This principle should be included at the beginning of any policies relating to children's access.

Library access policy for minors applies to all formats of information. This has been clarified in various *Library Bill of Rights* Interpretations. There are, of course, ongoing legal cases involving the Internet, and librarians should check with legal counsel. But they should also be reassured by the fact that many public libraries around the country are providing no-charge, nonfiltered Internet access for adults and minors alike. The Office for Intellectual Freedom can help librarians identify model libraries and policies.

The policy on children's Internet use could be constructed in two ways—as part of a general access policy or as part of a specific policy for children's access to libraries. Librarians should think about which approach would best apply to their situation. Academic libraries might not need such a policy, with the caveat that growing numbers of minors, as registered students or not, are using nearby college and university libraries.

An ideal complement to a children's Internet access policy is a document similar to the Illinois Library Association's *Cyberguide for Kids and Parents.* This four-page guide celebrates "the most innovative and exciting learning tool of the century," but also provides parents with definitions and "safety tips" (acknowledging that like the real world, the virtual world "contains some sites with sexual, violent, or other content that may not be appropriate for children"). There are predators who try to abduct children by setting up rendezvous over the Internet. This is a crime and children should know to report such threats to an adult, just as they would let a librarian or parent know if they were being stalked by a library patron. The ILA guide contains a list of more than eighty "Great Web Sites." These sites include everything from the Illinois State Police to "Sports Illustrated for Kids." This kind of document conveys the educational value of the Internet and automatically answers the question: Why does a library need the Internet for kids anyway?

The access policy for children should reflect the same positive tone. The policy itself should contain:

1. The library's mission for serving youth.
2. References to the *Cyberguide for Kids and Parents* or similar type of document prepared locally or regionally.
3. Information on whether the library's terminals are filtered, unfiltered or both. A parent can then decide if his or her child should go to the library alone or only accompanied by a parent. It should be emphasized that librarians do not act *in loco parentis.*
4. Emphasis on the importance of parents working with their children, not only to monitor their child's access, but also to enhance that access to information by using a format that most kids find fascinating and engaging—the Internet.
5. A statement, authorized by the library's legal counsel, that prohibits use of library equipment to access material that is legally defined as obscene, harmful to minors or child pornography.

Although the law in this area is still being developed, a library stands on far firmer ground with its user community and other officials if that library has demonstrated its awareness of community concern and its good-faith effort to comply with statutory obligations by posting a thoughtful written policy.

One informal solution to computer use problems is to group terminals in different arrangements if you have multiple terminals and lots of space. Some can be banked near a reference desk so that personal assistance is readily available. Some could have privacy screens or recessed screens. Some could be multiple-user workstations, while others could be single-user machines. Such diversity helps address the problem of users being offended by a neighbor's legal but nonetheless offensive screen display.

Remember that any suspected illegal behavior, such as destroying the hardware or software intentionally, should be handled by law enforcement officials, not librarians.

Privacy Policy for Minors

It is important to remember that the courts have upheld certain rights for children in regard to privacy and access to library resources. State confidentiality of library records laws apply to children as well, unless specified. Therefore, ALA has said that a librarian should not reveal circulation records to a parent or teacher or anyone else. While ALA supports this stance, the law is still being developed in this area, and there may be exceptions in regard to parents having access to children's information. Your policy will depend on whether you want to emphasize children's rights to privacy as part of a larger privacy policy or not.

Summary

In addressing issues of children in libraries, you must decide whether you wish to create a separate policy for children or to include children in a broader policy statement. In either case, you need to know that in the areas of content, access and privacy, the library profession continues to move in the direction of age-neutral policies. However, there are "harmful to minors" statutes and you need to know your state's laws in this regard. There may also be privacy laws giving parents certain rights. Further, you need to keep up-to-date on the unresolved issue of filters on public access terminals. The Supreme Court has said that content that is protected for adults cannot be abridged for the sake of minors. While navigating in these uncertain waters, you should know that many of your colleagues are offering unfiltered Internet access to minors successfully by offering supplemental information about kid-friendly sites and encouraging the parents to become involved. They follow the law, supported by written policies and a user-friendly, responsive environment.

The American Library Association's thirty-year stance on library services for minors is supported by the principal education associations in the United States, including the influential National Council of Teachers of English. All these organizations conduct or consider research on the impact of media on children. And although some research suggests a negative impact of television violence on children, it is not enough to motivate any teachers' or librarians' associations to revert to the days when children's library service was characterized by some as repressive.[15]

The very fact that the world is a more dangerous place, with more explicit and intense visual and aural expression, is all the more reason for libraries to provide information so that young adults, especially, gain the knowledge and critical skills to navigate in this environment. Recently, at a library conference, a high school librarian reported that a class came into the library to do "mermaid" reports that utilized the Web for at least some of the research. One can imagine the diversity of sites: from mythology and New Age religion to sexual fantasy. The librarian used this opportunity to teach the class how to evaluate each resource as appropriate to the assignment at hand. There were no protests or angry parents—just a class whose reports and learning experience were most certainly enhanced by the librarian grabbing this "teachable moment." Such professional approaches to the Internet and other resources will give children far better library experiences—not to mention life skills—than an Internet filter ever could.

Many libraries encourage their readers to suggest, in a provided journal or on cards, books they have enjoyed and recommend. This kind of unsolicited comment on books not only is a helpful informal selection tool, but it also communicates to the public that they have an impact on the library's selections. Such reader feedback can be a helpful indication of the pulse of the community regarding their library information and recreational needs.

CONTENT PERCEIVED TO LACK SCHOLARLY VALUE, ACCURACY OR LEGITIMACY

A common issue on college campuses in recent years has been the debate surrounding the "canon"—those works seen by traditionalists as the essential background of a college-educated person, but seen by others as an outdated assumption that all people should study the same thing. Critics believe that the canon tends to emphasize Western culture and white men. This furious debate has led to such related issues as "political correctness," or "PC." This term is used pejoratively by traditionalists, whose opponents reject the canon in order to include works and ideas by women and non-Western cultures. Critics of PC believe that diversity for its own sake has compromised the quality of the curriculum in the name of trendiness. This has also been described as part of the "culture wars," the title of James Hunter's influential book.[16]

Many believe that the culture wars and PC debate was sparked by Allan Bloom and Dinesh D'Souza, both of whom wrote books out of their concern that leftist thought was taking over campus discourse.[17] Although most PC critics concede that a college education should be open to all regardless of race, class or gender, many believe that individual merit should be the admission criterion, not group affirmative action. The same should hold true, they argue, for curricular topics and content, which should be based on quality and importance of the topic, not on what is fashionable. They argue that if left to chance, most campuses, including their libraries, tend to focus on liberal content and ideas, given the leftist bias of academe.

Several academics weighed in on this topic in "The Many Faces of Political Correctness," featured in *Educational Record.* Judith Eaton characterized the debate in this way: "One group believes that we must be coerced in order to be equitable; the other believes we need to be influenced to do what is right and then be left alone." She ironically tries to find common ground: "In two areas, the groups are on common ground. Their tolerance level for one another's ideas and issues is so low that civil discourse—to which both groups give much lip service—is infrequent. They also display an extraordinary distrust of each other. The 'politically correct' (PC) are convinced that the 'politically incorrect' (non-PC) seek only to retain the racism and sexism that characterize some of society. Conservatives are convinced that the liberal opposition is so committed to race and gender equity that it is willing to sacrifice fundamental American principles, including individual liberty and fairness."[18]

Of all the contributors, Yale's Benno Schmidt was the most insistent that freedom of expression be maintained on a campus, PC or not:

> Thus, universities themselves must summon up the clarity of purpose to defend the principles of liberty on which the academic mission rests. Perhaps the most important lesson universities can teach their students is to think and to search for truth in freedom. For most students, this lesson is not easy. They come to universities with little or no understanding of the theory and practice of freedom of thought. . . .

> Such pressures are perennial; what is troubling is how little academic values and principles are pushing back against these pressures in many universities. The problems of freedom on our campuses are thus part and parcel of a much larger problem on our campuses and throughout the larger society. It is hard to adhere to principle in a society (or an institution) that doubts its fundamental purposes. Adherence to principle requires a long view, and universities and their members are subjected to the hydraulic pressures of immediacy characteristic of our frenetic time. Moreover, universities have become the anvil on which young people—and often old, as well—beat out their resentments at the incompleteness of life. The economic and political insecurities of universities, from within and without, have produced a style of academic leadership that is averse to risk, queasy about defending academic values, and inclined to negotiate and propitiate about almost anything.
>
> Thus on some campuses there is little institutional resistance to growing pressure to suppress and to punish, rather than to answer, speech that offends notions of civility and community. These campuses are heedless of the oldest lesson in the history of freedom of expression, that offensive, erroneous, and obnoxious speech is the price of freedom. Offensive speech cannot be suppressed under open-ended standards without letting loose an engine of censorship that cannot be controlled.[19]

Other contemporary academics aren't so sure. In another anthology, such scholars as Henry Louis Gates Jr., Cass Sunstein and Edward Said discuss hate speech and other campus First Amendment problems. Some of them are hostile toward what they consider the "absolutist" position of some of their colleagues toward free speech, and contest the concept of content neutrality.[20]

Many academics renounce the scholarship of such Africanists as Leonard Jeffries, who was embroiled in controversy at City College of New York for anti-Semitic remarks and scholarship some believe is based on folklore rather than scholarly documentation. Librarians often add this controversial material to the collection, making sure to provide alternative views. The details of this and other controversies are well covered in *History on Trial: Culture Wars and the Teaching of the Past*, in which the authors also recount the attempt by the National Endowment for the Humanities to set voluntary standards in various academic disciplines to be applied to K–12 curricula.[21]

Here, despite the heat of the argument, there is some common ground among academics, and many academic librarians have successfully weathered the storm when they added controversial books to the collection. As with other controversial materials, politicians and faculty alike have been more accepting of the necessity of academic libraries collecting a variety of points of view. But with budgets so limited, there have been inevitable challenges, and librarians need to be prepared.

In the legal arena, most of the activity surrounding this issue has been directed toward group versus individual freedom. Some of the hate speech codes were overturned because the Supreme Court still bases speech decisions on the First Amendment, which protects individual speech and does not necessarily condemn speech that offends a particular group. Libraries, in sum, are still on firm First Amendment ground here. This is, of course, Catharine MacKinnon's complaint—that the First Amendment does not protect such oppressed groups as women, and that words do, indeed, hurt and should be controlled in some cases. But her point of view has not prevailed in the courts.

The American Library Association has made its position clear—in favor of balanced collections with diverse views. The *Intellectual Freedom Manual* offers suggestions on writing a collection policy. And librarians have never been responsible for the "truth" or content of materials purchased. It is, however, extremely tempting in an age of limited resources to dodge the issue in the name of money. We should all be aware of that tendency. At the same time, it is true that no research library can collect in the breadth and depth it once did.

It does seem, however, that the library should collect representative content for controversial new areas of scholarship and certainly books in demand for the current curriculum. Today's "trend" may well endure. Witness the field of gender studies. Those who want to buy retrospectively in the area of women's studies may find that early material is now prohibitively expensive. One could also argue that if some faculty members focus on cutting-edge scholarship, the library should balance it with "politically incorrect" ideas that may not be in fashion now, but may well reappear. Students should find refuge in one campus institution dedicated to preserving balanced views on all sides of a controversy. If a local classics department, for example, is so opposed to *Black Athena* that it will not present the topic in class, then the library should be doubly sure to buy that controversial title.[22]

In fact, the "culture wars" provide a rich opportunity for library programming—controversial speakers, panel discussions, exhibits. A rare book library with a "Little Black Sambo" collection might sponsor a panel discussion among children's literature specialists with diverse views. In a complementary exhibit, the narrative or objects could include the view opposing the collecting of books perceived today as racist.

Librarians should continue to strive for balance and diversity of collections, being sensitive to major controversies in which all sides should be represented. No separate policy about controversial materials is needed if the collection development policy is sound and ALA statements about diversity of views are heeded.

One of the most painful subjects that public and academic librarians alike have faced is Holocaust denial literature. Here is a case in which the deniers are members of organizations with anti-Semitic political agendas. Their often convoluted and politically motivated arguments are frustrating to anyone trained in traditional scholarly research methods.

It seems that libraries should consider meeting such challenges head-on. A good source of information with many perspectives represented is a panel discussion on the topic "Controversial Materials in the Jewish Library," which took place at the annual convention of the Association of Jewish Libraries in June 1986. Most libraries with any Jewish studies or history collecting responsibility would purchase at least a representative sampling of Holocaust denial literature. Many, however, would use catalog copy or separate shelving to segregate this literature from other Holocaust history. The discourse surrounding this difficult problem can be applied to any type of scholarship that is considered substandard by a majority of researchers in that field.

Skidmore College took an interesting approach to the ideas of Holocaust deniers. When the school newspaper received a requst, along with a check, to print an ad by a Holocaust denier (Committee for Open Debate on the Holocaust), staff members announced in an editorial that instead of printing the ad by itself, the paper would publish a special investigatory issue—"Why Are Holocaust Deniers Targeting College Campuses?"—and include the Holocaust denial ad as part of that issue. The editorial warned the campus to expect the special issue and that it might offend some readers. On April 21, 1994, the issue was published and received notice on National Public Radio. In addition, the American Jewish Committee printed 2,000 copies of the issue and sent one to the library of every four-year college in the United States.

Although this project was not related to the library, the editors' strategy could be adapted to controversial library materials. Instead of shying away from a controversial book, a library can arrange an exhibit around that book, including materials that oppose it. This highlights the library's commitment to intellectual freedom.

SAMPLE OUTLINE FOR POLICIES ON CONTENT

The following summary is a guide and may be adapted to fit your library's profile and needs. Librarians are urged to consult their legal counsel before distributing this or any policy with First Amendment implications. Remember, too, that the planning and follow-up stages are just as important as the policy itself. Implementation and operational procedures should accompany all policies.

Collection Development Policy

A current collection development policy is a library's basic document for decision making in the area of content. This policy should (1) reflect the library's mission, curricular or community needs and reader demand; and (2) promote intellectual freedom by incorporating the concepts in the following section. Numerous ALA groups and publications, including the *Intellectual Freedom Manual*, offer guidelines on how to write collection development policies that incorporate intellectual freedom–friendly principles.

Intellectual Freedom Concepts to Include

1. Selection is not necessarily censorship. Accompanied by a good collection development policy, selection of library materials demonstrates fiscal responsibility and recognition of the user community's priorities.
2. Selection becomes censorship when the library decides against a particular item—*even though it satisfies all the collection development policy criteria*—because:
   a. The material offends the librarian or other selector.
   b. The material is politically incorrect and might cause controversy.
   c. The material is sexually explicit but constitutionally protected.
   d. The material might be offensive to a particular age group, but is constitutionally protected.
   e. A faculty member or group, or a prominent community member or group, applies political pressure.

3. Decision-making criteria for selecting, weeding, and preserving materials should include sensitivity for maintaining a balanced and diverse collection.
4. Criteria for selecting materials should be format neutral. For example, the same intellectual freedom principles apply to a given photo, whether it is in a book or on the Internet. All formats should be included in the collection development policy.
5. Filtering Internet content on library public access terminals may unconstitutionally limit children's rights to access, not to mention those of adults. Legislation and litigation are pending and librarians must contact the Office for Intellectual Freedom for the latest information.
6. Selection doesn't preclude patron access to other information through the Internet, interlibrary loan or document delivery. If a request clearly does not fit into the library's collection development guidelines, the librarian should assist the patron in obtaining the material elsewhere. Interlibrary loan should never be used as a tactic for avoiding the purchase of a controversial book.
7. Selection should be age appropriate. Minors should be permitted to consult adult as well as juvenile holdings.
8. Sometimes a library will purchase a book perceived by some to lack scholarly value or to contain outdated or false information. The book may be requested for controversial research or course work; it may have garnered media attention and thus generated student or community demand; or it may be a retrospective purchase used to trace the history of a particular discipline or idea. Librarians aren't responsible for the "truth" or accuracy claims of any material.

Other Important Appended Documents

1. Consortial responsibilities for collecting in assigned areas.
2. ALA intellectual freedom policies regarding content, including the rights of minors.
3. Relevant state laws and local statutes. Check to see if your state association's intellectual freedom committee has compiled a manual.
4. Any policies regarding Internet use or content, including filtering policy.
5. A "tickler file" of pending legislation and litigation regarding content, to be updated regularly.

Procedures

1. Staff instructions for dealing with law enforcement officials or groups attempting to remove materials from the library.
2. Instructions on how to request removal or addition of a book, including forms.
3. Campus procedures for adding courses to the curriculum, with instructions and forms for library input.
4. Weeding or deaccessioning policies and procedures, including forms.
5. Preservation triage policies.
6. Procedure for regular review of the collection development policy.

NOTES

1. Miguel de Cervantes Saavedra, *Don Quijote*, trans. Burton Raffel (New York: Norton, 1995), p. 30.

2. David Shenk, *Datasmog: Surviving the Information Glut*, rev. ed. (New York: HarperCollins, 1997). See also Theodore Roszak, *The Cult of Information: A Neo-Luddite Treatise on High Tech, Artificial Intelligence, and the True Art of Thinking* (Berkeley: University of California Pr., 1994).

3. Robert Fogel and Stanley Engerman, *Time on the Cross: The Economics of American Negro Slavery* (New York: Norton, 1989).

4. "Development of a Materials Selection Policy," in *Intellectual Freedom Manual*, 5th ed. (Chicago: ALA, 1996), p. 204.

5. "Questions and Answers"—see appendix C.

6. A good book is Karen Schneider's *A Practical Guide to Internet Filters* (New York: Neal-Schuman, 1997). Another is *Access Denied: The Impact of Filtering Software on the Lesbian and Gay Community* (Washington, D.C.: Gay and Lesbian Alliance against Defamation, 1997).

7. See an explanation of the "marketplace of ideas" theory in Donald Gillmor et al., *Mass Communication Law: Concepts and Cases*, 5th ed. (St. Paul: West, 1990), pp. 5–7.

8. *Cyberguide for Kids and Parents* (Chicago: Illinois Library Association, 1997), p. 1; ila@ila.org.

9. *Intellectual Freedom Manual*, p. 85.

10. *Mainstream Loudoun* v. *Board of Trustees of the Loudoun County Library*, 1998 U.S. Dist. LEXIS 18479, at 25–29 (E.D.Va. 1998). For a comprehensive history, see *Tech Law Journal*'s Web site: http://www.techlawjournal.com.

11. Id. at 29.

12. Id. at 34.

13. Id. at 40–42.

14. Id. at 43.

15. See *Intellectual Freedom Manual*, pp. 86–94.

16. James D. Hunter, *Culture Wars: The Struggle to Define America* (New York: Basic Books, 1991).

17. Allan Bloom, *The Closing of the American Mind* (New York: Simon & Schuster, 1987); Dinesh D'Souza, *Illiberal Education: The Politics of Race and Sex on Campus* (New York: Free Pr., 1991).

18. Judith S. Eaton, "'PC' or Not 'PC': That Is Not the Question," *Educational Record* (winter 1992): 26.

19. Benno Schmidt, "The University and Freedom," *Educational Record* (winter 1992): 15.

20. *The Future of Academic Freedom*, ed. Louis Menand (Chicago: University of Chicago Pr., 1996).

21. Gary Nash, Charlotte Crabtree, and R. Dunn, *History on Trial: Culture Wars and the Teaching of the Past* (New York: Knopf, 1997).

22. An interesting debate surrounds this scholarship. See Martin Bernal, *Black Athena*, 2 vols. (New Brunswick, N.J.: Rutgers University Pr., 1987); and *Black Athena Revisited*, ed. Mary Lefkowitz and Guy M. Rogers (Chapel Hill: University of North Carolina Pr., 1996).

CHAPTER 22

Intellectual Freedom Policies for Access to Information

GENERAL CONSIDERATIONS

The right to access is not explicitly stated in the Bill of Rights; however, it has developed in the courts as a corollary to freedom of speech. The right to receive information was first articulated in Justice William Brennan's concurring opinion in *Lamont* v. *U.S. Postmaster General:* "The dissemination of ideas can accomplish nothing if otherwise willing addressees are not free to receive and consider them . . . [for] [i]t would be a barren marketplace of ideas that had only sellers and no buyers."[1] In *Griswold* v. *Connecticut,* the majority opinion restated this right: "The right of freedom of speech and press includes . . . the right to distribute, the right to receive, the right to read. . . . Without these peripheral rights the specific rights would be less secure."[2] Finally, in *Stanley* v. *Georgia,* the Court said: "The right to receive information and ideas, regardless of their social worth . . . is fundamental to our free society."[3] All these cases were cited as precedent in the recent *Reno* v. *ACLU* overturning of the Communications Decency Act (CDA).[4] Furthermore, the specific rights of minors to receive information are covered in *Pico* and *Tinker.*[5]

This corollary right to receive information having been solidly established, the American Library Association has tried through its policies to apply the right of access to information as widely as possible, regardless of "origin, age, background, or views," as stated in Article V of the *Library Bill of Rights;* economic status, as implied in the Interpretation "Economic Barriers to Information Access"; or gender or sexual orientation, as clarified in the Interpretation "Access to Library Resources and Services regardless of Gender or Sexual Orientation." Further, a "Resolution on

Access to the Use of Libraries and Information by Individuals with Physical or Mental Impairment" was passed by the ALA Council in 1988 specifically to address growing concern that HIV-positive patrons would experience discrimination in the use of public facilities. Finally, the Interpretation "Access to Electronic Information, Services and Networks" makes it clear that access applies to all formats. See appendixes C and I.

Many librarians have complained that the preceding interpretations are laundry lists. They are concerned that a group will unwittingly be excluded and thus denied full access to library services. This topic is frequently debated at meetings of the Intellectual Freedom Committee. Although the committee has always acknowledged the potential problem of laundry lists, ALA membership has time and again asked for very specific applications of the general philosophy of the *Library Bill of Rights*—often for the sake of library boards or the general public. This is the very kind of complex issue that arises if written policies get too specific. It brings to mind all the No Smoking policies that could not be applied when college students began chewing tobacco in the library and spitting in the wastebaskets. After that, many libraries changed their signs to read, "No use of tobacco products in the library."

The American Library Association has a long tradition of believing that publicly funded libraries and their information resources should be accessible to as wide a group of individuals as possible, in all formats. This is reinforced by legal precedent, which continues to move in that direction.

As a general principle, we have already established that in a limited public forum like a publicly funded library, certain limits can be legally imposed. These limitations must be equitably applied and content neutral. This principle should be reflected in any access policies.

FEES AS A BARRIER TO ACCESS: BUDGETING FOR INTELLECTUAL FREEDOM

> A fee arrangement is likely to create a climate in which concerns about cost will discourage communication and reduce the flow of information among members of the academic community [and] generate mechanisms for financial accountability through an analysis of Internet's use by students and faculty members that will inhibit free expression.
>
> —American Association of University Professors,
> Resolution passed at 1994 Annual Meeting

One of the most controversial Interpretations of the *Library Bill of Rights* has been "Economic Barriers to Information Access." Some legal theorists shy away from the concept of economic status as an individual right, and no legal precedents yet exist in this area pertaining to libraries. However, the traditional approach of publicly funded libraries in this country has been to avoid passing on additional costs of library services to the public who have already paid taxes for the library. In fact, some libraries are legally required to provide "free" services.[6] It was in this spirit, along with growing concern at the number of information resources that were being offered for a fee, that the ALA Council adopted the Interpretation regarding fees as a barrier to access.

I have witnessed a great deal of misunderstanding of this Interpretation, particularly among colleagues in academic libraries. Although excellent professional literature exists on the subject of fee-based services, the topic is rarely placed within the context of library professional ethics or intellectual freedom concerns.[7] This is one area for which the AAUP has considered the intellectual freedom implications more readily than their academic library colleagues.

Some of us think in relatively narrow terms about assessing fees. It is natural that the concept of fees for access be analogized to photocopy charges or, in the case of computer printers, to the skyrocketing costs of paper: "Printing a citation is like photocopying." It is also very tempting to add fee-based services rather than face a restructuring and reallocating of an entire library budget. Typically, financial decisions must be made more quickly now than in the past, depriving library administrators of the luxury of reviewing the budget as a whole on a regular basis. Further complicating the issue is the information explosion, the rising cost of journals and the increasing number of alternatives to subscriptions. And along with electronic technology comes the cost of maintenance and regular replacement of equipment. Murray Martin and Betsy Park offer the view that fees are inevitable in most situations, unless there is an extraordinary influx of donations, grants or new sources of funding. And yet the authors acknowledge that some libraries may have statutory considerations. Regardless, Martin and Park lay out a process of financial analysis that defines cost and benefit. The "economics of information" approach leaves the door open for those librarians who wish to avoid fees and need a way to break down their costs. Another helpful book in this regard is *Costing and Pricing in the Digital Age*, in which Herbert Snyder and Elizabeth Davenport show how to distinguish fixed and variable costs of digital information, and how to compare costs of traditional print sources to those of electronic sources.

Despite those experts who see fees as inevitable, there are several sound reasons, aside from intellectual freedom, to resist such a strategy.

First, if library administrators expect campus or municipal administrators to look at the library budget as a whole and understand it as such, it is better to apply the costs of library materials and services as a whole and make sure that no costs are transparent. Passing the cost on to the consumer of the information may hide the real cost of access in terms of the budget process. Such cost shifting makes it very difficult for the library to present a clear case to a faculty senate or to a library board that more funds are needed because electronic resources cost more than the print equivalent. If the library administration has passed on costs to the consumer and can't track them, it may have a difficult time justifying a budget increase. It is very important for the fiscal health of the library and for any long-range budget planning process to be able to (1) report the costs of providing particular information services and products and (2) do comparative cost-benefit analysis for various information service options. It is far too easy for the "library receipts" and similar pools of money to be absorbed or forgotten. It then becomes very difficult to sort out the real cost of a particular library service.

Second, if the limited public forum is to return to some semblance of equity of access, the charging of fees for value-added services is also a problem. Imagine the competitive environment of a top-notch undergraduate college. This type of education costs around $25,000 a year. For many, this is easily absorbed, but for a scholarship student, paying $25 for a journal article may simply be out of the question. If this extra article from a journal not owned by the college will enhance the quality of a term paper, a student who can use his or her credit card and pay for added value has a significant edge. During a tour of the Science, Industry, and Business Library of New York Public Library, in the heart of midtown Manhattan, a businessman was heard to comment, "But don't all Manhattan firms have their own database services? Why is this library necessary?" The fact is that many new small businesses with first-time owners do not have this luxury, and a public library is a necessity for them to be able to compete.

There are creative ways to finance information services for business. For example, if your state has an economic development program for small businesses, the library could seek a grant to offer services to these businesses and, at the same time, do valuable comparative studies for the state on the information service's impact on profitability. Faculty members who are seeking grants for their research might include in their proposals the costs of information services.

If one must assess fees for library service, one possibility is a campuswide library fee applied equitably. Similar fees are charged for science laboratory courses and for athletics. Although administrators and students understandably balk at the prospect of yet another fee, a library fee based on statistical studies of cost would alert the entire campus to the expense of the "electronic library of the future." It also raises the question of campuswide priorities when it comes to assessing fees.

A third issue to consider is the administrative cost of collecting money, and the cost of equipping machines to handle cash, credit cards or a universal ID, not to mention adjacent change machines. Which brings us back to the question of printers. Chances are that students are going to have the dime it takes to print out a bibliographic citation. But will they bother if the process is cumbersome? Will they scribble the citation on an envelope and present it to the circulation clerk, only to find that the call number they copied makes no sense to the desk clerk? These practical kinds of considerations should be part of the decision-making process.

Fourth, when adding any type of new format or service, librarians should ask themselves if there is a way to reallocate existing funds. Most campuses and municipal governments have increasingly rigorous processes for requesting additional funds; they force units to look at ways to reallocate existing monies first. For example, are you passing on the cost of remote-storage delivery of a book? Probably not. Ask yourself why some costs are absorbed and some are passed on. If the library cannot afford a particular journal title or cannot afford to store a particular journal title in the library building, both decisions are economic and should be compared. Some university libraries have canceled journals and put the savings into a pool to pay for document delivery. At the end of the year they compare "access versus ownership" costs. In most cases, libraries find that once the service becomes popular, the demand uses up the money more quickly each year. But the tactic does buy a year or two for some careful collection planning and for consulting with consortium partners about the situation.

Librarians can ask local schools to give scholarships for access to databases, or reward students' high grades with access instead of pizza. If vendors offer free demos, be sure to get the word out on campus. This will introduce students and faculty to the wonderful opportunities of electronic databases (which come at a cost!), help build patron demand and help the library make prudent selections.

Ask yourself if the campus computer network has to pass on any costs to the users when it adds services. If not, then why does the library? Finally, does the library receive the use of the money collected for fee-based services? Often this money goes to a general campus fund along with proceeds from vending machines. If that is the case, then for budgeting purposes the cost for library information is essentially hidden.

In summary, there are no intellectual freedom police who are going to censure a library for charging fees. But by applying intellectual freedom principles to the budget process, librarians often get a fresh perspective. Strategically, it may be far better to offer the services at no extra charge until the funds are depleted. The library then can measure the demand and ask for more money accordingly. The library can present alternatives, such as dropping other library materials or services. Budget requests based on fiscal realities, with no hidden costs, are excellent long-term planning tools.

If a library is forced to charge fees for some collections or services, the fees must be content neutral and must be equitable. (This, incidentally, argues for a campuswide fee.) The practice of offering humanities sources at no extra charge because they are inexpensive while charging for science journal articles to absorb exhorbitant cost is questionable. If one must charge, the fees should be spread as equitably as possible across all curricular fields. Fees should be posted and described very clearly for all types of materials and services.

It is well to keep in mind the musings of James Boyle:

> We have a loosely related cluster of issues, linked by several different connotations of the word "information." We have the information technology issues, the genetic information issues, the privacy issues, the dataflow issues, and the intellectual property issues. The justification for treating these together is precisely the homologization of forms of information, their liquidity, in the monetary sense of easy conversion from one form into another. The phrase "information wants to be free" has part of its force because it anthropomorphizes this liquidity, this conceptually, technologically, and economically driven tendency to float free of some particular form and context. One might even call it the universalizing logic of the information relation. The tendency is toward the economic and conceptual separation of the informational message from the medium—cells, diskettes, telephone directories, or whatever—and of the progressive devaluation (literally, the diminishing marginal cost) of the medium as compared with the message. As the information content is decontextualized, the location or form of the information comes to seem increasingly irrelevant—as irrelevant as the color of two books would be to a comparison of their arguments.[8]

The point to be gained is that we need to think creatively about budgeting and not automatically assume that a new format needs fees for cost recovery. And any kind of budgeting process or planning should incorporate the library's mission and ideals. An encouraging example of this kind of creative planning process is found in the guidebook and how-to manual, *Planning for Results: A Public Library Transformation Process*, by Ethel Himmel and Bill Wilson (Chicago: ALA, 1998).

FILTERS AS A BARRIER TO ACCESS

The controversy over filtering library public access terminals for content is ongoing. Information currently available is found in the "Children in the Limited Public Forum" section of chapter 21 because the filtering issue focuses on limiting access to minors.

SPECIAL ACCESS SITUATIONS

Foreign Nationals

During the FBI Library Awareness Program, librarians were asked to distinguish "foreign" library users from U.S. citizens. Neither the First Amendment nor resulting ALA policy has ever restricted speech on the basis of national origin or status. Librarians should simply be aware of this fact; it probably doesn't call for a special policy.

Classified Government Documents as a Barrier to Access

Many academic colleagues will eagerly collaborate with librarians in pressing the federal government for a more speedy, systematic way to declassify confidential government documents. In the early 1990s, the policy for declassification changed—if in doubt, the government kept the document secret. Before that, the policy had been the other way around! Within ALA the Government Documents Round Table (GODORT), the Legislative Committee and the Washington Office keep a close eye on this situation. So do such groups as the Organization of American Historians and the Society of American Archivists. Librarians should remain actively concerned about this very real barrier to access. It is a critical issue not only for scholars waiting to resolve certain issues before publishing a monograph, but also for veterans wanting information on health issues arising from the Gulf War. These are but two examples of why documents that are no longer security sensitive should be released on a timely and systematic basis.

Donor and Other Restrictions as a Barrier to Access in Special Collections

The issues covered briefly in this section are but a sampling of the highly complex issues facing special collections librarians, who have an especially difficult set of issues and values to weigh in providing access to unique materials, often in poor condition.

Special collections librarians frequently agonize over how many donor "conditions" are acceptable when soliciting and accepting a gift. It is truly a balancing act; personal papers, for example, may be incredibly valuable for scholars—if scholars can actually gain access to them within a reasonable period of time. The expense of processing papers with complex restrictions is another factor to consider. While all librarians do accept gifts of this kind and will continue to do so, they are advised when negotiating with the donor to narrow as much as possible both the number of restrictions and the length of time the restrictions apply, for the sake of scholars. Of course, with archival and other documents, sometimes legal confidentiality statutes apply. The applicable ALA policy is "Restricted Access to Library Materials," which states: "Because materials placed in restricted collections often deal with controversial, unusual, or 'sensitive' subjects, having to ask a librarian or circulation clerk for them may be embarrassing or inhibiting for patrons desiring the materials. Needing to ask for materials may pose a language barrier or a staff service barrier. Because restricted collections often are composed of materials which some library patrons consider 'objectionable,' the potential user may be predisposed to think of the materials as 'objectionable' and, therefore, [be] reluctant to ask for them."

Libraries should have clearly stated procedures for selecting items to be placed in or removed from a restricted collection. If books are kept in a special collection because they are controversial or frequently stolen, every effort should be made to provide circulating copies in the general stacks and to inform patrons why the book has been restricted. Many special collections items have a flyer explaining why the item is restricted. Reasons might include rarity, frequent theft or physical deterioration. A book should not be placed in a restricted collection for its content per se. Librarians should apply all their ethical and professional sensibilities to every decision to place any title in a restricted collection.

Another issue in special collections involves restricting access by maintaining closed stacks. As long as this restriction is applied equitably, such a policy for the security and physical condition of the materials is acceptable.

A stickier issue is that of content-based restrictions. Placing a book in special collections or behind a desk because of its content is a clear violation of the *Library Bill of Rights.* Often the very materials kept behind the desk are those that patrons are most reluctant to request. At one special collections library, a foreign student was insulted that a book on African marriage customs was kept behind the desk, as if such practices were somehow shameful. Libraries should be very careful about their motivation for placing books in closed collections.

However, if a book is rare or its physical condition renders it unusable, libraries have the right to restrict access. At the same time, librarians might make this particular item a high priority for preservation microfilming or buy a "surrogate" copy or facsimile of the book.

One should also consider serendipity, however. Often rare book libraries get requests from desperate students who must read a popular title and all copies have been checked out except the one in Rare Books. First, the rare book librarian should contact the faculty member to see if a reserve shelf can be set up or extra copies purchased. Second, unless the demand is such that the book would be destroyed, it might afford an opportunity to introduce a student to an early edition of a novel with contemporary illustrations and historical importance. This has happened numerous times at the University of Illinois and has resulted in several students returning to do lengthy papers on the publishing history of a particular title, or a history of the illustrations.

Access to Meeting Rooms and Exhibit Space

Policies regarding meeting rooms and exhibits are governed by the First and Fourteenth Amendments. We have studied how time, place and manner restrictions may be placed on such areas in a limited public forum. The key is that once an auditorium is open for piano recitals, for example, it is also open to the local garden club. The times can be scheduled and limited, but when rooms are made generally available, they are available on an equitable basis. The same applies to exhibitions. It is expected that there will be an exhibition schedule, and some libraries do not allow outside exhibitors. But once such exhibits are allowed, then all requests must be handled in an orderly way. If you have ten requests, it is reasonable to compile a waiting list or to hold a competition. But there should be clearly understood criteria for requesting exhibit space if the demand exceeds available space.

Cataloging as a Barrier to Access

Very little of the otherwise excellent literature on cataloging, classification and indexing addresses the inevitable cultural biases of such systems. It is far easier to link intellectual freedom principles to content. And yet, consider the previously cited dilemma accompanying Holocaust denial literature. Should a subject heading ("pseudo-history," for example) be created to separate that material from the accurate historical documentation of the period? How does this relate to the intellectual freedom principle of content neutrality or to the statement on labeling?

Sanford Berman, cataloger at Minnesota's Hennepin County Library, was one of the mavericks in this area, with the publication of *Prejudices and Antipathies* in 1971, and a few other cataloging theorists have grappled with the issue.[9] In researching this book, it became obvious to me that more research and scholarship are needed in this area.

SAMPLE OUTLINE FOR POLICIES ON ACCESS

Each library should consult with legal counsel for the latest information regarding Internet and other laws affecting access policy. Remember that planning and implementation are as important as the policies themselves. All policies should begin with a statement linking the library's mission to the policy.

Libraries should consider developing the following access policies incorporating intellectual freedom concerns.

1. Internet access policy or campus computer network policy as applied in the library or both. Intellectual freedom concerns include:
   a. The type of access allowed to children (check pending legislation and litigation).
   b. A scheduling policy for terminals that is based on "equitable time," not on the nature of the research being performed.
2. Policies regarding minors' access to information. It may be preferable to incorporate access for minors into a larger access policy, rather than create a separate document. Check with legal counsel.
3. Policies regarding fees. Intellectual freedom concerns include the potential chilling effect of economic barriers to access for low-income students and community members. If fees must be

assessed, there should be a public notice of all applicable charges. Any options to reduce or avoid the fees should also be listed. For example, can a student download a file instead of paying to have it printed out? Is there a free hard-copy alternative to the electronic text version of a document?

4. Policy regarding access to meeting rooms. Intellectual freedom concerns relate to limited public forum principles. Time, place and manner restrictions are acceptable, but content-based restrictions are not.
5. Policy regarding exhibition space. Same concerns as in item 4.
6. Policy on selection of materials to be kept in closed stacks (if any), in noncirculating collections or behind the desk. Intellectual freedom concerns: Be aware that "security concerns" are often inappropriately applied to books with controversial content. Books can be moved to closed stacks for reasons of cost, physical condition, uniqueness or unprocessed status—but not content.
7. Policies on patron behavior, if necessary. Librarians are urged to learn the issues surrounding the *Kreimer* v. *Morristown* case and plan accordingly. Intellectual freedom concerns: Be aware that some library behavior policies have faced court challenges because they are overly broad. Patron behavior policies must be applied consistently and equitably. They can't stifle speech based on content. In some cases, local ordinances and law enforcement will suffice and behavior policies specific to the library are unnecessary.

Appended Material

1. ALA intellectual freedom policies related to access, including the rights of children.
2. Any state intellectual freedom policies related to access, especially Internet access.
3. Pending legislation and court cases, in a tickler file.
4. Any access policies applicable to consortial membership.
5. Procedures for due process in case network privileges or any other library access privileges are suspended.
6. Procedures for regular review of all access policies.
7. Staff procedures for contacting local law enforcement in case of violations of the patron conduct policy.

NOTES

1. 381 U.S.301 (1965).

2. 381 U.S. 479 (1965) at 1680–81.

3. 394 U.S. 557 (1969).

4. *Reno et al.* v. *American Civil Liberties Union et al.*, 138 L.Ed 2d 874 1997.

5. *Board of Education, Island Trees (New York) Union Free School District 26* v. *Pico*, 457 U.S. 853 (1982); and *Tinker* v. *Des Moines Independent Community School District*, 393 U.S. 503 (1969).

6. See Pete Giacoma, *The Fee or Free Decision: Legal, Economic, Political, and Ethical Perspectives for Public Libraries* (New York: Neal-Schuman, 1989). He includes an appendix that analyzes, state by state, any legal or other statutory obligations regarding the charging of additional fees for library service. This valuable chart is, regrettably, quite old, and someone should update it.

7. Exceptions include Giacoma, *The Fee or Free Decision;* Herbert Snyder and Elizabeth Davenport, *Costing and Pricing in the Digital Age* (New York: Neal-Schuman, 1997); and Murray Martin and Betsy Park, *Charging and Collecting Fees and Fines: A Handbook for Libraries* (New York: Neal-Schuman, 1998), which has far more philosophical perspective than the title would suggest.

8. James Boyle, *Shamans, Software, and Spleens: Law and the Construction of the Information Society* (Cambridge, Mass.: Harvard University Pr., 1996), p. 7.

9. Sanford Berman, *Prejudices and Antipathies: A Tract on the LC Subject Heads concerning People* (Metuchen, N.J.: Scarecrow, 1971); Allan Wilson, "The Hierarchy of Belief: Ideological Tendentiousness in Universal Classification," in *Classification Research for Knowledge Representation and Organization*, Proceedings, Fifth International Study Conference on Classification Research, 1991 (Amsterdam: Elsevier, 1992), pp. 389–97. Also refer to the earlier account of Jewish libraries' difficult decisions regarding Holocaust denial literature.

CHAPTER 23

Intellectual Freedom Policies for Privacy

GENERAL CONSIDERATIONS

What is a librarian's role in protecting privacy rights in a limited public forum? Often the concept of privacy seems to be at odds with librarians' efforts to provide access to a wide variety of resources. It is helpful to view, as a necessary complement to a public forum, what Thomas Emerson called "a sphere of space that has not been dedicated to public use or control."[1] When a library user checks out a book, puts a hold on a book, asks a reference question or searches on a terminal, the transaction must be protected as part of that individual's right to privacy.

Chapter 10 described how privacy became a constitutional and library intellectual freedom concern. Chapter 19's analysis of the FBI Library Awareness Program showed how a government agency's action became a catalyst for a concerted response by the library profession. It was also a wake-up call to academic librarians—their institutions, too, could be the targets of government intervention.

This chapter will build on chapter 10's legal history of the evolution of the right to privacy and offer policy-making strategies for confidentiality of library records and computer network use. It includes a study of the Jake Baker case at the University of Michigan, which brought privacy issues into direct conflict with a university's decision to punish what they believed to be inappropriate use of the campus network.

THE WIDE VARIETY OF LIBRARY PRIVACY SITUATIONS

Library privacy policy consists of laws, ALA policies and, very importantly, a trained, sensitive library staff. Arguably the last is more important for protecting privacy than any other factor. This is because many people think of privacy in a limited way. An experienced, well-trained librarian or staff member knows that the following situations are potential violations of user privacy:

1. A journalist asks for library circulation records of a public official under investigation.
2. A tenure review committee asks for circulation records to review a candidate's reading history.
3. A campus committee reviewing a plagiarism case asks to see records of what the accused student has checked out or read on reserve.
4. A faculty member asks to see the circulation records for his or her reserve list to assign grades according to which students read the most.
5. A reference librarian asks for confirmation of residency, status or address before providing service. Or, the librarian asks for a name and phone number to call the user back after searching for the answer. Or, the librarian uses a two-way speakerphone that makes the patron's query audible to anyone near the reference desk.
6. Postcards are used to notify patrons of overdue books or fines.
7. Paper with lists of overdue notices or other privacy-protected library information on one side is reused as scratch paper.
8. To save money on database development, a library vendor offers fewer levels of security for library staff using the system. This leads to student workers being assigned inappropriately high security levels, giving them access to names of fellow students and the books they have checked out. (Peer pressure has tempted more than one student worker to erase fines for a friend or reveal confidential circulation information.)
9. A parent asks to see what his or her child has checked out.
10. The FBI visits a university library and asks what types of database searches the university's foreign nationals have requested recently.
11. Special collections libraries ask for fairly detailed patron registration information in the interest of security. (They want the

capability of tracing the last user of a book, should it be discovered that the book has been mutilated or is missing pages.)

12. A scholar may ask a rare book librarian if any other scholar is doing work with the same material, in order to "stake out a claim" for a future publication project.
13. A flag listing each user's name is kept with reserve materials.
14. While investigating a bizarre violent crime at the local high school, city police officers ask for circulation records for any patron who has checked out books on the occult.
15. A thief convicted for stealing thousands of books from libraries nationwide has just been released from prison. An Internet security group has posted this information to alert librarians. Librarians are posting a photograph of this convicted felon in their library reading rooms.
16. A small public library has only one public access terminal located in the center of the reading room. A teenage patron wants to look up information on abortion on the World Wide Web, but is afraid someone might pass by and see what she is doing.
17. Journals on controversial topics like euthanasia and gay rights are kept behind the periodicals circulation desk and can be obtained only by showing an ID card.

THE PUBLIC POLICY ARENA FOR PRIVACY

In addition to federal statutes, much data privacy and user confidentiality legislation is decided at the state and local levels of government. It is thus important that librarians contact their local legal counsel before writing any policy in the area of privacy.

In our relatively open society, especially in a library, it is easy to forget about privacy. When a teenager is checking out a book on a sensitive topic, a librarian can simply check it out—or remark, "Do your parents know you're reading this?" Such a remark could have a chilling effect. *Training should be required of all employees,* not only to learn privacy laws, but also to become aware of the more subtle ways of assuring a reader's sense of privacy.

We have already covered the multitude of legislative and judicial actions relating to confidentiality of patrons' use of library resources and services. It is safe to say that in the area of privacy and confidentiality, there is a great deal of public consensus regarding the increased need to be vigilant. Legislators have responded, and almost all states now have confidentiality of library records statutes. Though the general public may not understand immediately how a particular library policy is related to privacy rights, once it is explained they may well react sympathetically. This may not be true of law enforcement officials, however, and librarians need to be prepared.

A number of organizations could serve as useful coalition partners on issues of privacy. The Electronic Privacy Information Center (EPIC) is a terrific source for the latest news updates, full texts of court cases and other important documents. This group is a project of the Fund for Constitutional Government. The Electronic Frontier Foundation is another responsive organization, and the ACLU has a special Privacy Project initiative.

The controversial question is whether there can even be such a thing as privacy in the online environment of the new millennium. Some libraries are simply warning their users up front that privacy on the Internet cannot be guaranteed, while others try to find strategies to protect privacy.

LEGAL AND POLICY ISSUES TO KEEP IN MIND

It is essential that librarians understand applicable federal, state and local ordinances, and the amount of protection they afford to libraries and librarians. Almost every state has a confidentiality of library records statute. The first legislation of this type tended to cover confidentiality of circulation records only; later statutes included reference queries and other information transactions. Many librarians still have a limited understanding of the scope of situations covered by this type of legislation. In many states the right to privacy in a publicly funded library—in a limited public forum—includes confidentiality of any personally identifiable information. ALA has supported this principle with its "Policy concerning Confidentiality of Personally Identifiable Information about Library Users" (included in appendix J).

Generally minors are afforded the same library privacy rights as adults. Librarians should be aware of the 1974 Buckley Amendment (20 U.S.C. 1232g), however, because its applicability to school library circulation records of people under eighteen years of age is still untested. This amendment to the Family Education and Privacy Rights Act gives parents the right to see their minor children's school records. Although the amendment probably would not be applied to circulation records of public and academic libraries, librarians should seek legal advice on this issue.

Foreign nationals have traditionally had First Amendment rights extended to them.

The identity of convicted felons who have been released from prison, or of library patrons suspected of theft, is frequently shared among librarians on security newsgroups or Web sites. Photographs or descriptions should not be in the general public view. It is even questionable whether they should be posted at all, but this common practice has never been challenged in court.[2]

Reference queries are generally covered by state privacy laws. This means that reference questions must be kept confidential. If a librarian consults with colleagues, the name of the patron should be separated from the question. If a patron needs to be called back, he or she should be offered the option of calling the desk at a particular time, rather than being forced to leave a phone number. Librarians are beginning to use the computer networks for reference service; some are experimenting with face-to-face visual inquiry on the screen. Such systems are excellent ways to personalize reference service, but should be scrutinized for privacy considerations.

The placement of public access terminals is an important privacy issue. Now that content on Web pages is clearly visible from a distance, a great deal of public attention has been focused on those patrons who display images that are offensive to some people, sometimes intentionally to provoke. Rather than filter out potentially offensive Web sites, create ways to offer a diversity of seating options. Special screen shades and computer study tables with privacy walls are available. For those libraries with the luxury of space, some computers can be placed in banks near the reference or user-training desk; patrons who choose this seating understand that their research is visible and that they are close to a reference librarian should they need assistance. For more experienced users who want their privacy, the library could place some terminals individually in more private areas. This kind of creative arrangement is the same as buying various kinds of library furniture, from study tables to couches, for different use patterns.

Placement of terminals is an example of a practical solution that might help a library avoid the extreme step of mounting filtering software on the public workstations. Often these kinds of gestures show patrons that you respect a variety of user preferences for study. At the same time you are not abridging the freedom of access to information. In a litigious society like ours, such gestures can often avoid costly legal or public relations battles.

CONFIDENTIALITY OF LIBRARY RECORDS

In addition to this chapter, librarians are again urged to consult the excellent series, *Confidentiality in Libraries: An Intellectual Freedom Modular Education Program*, published by the Office for Intellectual Freedom. This series is designed not only for giving workshops, but also for learning the steps in writing policy to address real-world situations librarians are likely to encounter.

Guidelines for Writing Confidentiality of Library Records Policies

The following considerations when writing confidentiality policies are adapted from the modular education program. Before running policy drafts past the thirteen considerations listed in this section, the drafting team should decide two general questions. First, will the policy warn users that some electronic information—especially e-mail—cannot be guaranteed privacy? On the other hand, patrons should not be given the impression that their transactions are being monitored or unduly scrutinized. Second, do librarians understand the distinction between legal and illegal activity on the Internet? Some forms of hacking are illegal. Downloading proprietary information is illegal. Although librarians have always tried to respect the privacy of user research activity, signs should be posted at public workstations with warnings of the illegality of certain activities. The following Confidentiality Inventory is presented in the "Trainer's Manual."

1. Does your policy statement make clear the role of confidentiality in protecting intellectual freedom?
2. Is the information to be protected listed: reference requests, information services provided, circulation records, registration records, other patron information? Have you included language to deal with unforeseen circumstances, like "including, but not limited to . . ."?
3. Do you state who may or may not have access to patron information?
4. Do you outline the specific conditions under which access may be granted?: with a court order *after* good cause has been demonstrated?
5. Who is responsible for responding to inquiries? What is the "chain of command"?

6. Is the procedure for handling confidentiality inquiries outlined in a clear, step-by-step manner? Does it include reporting the incident to the ALA's Office for Intellectual Freedom?
7. How is the procedure to be taught and to whom?
8. Do you list the procedure for adopting the policy?
9. Are there provisions for notifying the public of the policy?
10. Are exemptions, exceptions, or special conditions enumerated? Do you address needs unique to your library environment?
11. If your library is part of a cooperative, automated computer system, are there provisions for coordination with the other libraries in your system?
12. Is the procedure for responding to a court order outlined?
13. Are the Library Bill of Rights, Statement on Professional Ethics, ALA Policy on the Confidentiality of Library Records, and state laws (where applicable) mentioned or acknowledged? Does your policy conform to these supporting documents?[3]

Necessary Procedures to Accompany Confidentiality of Library Records Policies

If law enforcement officials demand to see library patron records, a librarian should not panic or assume that a subpoena requires instantaneous relinquishing of the requested information. The following is the procedure recommended in the training module, "Policy Development":

> Procedures for dealing with a subpoena should be identified, including referring the subpoena to the library director and then immediately to legal counsel, who should have been prepared by the librarian to defend professional ethics and First Amendment rights in a motion to quash the subpoena, or a motion for a protective order. The officers should be required to make a showing of good cause before a judge. The library should argue that the subpoena threatens First Amendment rights to use a library and have access to information without fear of surveillance. Subject to the advice of the library's counsel, the library should comply only if the court issues an order enforcing the subpoena.[4]

In the case of administrative records, ALA argues, quite legitimately, that circulation records are kept for administrative control only, not to chart student progress or reading habits of patrons. Therefore, such records should be destroyed when their role in the work-flow cycle is complete. If they are used for user studies or other statistical purposes, care should be exercised to obliterate any link between a personal name and the information gathered. Librarians should work with the archivist or records manager on exceptions for this kind of sensitive information, which should not be retained, even for the sake of a comprehensive archival record.

Many breaches of confidentiality can be avoided with such simple clerical details as using envelopes instead of postcards for overdue notices, and crossing out the names of previous borrowers on a circulation card. These problems are often easily addressed in staff brainstorming sessions to identify and change any objectionable practices.

Library system vendors sometimes do not hear about privacy concerns when requests for proposals (RFPs) are crafted and negotiated. It is the responsibility of the library community to recognize these potential problems before it is too late to change the contract. In fact, it is wise to assign one librarian the responsibility of scrutinizing all RFPs, line by line, to identify potential intellectual freedom concerns.

A library system typically has various levels of security. Some security is based on user passwords. When a library worker or user signs on, that individual's password defines the functions and menus he or she will be able to access. Another kind of security control can be assigned to a physical terminal, which is limited to specific functions regardless of the user's password. Yet another type of security is afforded by "fire wall" software, which protects systems from experienced users who might be able to hack through the security measures. Following are some very specific considerations to ask of any system vendor:

> What capability does your system (or prospective system) have to protect the confidentiality of library records? Password access? Separate computer for patron records?
>
> Does your system obliterate the circulation records when materials are returned by the patron? Can the record be reconstructed once deleted?
>
> Is your system able to associate retrospective data with an individual user? Has this been done or is it done on a regular basis? . . .
>
> Are coded user records easily decoded?
>
> How secure is the system from access by unauthorized persons?
>
> What antivirus protection does the system have, if any?
>
> How long in real time must records be stored in the computer for the system to work?
>
> Can records be immediately deleted when they are no longer needed or current? . . .

Are products such as overdue notices printed on forms that protect the identity of the patron?[5]

COMPUTER NETWORKS: CONTENT, ACCESS AND CONFIDENTIALITY CONCERNS

> There is a growing consensus that if the jumble of state and federal statutes, consumer pressure, and self-help is to be unified into meaningful privacy protection in the digital age, then we will have to do more than pass a law. The law in general, and each of us in particular, will have to make some fundamental adjustments in the way we think of personal information and electronic communication. . . . With so much information available at a keystroke, it is now inescapable that there will be times when what is whispered in the closet will indeed be shouted from the rooftops.
>
> —Caroline Kennedy and Ellen Alderman[6]

Computer networks have not yet been added to the "limited public forum." Their legal status is likely to continue to evolve. It is particularly critical for librarians to be involved in any kind of decision-making process affecting the design or maintenance of the library's computer network.

At a college or university, the organization of the campus computer system usually involves a central office for computer services. Depending on the size and complexity of the institution, this office might be subdivided into administrative and academic computing functions. Generally, library activities report to the academic side, but this is by no means always true. Some libraries have their own library systems office, which is usually coordinated with the larger campus systems operation. And in many situations the university librarian is also the chief information officer.

Public libraries may have their own system or may be linked through a municipal or regional consortium. Some public libraries have an on-site network administrator. The job can be full- or part-time depending on the size and complexity of the network. If the computer network administrator is not a librarian, the library administration should provide him or her with the ethical and intellectual freedom contexts in which such systems are viewed and used by librarians and their patrons.

When individuals from other professional backgrounds do get involved in network administration, librarians need to remember that computer professionals' organizations have their own missions and codes of ethics that may conflict with those of the library profession. Some librarians, in fact, find themselves subject to two ethical codes. A good example is the Bill of Rights and Responsibilities for Electronic Learners, developed in the early 1990s by EDUCOM. This was a smaller subset of an impressive program to discuss ethics among librarians and computer professionals. Because EDUCOM is supported by many types of education professionals, the program was an ideal way to discover where ideas might clash. For example, early drafts of the Bill of Rights emphasized responsibilities, more than rights, of network users, while the ALA policies were somewhat opposite. ALA's Intellectual Freedom Committee corresponded with EDUCOM about this potential conflict, and the EDUCOM document subsequently was revised to incorporate the library profession's concerns.

In order to make good policy, librarians should know exactly how the network operates. For example, how does anonymous e-mail work? The justices of the Supreme Court reportedly were given a comprehensive orientation to the Internet before they deliberated on the Communications Decency Act.

Content on Computer Networks

Generally, computer network administrators are painfully aware of their challenge: to provide ever-expanding access with increasingly limited resources. As a result, they may make decisions to restrict access, not with the intent to censor, but to allocate resources in a way they believe to be fair. It is understandable, then, why systems administrators might block newsgroups (like the "alt." series, which often have countercultural or alternative-lifestyles content) if such content is not directly related to the mission of the institution. Unfortunately, this policy has been used in some cases to censor material the network administrator decides is offensive. Some librarians might argue that this type of access restriction conflicts with the library's collection development mandate and violates other ALA intellectual freedom policies. This is but one of many reasons that a librarian should be appointed to any kind of campus network oversight committee so that these issues are at least brought to the table.

Access to Computer Networks

Access of minors to computer networks was discussed in chapter 21. Libraries are likely to have widely varying access policies. For example, many academic libraries identify a "primary user group" receiving a full complement of services and access, and a secondary group limited to "guest" status on workstations. Many libraries have vendor licensing agreements mandating a strictly limited user base. In such cases, librarians may have little choice; in negotiating with the vendor, however, they should make every effort to reach a contractual agreement that offers optimal access to the largest possible user group. I am unaware of any patron legal action regarding the various levels of user access found in most academic libraries.

If access is governed by a set of policies, any rescinding of a user's access should be accompanied by due process—for example, an appeal before a student affairs or similar committee.

Privacy on Computer Networks

ANONYMOUS E-MAIL

If a library offers public access terminals and has an e-mail server on its network, it may contend with problems of anonymous e-mail. E-mail can be sent in one of two ways: from a user's account or from a Web browser on a public access terminal. If e-mail is sent from a user's account, the message carries with it the e-mail address of the sender. However, if e-mail is sent from a Web browser, the mail server cannot verify the sender's e-mail identity, so the sender can remain anonymous. The return address of anonymous e-mail is determined by the system administrator who sets up the ability to send e-mail from a browser. This person can trace such a message to a particular terminal and to the time it was sent, but cannot identify the sender. This opens up the potential for an anonymous correspondent to send harassing, threatening or obscene e-mail to an unsuspecting receiver. In other words, people can send messages that can't be traced to them, rendering this kind of access ripe for abuse.

Why would a library want to permit anonymous e-mail? Because many Web sites request feedback when people are cruising the Web and provide e-mail to get that feedback. Or the library may want to let a user ask a reference question from a public terminal. It is a convenience allowing users to send correspondence without signing off and then on to their own e-mail account. And in a public library it is highly likely that a large percentage of users do not have an e-mail account. An anonymous account, in other words, protects the privacy of inquiry and is a convenience or a financial necessity for some patrons to obtain maximum access to information.

There are several down sides to providing anonymous e-mail. One is that if the sender expects a reply, his or her own e-mail address must be included in the body of the message, since the default return address selected by the system administrator will cause a reply to either bounce back to the sender (if it is an invalid address) or go to an account that all anonymous users share. Another problem is, of course, the potential for abuse. If any illegal messages are sent using anonymous e-mail, the library or its governing body may be held legally liable for such messages or accused of abuse of state funds. A third problem is the lack of privacy afforded such communication. By default, Web browsers save all outgoing mail messages to the local hard drive. Unless special precautions are taken by the system administrator to prevent the storage and retrieval of all e-mail messages, any subsequent user of the browser will be able to view all anonymous e-mail messages that have not been purged from the hard drive.

There are solutions to this problem. One is to ask people who want to send messages from a public terminal to provide a log-on or password for a session. This password could be derived from their library card or other means, but it would enable a network administrator, if necessary, to trace a particular patron's activity on the Internet. In most cases, network administrators do not have the time to check logs systematically. However, if a law enforcement officer or agency requested such logs, they would be available. On a large network, such a log search might require either special software or a lot of time, but technologically such a breach of privacy is possible. It is up to the network administrator to determine how long these logs are kept, just as it is up to a library to determine how long to keep circulation records. Both are similar, and extremely important, privacy policy issues.

To solve the awkwardness of making and responding to inquiries using anonymous e-mail, many organizations are now providing Web forms for this activity. Using a form makes clear to both sender and receiver the identity of the communicators. However, the identity of the sender is still only as reliable as the information provided by that sender. I know of no litigation regarding this problem, but the potential—either for invasion of privacy or for abuse of an anonymous account—is certainly there. This is legally uncharted territory. Some argue that patron privacy must be absolute. Others argue that if patrons must be identified in order to check out a library book, they should be required to reveal their identity to use network resources.

One solution might be to allow anonymous e-mail and carefully monitor frequency of abuses or inappropriate communications as measured by the number of replies sent to the default return address. Another would be to require some sort of sign-in procedure with erasure of identity after a certain period—similar to a circulation system for library materials. This book does not advocate one solution over another, but librarians are urged to keep abreast of legal and technical developments in this area.

In making a decision about anonymous e-mail on library terminals, pertinent questions include the following:

Has any actual abuse occurred? Is there a history of abuse of your network? Has the speech been simply offensive to some or truly illegal?

In the case of computer network abuse, who is legally liable—the library providing the access? The individual librarian? The university? The municipality? Only the perpetrator, if he or she can be identified?

What are the options for patron identification? Can this information be erased once the patron activity has ceased and the record is no longer necessary for library operations? How long are logs kept? Are they monitored regularly or only if requested by a law enforcement agency?

In all cases, the policy should include the caveat that e-mail is not private. Hackers and others have proven this to be true.

CRIMINAL ACTIVITY ON THE NETWORK

Computer network administrators tell of the rising problem of illegal activity on shared computer networks. Illegal activity includes, among other offenses, some types of hacking, harassment and downloading of proprietary software or content. If the network administrator suspects any kind of illegal activity, he or she will probably contact a network security officer or, in the case of a public library, a local law enforcement agency. Suspicious activity is usually detected during routine monitoring if a particular Web site is very busy or if someone reports being harassed. (Libraries should never allow staff to copy proprietary software, either.)

Librarians have several important issues to consider. Because librarians do not routinely monitor the research habits or activities of library users, we may not be aware of illegal activity. However, copies of campus computer network use policies should be prominently posted so that everyone using public access terminals is aware of the definition of various types of illegal activity and the consequences if knowingly breaking the law or the policies.

Pedophiles who stalk children on the Internet are criminals, and any such activity will be investigated by the FBI. This crime is an example of "speech-action," for which there is no First Amendment protection. Librarians who oppose filtering have been falsely accused of being promoters of illegal Internet activity. It is essential that the public understand that librarians are not promoting or protecting criminal activity.

Individual computer network users should be aware that computer center officials can monitor use, night or day. They can observe who is accessing alt.sex at 2:00 A.M., for example, and from what machine. In most libraries and on most campuses, this information is highly privileged and is available only to a few administrators, in the same way that library circulation records are available only to a limited number of staff. The national news has been filled with examples of hard drives being hauled into court as evidence. Users should be aware of the capability of computer networks to store this kind of information. A legitimate question for a librarian to ask computer center administrators is: How long does this information really need to be archived?

Suspension of computer privileges for misconduct is an area that begs for librarians' involvement, especially if that suspension severs patron access to library holdings records or content. ALA policy calls for due process when investigating this type of alleged misconduct. On a campus, due process might consist of a hearing before a student affairs committee with students, faculty and administrators involved in individual appeals. The Jake Baker case discussed later in this chapter is a sobering reminder of the importance of proper procedures. Officials should remember that wrongfully accused students could bring suit themselves in defense of their right to privacy and access.

USER STUDIES

Increasingly libraries are conducting online user studies to determine priorities for library services, or to determine how well various search strategies are working. In all such cases, users should remain anonymous. If a reward or some other kind of incentive is being offered, participants in the study should be alerted by an on-screen message or other means that in order to receive the reward, confidentiality might be breached.

Issues for Library Networks

The following questions summarize the concerns already discussed, and can be used to develop comprehensive policies for the use of library networks:

1. Assuming that allocation of limited computer resources is a fact of life, many policies are based on an available resources rationale. How do you avoid using this as an excuse to block certain types of information? Can the decision to block certain information be made in a content-neutral manner?
2. Does the library collection development officer participate in the determination of which resources are blocked?
3. Does the procedure for dealing with a person suspected of violating computer network use policies involve due process?
4. When performing network maintenance, is security breached? If so, is it systematic?
5. How long are various types of data (especially the logs linking a particular user to a particular use) kept?
6. How is anonymous e-mail regulated? Is it allowed? Is there any liability if it is abused?
7. What avenues of cross communication are in place to ensure that network use policies do not conflict with other policies?
8. Is there—should there be—a warning that e-mail is not confidential?
9. Does the policy state a commitment to the First Amendment, to policies of ALA and other professional organizations, to the Electronic Communications Privacy Act and to applicable local and state laws and statutes?
10. Does the policy emphasize that information in electronic format is protected by the same laws and policies as are other formats and other forms of speech on campus?
11. Under what circumstances would electronic media information be disclosed to law enforcement officials? What is the process?
12. How does the policy of privacy relate to other laws—for example, the Freedom of Information Act? What happens when law enforcement officials want to see logs? What are the disclosure

policies and laws? It is very important to include this information so that users understand that they don't have absolute assurance of privacy on the network.

13. How does network security relate to individual users? For example, how does authentication of users work? How many people have access to the highest levels of security clearance?
14. What are the limitations? If a policy is governed by limitations, are they explained to the users? For example, what is the network bandwidth campus users can expect? Does it extend to dormitory rooms? Fraternity houses? Home access to a public library?

In addition, a computer network use policy should contain:

A statement about the primary purpose of the computer network. This should be made in positive terms, to promote use.

A clear definition of the user group to whom the policy applies.

The principles underlying network use (for example, the rights versus responsibilities dichotomy).

A statement of the principles of intellectual and academic freedom. The policy should also include related statutes and local policy. It should be consistent with existing policy. Many campuses have had great luck raising awareness of students about problems with "flaming" (transmission of abusive language on the Internet, directed at other persons), copyright problems and other issues that students may not think about until it's too late. Some networks post "netiquette" guidelines to promote civility and to prevent abuse.

A definition of the network, who is in charge of it and who makes policy.

The process for appeal if a person's network access is suspended.

The Jake Baker Case: Content, Access and Privacy on a Campus Computer Network

Although no library was involved in the Jake Baker case at the University of Michigan, it is entirely possible that a similar situation could involve library materials or anonymous e-mail from a library terminal. I am indebted to Mike Godwin for his thoughtful and legally astute account of this case.[7]

In October 1994, twenty-year-old Jake Baker, a sophomore at the University of Michigan, posted "Gone Fishin'" on the alt.sex.stories newsgroup. This fictional fantasy—though some would contend it was too real to dismiss as fiction—involved a teenage boy and girl who were raped, tortured and then murdered. Though some readers protested the distasteful violence permeating Baker's stories, he continued to post them. One "cyberfan" was Arthur Gonza, with whom Baker began a private conversation, sharing sexual kidnapping fantasies.

Baker crossed a line when, on January 9, 1995, he posted a sadistic story about a woman character with the same name as a fellow student on campus. The story was so disturbing that a Moscow teenager shared it with her father, who complained to his friend—a Michigan alum—about this disgusting use of university resources.

When the campus police arrived at his dormitory room the next day, Jake Baker consented to the search of his room. Though he thought that his cooperation would help his situation, in fact it led authorities to his undeleted e-mail chats with Arthur Gonza. Because these fantasies were written in a style that suggested the planning of real murders of women, the university didn't feel it could take a chance. Accordingly, officials suspended Baker and turned over his e-mail to federal law enforcement authorities. Next, the FBI arrested Jake Baker for violating Title 18, U.S. Code 875(c), which prohibits communicating the threat of kidnapping through interstate commerce.

Originally, the government had contemplated using the federal obscenity statutes (18 U.S.C. 1465 or 47 U.S.C. 223), but neither suited the nature of this incident. They hoped that the word *threat* would be interpreted broadly in the courts. Legally, the government did not need to prove that Baker intended to threaten a person, only that he communicated speech that could be construed by a "reasonable person" as a threat. The problem, of course, was that Baker stated that his stories were fiction. Further, a court-appointed psychiatrist declared him not to be a threat. This situation is similar to that in airports when passengers are warned not to express, even jokingly, any intent to hijack a plane.

The judge did not accept the government's argument, however, and granted the defendant's motion to dismiss on May 26, 1995. The case never went to trial.

One of the most relevant aspects of Godwin's analysis is his speculation on how hard it is to write a law to address Baker's type of speech, which a judge decided was legally protected even though it was disturbing to many. One approach is to target speech that would make a "reasonable person" *feel* threatened (even if the speech was not a *true* threat). The problem is that courts call this kind of law "overly broad"; that is, as explained in section II, it might overextend into constitutionally protected speech. For example, an overly broad law might be wrongfully applied to speech in a mystery novel plot that reveals a clever way to cover up a rape incident; it could even apply to the speech in a letter explaining an employee pension plan change that makes an employee feel threatened by the prospect of a bleak retirement. Such a law would therefore have a chilling effect on speech not yet spoken. A mystery novelist, for example, might hesitate to write a book because of potential punitive results.

So why not try another strategy—to narrow the law by stating that any speech using a person's actual name in a threatening way is unprotected. As Godwin points out, however, that wouldn't work because shrewd writers already know how to avoid such a law by changing a real name ever so slightly. Godwin concludes:

> Beginning to see how difficult it is to write the "right" kind of speech-restricting law? You know: a law that prohibits speech that just about everybody finds troubling even as it protects those speakers who (we may think) deserve First Amendment protection far more than Baker does?
>
> Do you notice how, as we walk through the effort it takes to write a law that we hope is narrow enough not to infringe on our freedom yet is broad enough to criminalize a kind of speech or behavior we disapprove of, what we write looks more and more like a statute? That it gets harder and harder to avoid sounding like a lawyer or legislator? What we're doing is going through a thinking process very similar to what legislators—or at least the competent ones—go through when they write a statute. Sometimes going through that process means you can't avoid the conclusion that *no* statute could be written that criminalizes Baker's speech without also criminalizing speech that even the prosecutors in the *Baker* case would have to agree deserves First Amendment protection.
>
> Don't get me wrong—I'm not trying to argue that speech can never be banned or restricted. I have no trouble with laws punishing perjury or fraud or blackmail or "true threats," for example, and all four crimes center on the speech.
>
> But the *Baker* case tells us that when we try to classify some kind of offensive speech as *essentially* an act merely because of the psychological effect it has on us—I believe this is what Professor MacKinnon asks of us in *Only Words* and elsewhere—we come across just the kinds of difficulty we found here when we tried to base a law on the *Jake Baker* case. That is, we end up criminalizing either too much of the speech we want to protect or too little of the kind we are

> certain should be banned. I believe that whenever we come across this degree of difficulty in responding to troubling speech, it's a sign that passing a new law is the wrong way to go and that we should ask instead whether other mechanisms are in place that give us all the protection we need.[8]

And then Godwin points out what for librarians may be the most important idea—that most jury members are network users themselves. Many users had already decided at the time of the Baker posting that his stories had crossed a line—not a legal line, but one that breached an informally shared code of decency. Godwin speculates that eventually the Net would have taken care of the problem. This idea, which some believe is naive, is reminiscent of Brandeis and Holmes's "marketplace of ideas." At the very least, it reminds us to try a variety of conflict resolution strategies before resorting to the formal legal process.

Also important for librarians is Godwin's observation that prosecutors tried to tailor a prosecution to Jake Baker and couldn't get it to fit. This should have been a clue that perhaps Baker's speech wasn't criminal. In a similar fashion, tailoring policy to fit a particular person or incident becomes fraught with hazards.

LIBRARY PATRON AND EMPLOYEE RIGHTS

Although the *Kreimer* v. *Morristown* decision explicitly refused to judge Kreimer's behavior, the case's narrative did describe the kinds of problematic patron behaviors with which public and academic librarians are familiar. Whether in a reading room or at a computer terminal, library patron behavior in a limited public forum can be subject to time, place and manner regulations that library administrators feel are necessary to carry out the library's mission. These regulations must balance rights and responsibilities of users, must be content neutral and must apply equitably to all library users. The guidelines and practical suggestions in section I, including the explication of *Kreimer* v. *Morristown*, should help librarians develop good policies for patron behavior. Also particularly helpful is the Intellectual Freedom Committee's publication "Guidelines for the Development of Policies and Procedures regarding User Behavior and Library Usage" (appendix B). Another invaluable source is a memorandum, "Civil liability for an alleged hostile work environment related to patron or employee Internet use," written by Jenner & Block and available on the ALA/OIF Web site (http://www.ala.org).

Library professional discourse needs to pay closer attention to library employees who, like some patrons, are sometimes offended by library content or other activities in the public forum. How does a library manager distinguish between library activity protected by the First Amendment and library activity that may be fostering workplace harassment? What about the staff member who turns on the terminals every morning and is faced with obscene screen-savers presumably set the night before by the last workstation user? What about the cataloger who refuses to catalog materials that offend him or her? And what about employees who do not want their terminal use monitored?

The answers may vary. Librarians are urged to keep current with the rapidly changing workplace harassment law, which may sometimes collide with the constitutional protections of speech in a public forum.[9] Although the courts decided in *Kreimer* that body odor could disrupt the limited public forum, what about employees and patrons who have diseases that cause odor they can't control?

According to Robert O'Neil of the Jefferson Center for Protection of Freedom of Expression, "When it comes to laws such as those that would bar using state computers to access explicit material, the test should be whether government can tell a state worker not to bring to the workplace a personal copy of *Penthouse* or *Hustler* to read during lunch hour and coffee breaks. (Of course public employee use of state equipment—computers along with telephones, copiers, and the like—may be confined to official business, but such a constraint addresses activity, not content.)"[10]

O'Neil's point provides an approach to employee issues regarding electronic network access. The Internet is really just another medium. One may well argue that staff should not abuse e-mail; in fact, network filters are in demand as much for workplace control as for library control of minors! O'Neil's argument is that content should not and need not be the issue. Use of state property can be more easily subjected to limits through an equitable policy that is truly content neutral.

The following illustrates how employee workplace regulations collide with First Amendment rights. What happens when an art exhibition mounted in the library contains a freeze-dried dead kitten? In this case, the library director weighed the First Amendment against the employees' right to a healthy workplace. After consultation with attorneys and state health officials, he decided to maintain the exhibit. More important was the library director's offer of display space for the offended employees to mount their counterexhibit, which focused on kittens as live house pets.[11]

When new librarians and staff are hired, they should be informed that, contrary to the stereotype, a library is not a sheltered environment. Employees must be assured of their legal right to a safe, healthy workplace, with all laws strictly enforced regarding equal opportunity and protections against harassment and workplace violence. But because publicly funded libraries afford a high level of protection for the First Amendment, potential workers should be aware that given the nature of information and public discourse, they are quite likely to catalog or otherwise encounter material that is offensive to them.

In summary, employee First Amendment complaints should be handled with just as much respect and attention as those of patrons. Often the same principles apply. An opportunity for an employee to voice an opposing view will often suffice, as long as it isn't just a token gesture by management. If an employee is being disturbed by a patron or fellow employee, there may well be workplace laws to protect him or her. Just like those library users who wish that the limited public forum weren't quite so "robust," those for whom that forum is their workplace may sometimes feel uncomfortable, too.

SAMPLE OUTLINE FOR POLICIES ON PRIVACY

Libraries should consult with legal counsel before implementing any privacy policies. They should also have a copy of the *OIF Confidentiality in Libraries Modular Education Program*. Libraries should consider developing the following privacy policies incorporating intellectual freedom concerns.

1. Use of campus network or Internet at library workstations. The library confidentiality statute must be incorporated into the campus network policy. Users should be aware of which transactions are confidential and which, if any, are not. Library policies must conform to any state library confidentiality statutes.
2. Children's privacy rights. This document should clarify the differing roles of parents and librarians regarding children's access to library materials and services. For example, librarians do not serve *in loco parentis*.
3. Employee rights in regard to privacy in the workplace. Employee First Amendment rights must be protected at the same time that workplace laws are enforced. Sometimes these clash. Consult legal counsel.

Appended Materials

1. A copy of your state's library confidentiality statute.
2. A tickler file of pending privacy legislation and litigation.
3. Strict security and privacy policies for using the library's automated system. Make sure all staff have adequate training to assure patron privacy rights.

NOTES

1. Thomas Emerson, *The System of Freedom of Expression* (New York: Random House, 1970), p. 562.

2. Barbara M. Jones, "Should Libraries Post Suspect Notices? A First Amendment Perspective," in *Symposium on Identifying Cultural Property Protection Needs for the Twenty-first Century*, sponsored by the Smithsonian Institution, Arlington, Va., 1995, from published proceedings, pp. 77–82.

3. "Confidentiality Inventory," in *Confidentiality in Libraries: An Intellectual Freedom Modular Education Program Trainer's Manual* (Chicago: ALA, 1993), p. 30.

4. "Policy Development," in *Confidentiality in Libraries*, pp. 25–26.

5. *Confidentiality in Libraries*, Module II, p. 16.

6. Caroline Kennedy and Ellen Alderman, *The Right to Privacy* (New York: Knopf, 1995), p. 332.

7. Mike Godwin, *CyberRights: Defending Free Speech in the Digital Age* (New York: Random House, 1998). See also Charles Platt, *Anarchy Online: Net Crime, Net Sex* (New York: Harper, 1997).

8. Godwin, *CyberRights*, pp. 130–31.

9. Readers are advised to consult Marcy Edwards et al., *Freedom of Speech in the Public Workplace: A Legal and Practical Guide to Issues Affecting Public Employment* (Chicago: American Bar Association, 1998).

10. Robert O'Neil, "Protecting Free Expression in Electronic Communications," *EDUCOM Review* 31 (May/June 1996): 18.

11. Lois Walker et al., "Employee Rights versus the First Amendment," *American Libraries* 29 (May 1998): 60–61.

APPENDIX A

U.S. *Bill of Rights* *and Amendment* XIV

AMENDMENT I

Congress shall make no law respecting an establishment of religion, or prohibiting the free exercise thereof; or abridging the freedom of speech, or of the press; or the right of the people peaceably to assemble, and to petition the Government for a redress of grievances.

AMENDMENT II

A well regulated Militia, being necessary to the security of a free State, the right of the people to keep and bear Arms, shall not be infringed.

AMENDMENT III

No Soldier shall, in time of peace be quartered in any house, without the consent of the Owner, nor in time of war, but in a manner to be prescribed by law.

AMENDMENT IV

The right of the people to be secure in their persons, houses, papers, and effects, against unreasonable searches and seizures, shall not be violated, and no Warrants shall issue, but upon probable cause, supported by Oath or affirmation, and particularly describing the place to be searched, and the persons or things to be seized.

AMENDMENT V

No persons shall be held to answer for a capital, or otherwise infamous crime, unless on a presentment or indictment of a Grand Jury, except in cases arising in the land or naval forces, or in the Militia, when in actual service in time of War or public danger; nor shall any person be subject for the same offence to be twice put in jeopardy of life or limb; nor shall be compelled in any criminal case to be a witness against himself, nor be deprived of life, liberty, or property, without due process of law; nor shall private property be taken for public use, without just compensation.

AMENDMENT VI

In all criminal prosecutions, the accused shall enjoy the right to a speedy and public trial, by an impartial jury of the State and district wherein the crime shall have been committed, which district shall have been previously ascertained by law, and to be informed of the nature and cause of the accusation; to be confronted with the witnesses against him; to have compulsory process for obtaining witnesses in his favor, and to have the Assistance of Counsel for his defence.

AMENDMENT VII

In Suits at common law, where the value in controversy shall exceed twenty dollars, the right of trial by jury shall be preserved, and no fact tried by a jury, shall be otherwise re-examined in any Court of the United States, than according to the rules of the common law.

AMENDMENT VIII

Excessive bail shall not be required, nor excessive fines imposed, nor cruel and unusual punishments inflicted.

AMENDMENT IX

The enumeration of the Constitution, of certain rights, shall not be construed to deny or disparage others retained by the people.

AMENDMENT X

The powers not delegated to the United States by the Constitution, nor prohibited by it to the States, are reserved to the States respectively, or to the people.

AMENDMENT XIV

Section 1. All persons born or naturalized in the United States, and subject to the jurisdiction thereof, are citizens of the United States and of the State wherein they reside. No State shall make or enforce any law which shall abridge the privileges or immunities of citizens of the United States; nor shall any State deprive any person of life, liberty, or property, without due process of law; nor deny to any person within its jurisdiction the equal protection of the laws.

Section 2. Representatives shall be apportioned among the several States according to their respective numbers, counting the whole number of persons in each State, excluding Indians not taxed. But when the right to vote at any election for the choice of electors for President and Vice President of the United States, Representatives in Congress, the Executive and Judicial officers of a State, or the members of the Legislature thereof, is denied to any of the male inhabitants of such State, being twenty-one years of age, and citizens of the United States, or in any way abridged, except for participation in rebellion, or other crime, the basis of representation therein shall be reduced in the proportion which the number of such male citizens shall bear to the whole number of male citizens twenty-one years of age in such State.

Section 3. No person shall be a Senator or Representative in Congress, or elector of President and Vice President, or hold any office, civil or military, under the United States, or under any State, who, having previously taken an oath, as a member of Congress, or as an officer of the United States, or as a member of any State legislature, or as an executive or judicial officer of any State, to support the Constitution of the United States, shall have engaged in insurrection or rebellion against the same, or given aid or comfort to the enemies thereof. But Congress may by a vote of two-thirds of each House, remove such disability.

Section 4. The validity of the public debt of the United States, authorized by law, including debts incurred for payment of pensions and bounties for services in suppressing insurrection or rebellion, shall not be questioned. But neither the United States nor any State shall assume or pay any debt or obligation incurred in aid of insurrection or rebellion against the United States, or any claim for the loss or emancipation of any slave; but all such debts, obligations and claims shall be held illegal and void.

Section 5. The Congress shall have power to enforce, by appropriate legislation, the provisions of this article.

APPENDIX B

Guidelines for the Development of Policies and Procedures regarding User Behavior and Library Usage

Libraries are faced with problems of user behavior that must be addressed to insure the effective delivery of service and full access to facilities. Library governing bodies must approach the regulation of user behavior within the framework of the ALA "Code of Ethics," the *Library Bill of Rights* and the law, including local and state statutes, constitutional standards under the First and Fourteenth Amendments, due process and equal treatment under the law.

Publicly supported library service is based upon the First Amendment right of free expression. Publicly supported libraries are recognized as limited public forums for access to information. At least one federal court of appeals has recognized a First Amendment right to receive information in a public library. Library policies and procedures that could impinge upon such rights are subject to a higher standard of review than may be required in the policies of other public services and facilities.

There is a significant government interest in maintaining a library environment that is conducive to all users' exercise of their constitutionally protected right to receive information. This significant interest authorizes publicly supported libraries to maintain a safe and healthy environment in which library users and staff can be free from harassment, intimidation, and threats to their safety and well-being. Libraries should provide appropriate safeguards against such behavior and enforce policies and procedures addressing that behavior when it occurs.

In order to protect all library users' right of access to library facilities, to ensure the safety of users and staff, and to protect library resources and facilities from damage, the library's governing authority may impose reasonable restrictions on the time, place, or manner of library access.

GUIDELINES

The American Library Association's Intellectual Freedom Committee recommends that publicly supported libraries use the following guidelines, based upon constitutional principles, to develop policies and procedures governing the use of library facilities:

1. Libraries are advised to rely upon existing legislation and law enforcement mechanisms as the primary means of controlling behavior that involves public safety, criminal behavior, or other issues covered by existing local, state, or federal statutes. In many instances, this legal framework may be sufficient to provide the library with the necessary tools to maintain order.
2. If the library's governing body chooses to write its own policies and procedures regarding user behavior or access to library facilities, services, and resources, the policies should cite statutes or ordinances upon which the authority to make those policies is based.
3. Library policies and procedures governing the use of library facilities should be carefully examined to insure that they are not in violation of the *Library Bill of Rights.*
4. Reasonable and narrowly drawn policies and procedures designed to prohibit interference with use of the facilities and services by others, or to prohibit activities inconsistent with achievement of substantial library objectives, are acceptable.
5. Such policies and the attendant implementing procedures should be reviewed regularly by the library's legal counsel for compliance with federal and state constitutional requirements, federal and state civil rights legislation, all other applicable federal and state legislation, and applicable case law.
6. Every effort should be made to respond to potentially difficult circumstances of user behavior in a timely, direct, and open manner. Common sense, reason and sensitivity should be used to resolve issues in a constructive and positive manner without escalation.
7. Libraries should develop an ongoing staff training program based upon their user behavior policy. This program should include

training to develop empathy and understanding of the social and economic problems of some library users.

8. Policies and regulations that impose restrictions on library access:
   a. should apply only to those activities that materially interfere with the public's right of access to library facilities, the safety of users and staff, and the protection of library resources and facilities;
   b. should narrowly tailor prohibitions or restrictions so that they are not more restrictive than needed to serve their objectives;
   c. should attempt to balance competing interests and avoid favoring the majority at the expense of individual rights, or allowing individual users' rights to supersede those of the majority of library users;
   d. should be based upon actual behavior and not upon arbitrary distinctions between individuals or classes of individuals. Policies should not target specific users or groups of users based upon an assumption or expectation that such users might engage in behaviors that could disrupt library service;
   e. should not restrict access to the library by persons who merely inspire the anger or annoyance of others. Policies based upon appearance or behavior that is merely annoying or which merely generates negative subjective reactions from others, do not meet the necessary standard unless the behavior would interfere with access by an objectively reasonable person to library facilities and services. Such policies should employ a reasonable, objective standard based on the behavior itself;
   f. must provide a clear description of the behavior that is prohibited so that a reasonably intelligent person will have fair warning and must be continuously and clearly communicated in an effective manner to all library users;
   g. to the extent possible, should not leave those affected without adequate alternative means of access to information in the library;
   h. must be enforced evenhandedly, and not in a manner intended to benefit or disfavor any person or group in an arbitrary or capricious manner.

The user behaviors addressed in these Guidelines are the result of a wide variety of individual and societal conditions. Libraries should take advantage of the expertise of local social service agencies, advocacy groups, mental health professionals, law enforcement officials, and other community resources to develop community strategies for addressing the needs of a diverse population.

Adopted January 24, 1993, by the Intellectual Freedom Committee.

APPENDIX C

The Library Bill of Rights and Its Interpretations

The *Library Bill of Rights*

The American Library Association affirms that all libraries are forums for information and ideas, and that the following basic policies should guide their services.

I. Books and other library resources should be provided for the interest, information, and enlightenment of all people of the community the library serves. Materials should not be excluded because of the origin, background, or views of those contributing to their creation.

II. Libraries should provide materials and information presenting all points of view on current and historical issues. Materials should not be proscribed or removed because of partisan or doctrinal disapproval.

III. Libraries should challenge censorship in the fulfillment of their responsibility to provide information and enlightenment.

IV. Libraries should cooperate with all persons and groups concerned with resisting abridgment of free expression and free access to ideas.

V. A person's right to use a library should not be denied or abridged because of origin, age, background, or views.

VI. Libraries which make exhibit spaces and meeting rooms available to the public they serve should make such facilities available on an equitable basis, regardless of the beliefs or affiliations of individuals or groups requesting their use.

Adopted June 18, 1948. Amended by the ALA Council February 2, 1961; June 27, 1967; and January 23, 1980; reaffirmed January 23, 1996.

Access for Children and Young People to Videotapes and Other Nonprint Formats

An Interpretation of the *Library Bill of Rights*

Library collections of videotapes, motion pictures, and other nonprint formats raise a number of intellectual freedom issues, especially regarding minors.

The interests of young people, like those of adults, are not limited by subject, theme, or level of sophistication. Librarians have a responsibility to ensure young people have access to materials and services that reflect diversity sufficient to meet their needs.

To guide librarians and others in resolving these issues, the American Library Association provides the following guidelines.

Article V of the *Library Bill of Rights* says, "A person's right to use a library should not be denied or abridged because of origin, age, background, or views."

ALA's Free Access to Libraries for Minors: An Interpretation of the *Library Bill of Rights* states:

> The "right to use a library" includes free access to, and unrestricted use of, all the services, materials, and facilities the library has to offer. Every restriction on access to, and use of, library resources, based solely on the chronological age, educational level, or legal emancipation of users violates Article V.
>
> . . . [P]arents—and only parents—have the right and the responsibility to restrict the access of their children—and only their children—to library resources. Parents or legal guardians who do not want their children to have access to certain library services, materials, or facilities should so advise their children. Librarians and governing bodies cannot assume the role of parents or the functions of parental authority in the private relationship between parent and child. Librarians and governing bodies have a public and professional obligation to provide equal access to all library resources for all library users.

Policies which set minimum age limits for access to videotapes and/or other audiovisual materials and equipment, with or without parental permission, abridge library use for minors. Further, age limits based on the cost of the materials are unacceptable. Unless directly and specifically prohibited by law from circulating certain motion pictures and video productions to minors, librarians should apply the same standards to circulation of these materials as are applied to books and other materials.

Recognizing that libraries cannot act *in loco parentis*, ALA acknowledges and supports the exercise by parents of their responsibility to guide their own children's reading and viewing. Published reviews of films and videotapes and/or reference works which provide information about the content, subject matter, and recommended audiences can be made available in conjunction with nonprint collections to assist parents in guiding their children without implicating the library in censorship. This material may include information provided by video producers and distributors, promotional material on videotape packaging, and Motion Picture Association of America (MPAA) ratings *if they are included on the tape or in the packaging by the original publisher* and/or if they appear in review sources or reference works included in the library's collection. Marking out or removing ratings information from videotape packages constitutes expurgation or censorship.

MPAA and other rating services are private advisory codes and have no legal standing*. For the library to add such ratings to the materials if they are not already there, to post a list of such ratings with a collection, or to attempt to enforce such ratings through circulation policies or other procedures constitutes labeling, "an attempt to prejudice attitudes" about the material, and is unacceptable. The application of locally generated ratings schemes intended to provide content warnings to library users is also inconsistent with the *Library Bill of Rights*.

*For information on case law, please contact the ALA Office for Intellectual Freedom. *See also* "Statement on Labeling" and "Expurgation of Library Materials," Interpretations of the *Library Bill of Rights*.

Adopted June 28, 1989, by the ALA Council; the quotation from "Free Access to Libraries for Minors" was changed after Council adopted the July 3, 1991, revision of that Interpretation.

Access to Electronic Information, Services and Networks

An Interpretation of the *Library Bill of Rights*

The world is in the midst of an electronic communications revolution. Based on its constitutional, ethical, and historical heritage, American librarianship is uniquely positioned to address the broad range of information issues being raised in this revolution. In particular, librarians address intellectual freedom from a strong ethical base and an abiding commitment to the preservation of the individual's rights.

Freedom of expression is an inalienable human right and the foundation for self-government. Freedom of expression encompasses the freedom of speech and the corollary right to receive information. These rights extend to minors as well as adults. Libraries and librarians exist to facilitate the exercise of these rights by selecting, producing, providing access to, identifying, retrieving, organizing, providing instruction in the use of, and preserving recorded expression regardless of the format or technology.

The American Library Association expresses these basic principles of librarianship in its *Code of Ethics* and in the *Library Bill of Rights* and its Interpretations. These serve to guide librarians and library governing bodies in addressing issues of intellectual freedom that arise when the library provides access to electronic information, services, and networks.

Issues arising from the still-developing technology of computer-mediated information generation, distribution, and retrieval need to be approached and regularly reviewed from a context of constitutional principles and ALA policies so that fundamental and traditional tenets of librarianship are not swept away.

Electronic information flows across boundaries and barriers despite attempts by individuals, governments, and private entities to channel or control it. Even so, many people, for reasons of technology, infrastructure, or socio-economic status, do not have access to electronic information.

In making decisions about how to offer access to electronic information, each library should consider its mission, goals, objectives, cooperative agreements, and the needs of the entire community it serves.

THE RIGHTS OF USERS

All library system and network policies, procedures, or regulations relating to electronic resources and services should be scrutinized for potential violation of user rights. User policies should be developed according to the policies and guidelines established by the American Library Association, including "Guidelines for the Development and Implementation of Policies, Regulations and Procedures Affecting Access to Library Materials, Services and Facilities."

Users should not be restricted or denied access for expressing or receiving constitutionally protected speech. Users' access should not be changed without due process, including, but not limited to, formal notice and a means of appeal.

Although electronic systems may include distinct property rights and security concerns, such elements may not be be employed as a subterfuge to deny users' access to information. Users have the right to be free of unreasonable limitations or conditions set by libraries, librarians, system administrators, vendors, network service providers, or others. Contracts, agreements, and licenses entered into by libraries on behalf of their users should not violate this right. Users also have a right to information, training, and assistance necessary to operate the hardware and software provided by the library.

Users have both the right of confidentiality and the right of privacy. The library should uphold these rights by policy, procedure, and practice. Users should be advised, however, that because security is technically difficult to achieve, electronic transactions and files could become public.

The rights of users who are minors shall in no way be abridged.[1]

EQUITY OF ACCESS

Electronic information, services, and networks provided directly or indirectly by the library should be equally, readily, and equitably accessible to all library users. American Library Association policies oppose the charging of user fees for the provision of information services by all libraries and information services that receive their major support from public funds (50.3; 53.1.14; 60.1; 61.1). It should be the goal of all libraries to develop policies concerning access to electronic resources in light of "Economic Barriers to Information Access: An Interpretation of the *Library*

Bill of Rights" and "Guidelines for the Development and Implementation of Policies, Regulations and Procedures Affecting Access to Library Materials, Services and Facilities."

INFORMATION RESOURCES AND ACCESS

Providing connections to global information, services, and networks is not the same as selecting and purchasing material for a library collection. Determining the accuracy or authenticity of electronic information may present special problems. Some information accessed electronically may not meet a library's selection or collection development policy. It is, therefore, left to each user to determine what is appropriate. Parents and legal guardians who are concerned about their children's use of electronic resources should provide guidance to their own children.

Libraries and librarians should not deny or limit access to information available via electronic resources because of its allegedly controversial content or because of the librarian's personal beliefs or fear of confrontation. Information retrieved or utilized electronically should be considered constitutionally protected unless determined otherwise by a court with appropriate jurisdiction.

Libraries, acting within their mission and objectives, must support access to information on all subjects that serve the needs or interests of each user, regardless of the user's age or the content of the material. Libraries have an obligation to provide access to government information available in electronic format. Libraries and librarians should not deny access to information solely on the grounds that it is perceived to lack value.

In order to prevent the loss of information, and to preserve the cultural record, libraries may need to expand their selection or collection development policies to ensure preservation, in appropriate formats, of information obtained electronically.

Electronic resources provide unprecedented opportunities to expand the scope of information available to users. Libraries and librarians should provide access to information presenting all points of view. The provision of access does not imply sponsorship or endorsement. These principles pertain to electronic resources no less than they do to the more traditional sources of information in libraries.[2]

NOTES

1. See "Free Access to Libraries for Minors"; "Access to Resources and Services in the School Library Media Program"; and "Access for Children and Young People to Videotapes and Other Nonprint Formats."

2. See "Diversity in Collection Development."

Adopted by the ALA Council, January 24, 1996.

Questions and Answers: Access to Electronic Information, Services and Networks

An Interpretation of the *Library Bill of Rights*

In January of 1996, the American Library Association (ALA) approved *Access to Electronic Information, Services and Networks: An Interpretation of the* Library Bill of Rights. ALA's Intellectual Freedom Committee then convened to produce a sample set of questions and answers to clarify the implications and applications of this Interpretation.

Many of the following questions will not have a single answer. Each library must develop policies in keeping with its mission, objectives, and users. Librarians must also be cognizant of local legislation and judicial decisions that may affect implementation of their policies. All librarians are professionally obligated to strive for free access to information.

INTRODUCTION

1. *What are the factors that uniquely position American librarianship to provide access to electronic information?*

Electronic media offer an unprecedented forum for the sharing of information and ideas envisioned by the Founding Fathers in the U.S. Constitution. Their vision cannot be realized unless libraries provide free access to electronic information, services, and networks.

Thomas Jefferson, James Madison, and others laid the basis for a government that made education, access to information, and toleration for dissent cornerstones of a great democratic experiment. With geographic expansion and the rise of a mass press, American government facilitated these constitutional principles through the creation of such innovative institutions as the public school, land grant colleges, and the library. By the close of the 19th century, professionally trained librarians developed specialized techniques in support of their democratic mission. In the 1930's, the *Library Bill of Rights* acknowledged librarians' ethical responsibility to the Constitution's promise of access to information in all formats to all people.

2. *What is the library's role in facilitating freedom of expression in an electronic arena?*

Libraries are a national information infrastructure providing people with access and participation in the electronic arena. Libraries are essential to the informed debate demanded by the Constitution and for the provision of access to electronic information resources to those who might otherwise be excluded.

3. *Why should libraries extend access to electronic information resources to minors?*

Those libraries with a mission that includes service to minors should make available to them a full range of information necessary to become thinking adults and the informed electorate envisioned in the Constitution. The opportunity to participate responsibly in the electronic arena is also vital for nurturing the information literacy skills demanded by the Information Age. Only parents and legal guardians have the right and responsibility to restrict their children's and only their own children's access to any electronic resource.

4. *Do ALA intellectual freedom and ethics policies apply to the provision of access to electronic information, services and networks?*

Yes, because information is information regardless of format. Library resources in electronic form are increasingly recognized as vital to the provision of information that is the core of the library's role in society.

5. *Does the ALA require that libraries adopt the* Library Bill of Rights *or the ALA* Code of Ethics?

No. ALA has no authority to govern or regulate libraries. ALA's policies are voluntary and serve only as guidelines for local policy development.

6. *Does ALA censure libraries or librarians who do not adhere to or adopt the* Library Bill of Rights *or the ALA* Code of Ethics?

No.

7. *Do libraries need to develop policies about access to electronic information, services, and networks?*

Yes. Libraries should formally adopt and periodically reexamine policies that develop from the missions and goals specific to their institutions.

RIGHTS OF USERS

8. *What can we do when vendors/network providers/licensors attempt to limit or edit access to electronic information?*

Librarians should be strong advocates of open access to information regardless of storage media. When purchasing electronic information resources, libraries should thus attempt to empower themselves during contract negotiations with vendors/network providers/licensors to ensure the least restrictive access in current and future products.

Libraries themselves along with any parent institution and consortia partners should also communicate their intellectual freedom concerns and public responsibilities in the production of their own electronic information resources.

9. *How can libraries help to ensure library user confidentiality in regard to electronic information access?*

Librarians must be aware of patron confidentiality laws on library records for their particular state and community. In accordance with such laws and professional ethical responsibilities, librarians should ensure and routinely review policies and procedures for maintaining confidentiality of personally identifiable use of library materials, facilities, or services. These especially include electronic circulation and online use records. Hence, libraries and their consortiums should ensure that their automated circulation systems, other electronic information resources, and outside provider services strive to conform to applicable laws and the library's ethical duty to protect confidentiality of users. Electronic records on individual use patterns should also be strictly safeguarded. Software and protocols should be designed for the automatic and timely deletion of personal identifiers from the tracking elements within electronic databases. System access to computer terminals or other stations should also be designed to eliminate indicators of the research strategy or use patterns of any identifiable patron. For example, the efforts of the last user of a terminal or program should not remain on the monitor or be easily retrievable from a buffer or cache by subsequent users. Library or institutional monitoring for reserving time on the machines and the amount of time spent in electronic information resources should be similarly circumspect in protecting the patron's privacy rights.

Libraries and their institutions should provide physical environments that facilitate user privacy for accessing electronic information. For instance, libraries should consider placing terminals, printers, and access stations so that user privacy is enhanced. Where resources are limited, libraries should consider time, place and manner restrictions.

Finally, libraries must be sensitive to the special needs for confidential access to electronic information sources of physically challenged patrons.

10. *Our library is just one of many autonomous institutions in a consortium. How can we be sure that our cooperating partners honor the confidentiality of our library users in a shared network environment?*

This is a contractual and legal matter. The importance of confidentiality of personally identifiable information about library users transcends individual institutional and type of library boundaries. Libraries should establish and regularly review interlibrary and interagency cooperative agreements to ensure clear confidentiality policies and procedures, which obligate all members of a cooperative, or all departments and branches within a parent institution.

11. *Do libraries need an "acceptable use policy" for electronic information access? If so, what elements should be considered for inclusion?*

Access questions are rooted in Constitutional mandates and a *Library Bill of Rights* that reach across all media. These should be professionally interpreted through general service policies that also relate to the specific mission and objectives of the institution. Such general policies can benefit from the legacy and precedents within the ALA's *Intellectual Freedom Manual*, including new interpretations for electronic resources.

Reasonable restrictions placed on the time, place, and manner of library access should be used only when necessary to achieve substantial library managerial objectives and only in the least restrictive manner possible. In other words, libraries should focus on developing policies that ensure broad access to information resources of all kinds, citing as few restrictions as possible, rather than developing more limited "acceptable use" policies that seek to define limited ranges of what kinds of information can be accessed by which patrons and in what manner.

12. *Why shouldn't parental permission be required for minor access to electronic information?*

As with any other information format, parents are responsible for determining what they wish their own children to access electronically. Libraries may need to help parents understand their options during the evolving information revolution, but should not be in the policing position of enforcing parental restrictions within the library. In addition, libraries cannot use children as an excuse to violate their Constitutional duty to help provide for an educated adult electorate.

The *Library Bill of Rights*—its various Interpretations (especially *Free Access to Libraries for Minors; Access for Children and Young People to Videotapes and Other Nonprint Formats*), and ALA's *Guidelines for the Development and Implementation of Policies, Regulations and Procedures Affecting Access to Library Materials, Services and Facilities*—also endorse the rights of youth to library resources and information as part of their inalienable rights and the passage to informed adulthood. Electronic information access is no different in these regards.

13. *Does our library have to make provisions for patrons with disabilities to access electronic information?*

Yes. The Americans With Disabilities Act and other federal and state laws forbid providers of public services, whether publicly or privately governed, from discriminating against individuals with disabilities. All library information services, including access to electronic information, should be accessible to patrons regardless of disability.

Many methods are available and under development to make electronic information universally accessible, including adaptive devices, software, and human assistance. Libraries must consider such tools in trying to meet the needs of persons with disabilities in the design or provision of electronic information services.

EQUITY OF ACCESS

14. *My library recognizes different classes of users. Is this a problem?*

The mission and objectives of some libraries recognizes distinctions between classes of users. For example, academic libraries may have different categories of users (e.g., faculty, students, others). Public libraries may distinguish between residents and non-residents. School library media centers embrace curricular support as their primary mission; some have further expanded access to their collections. Special libraries vary their access policies depending on their definition of primary clientele. Establishing different levels of users should not automatically assume the need for different levels of access.

15. *Does the statement that "electronic information, services, and networks provided directly or indirectly by the library should be equally, readily, and equitably available to all library users" mean that exactly the same service must be available to anyone who wants to use the library?*

No. It means that access to services should not be denied on the basis of an arbitrary classification, for example, age or physical ability to use the equipment. This phrase, from *Economic Barriers to Information Access: An Interpretation of the Library Bill of Rights*, clarifies that simply making printed information sources available to those unable to pay while charging for electronic information sources abridges the principles of equality and equity.

16. *Which is a higher priority to offer more information or not to charge fees? Does this mean my library cannot charge fees?*

The higher priority is free services. Charging fees creates barriers to access. That is why ALA has urged librarians, in *Economic Barriers to Information Access*, to "resist the temptation to impose user fees to alleviate financial pressures, at long term cost to institutional integrity and public confidence in libraries."

17. *Does "provision of information services" include printouts?*

Whenever possible, all services should be without fees. Any decision to charge for service should be based on whether the fee creates a barrier to access. For example, some libraries have long provided free access to printed magazines while charging for photocopies. Translated to the electronic environment, this means that some libraries will provide the text on the screen at no charge, but might charge for printouts.

18. *If my library has no "major support from public funds," can we then charge fees?*

Yes, but ALA advocates achieving equitable access and avoiding and eliminating barriers to information and ideas whenever possible.

19. *What do you do if one person monopolizes the equipment?*

This is a policy issue to be established within each library according to its mission and goals. Time, place, and manner restrictions should be applied equitably to all users.

INFORMATION RESOURCES AND ACCESS

20. *How does providing connections to "global information, services, and networks" differ from selecting and purchasing material for an individual library?*

Selection begins with the institution's mission and objectives. The librarian performs an initial selection from available resources, and then the user makes a choice from that collection. Many electronic resources, such as CDs, are acquired for the library's collection in this traditional manner. Collections consist of fixed discrete items.

When libraries provide Internet access, they provide a means for people to use the wealth of information stored on computers throughout the world, whose ever-changing contents are created, maintained and made available beyond the library. The library also provides a means for the individual user to choose for him- or herself the resources accessed and to interact electronically with other computer users throughout the world.

21. *How can libraries use their selection expertise to help patrons use the Internet?*

Libraries should play a proactive role in guiding parents to the most effective locations and answers. Library websites are one starting place to the vast resources of the Internet. All libraries are encouraged to develop websites, including links to Internet resources, to meet the information needs of their users. These links should be made within the existing mission, collection development policy and selection criteria of the library.

22. *Should the library deny access to Constitutionally protected speech on the Internet in order to protect its users or reflect community values?*

No. The library should not deny access to constitutionally-protected speech. People have a right to receive constitutionally-protected speech, and any restriction of those rights imposed by a library violates the U.S. Constitution.

23. *Does using software that filters or blocks access to electronic information resources on the Internet violate this policy?*

The use of filters implies a promise to protect the user from objectionable material. This task is impossible given current technology and the inability to define absolutely the information to be blocked.

The filters available would place the library in a position of restricting access to information. The library's role is to provide access to information from which individuals choose the material for themselves.

Technology could be developed that would allow individual users of public terminals to exercise a choice to impose restrictions on their own searches. If these types of filters become available, libraries should carefully scrutinize them in light of their mission and goals.

24. *Why do libraries have an obligation to provide government information in electronic format?*

The role of libraries is to provide ideas and information across the spectrum of social and political thought and to make these ideas and this information available to anyone who needs or wants it. In a democracy libraries have a particular obligation to provide library users with information necessary for participation in self-governance. Because access to government information is rapidly shifting to electronic format only, libraries should plan to continue to provide access to information in this format, as well.

25. *What is the library's role in the preservation of electronic formats?*

The online electronic medium is ephemeral and information may disappear without efforts to save it. When libraries create information, they have the responsibility to preserve and archive it, if it meets the library's mission statement.

26. *Does "must support access to information on all subjects . . ." mean a library must provide material on all subjects for all users, even if those users are not part of the library's community of users or the material is not appropriate for the library?*

The institution's mission and objectives will drive these decisions.

27. *The Interpretation states that libraries should not deny access to resources solely because they are perceived to lack value. Does this mean the library must buy or obtain every electronic resource available?*

No. The institution's mission and objectives will drive these decisions.

28. *How can the library avoid becoming a game room and still provide access to this material?*

Libraries sometimes seek to prohibit the playing of computer games because the demand for terminals exceeds the supply. The libraries impose time, place or manner restrictions to the use of electronic equipment and resources. Such restrictions should not be based on the viewpoint expressed in the information being accessed.

29. *Do copyright laws apply to electronic information?*

Yes. Librarians have an ethical responsibility to keep abreast of copyright and fair use rights. This responsibility applies to:

1. the library's own online publications,
2. contractual obligations with authors and publishers,
3. informing library users of copyright laws which apply to their use of electronic information.

June 5, 1997

Access to Library Resources and Services regardless of Gender or Sexual Orientation

An Interpretation of the *Library Bill of Rights*

American libraries exist and function within the context of a body of laws derived from the United States Constitution and the First Amendment. The *Library Bill of Rights* embodies the basic policies which guide libraries in the provision of services, materials, and programs.

In the preamble to its *Library Bill of Rights*, the American Library Association affirms that *all* [emphasis added] libraries are forums for information and ideas. This concept of *forum* and its accompanying principle of *inclusiveness* pervade all six Articles of the *Library Bill of Rights*.

The American Library Association stringently and unequivocally maintains that libraries and librarians have an obligation to resist efforts that systematically exclude materials dealing with any subject matter, including gender, homosexuality, bisexuality, lesbianism, heterosexuality, gay lifestyles, or any facet of sexual orientation:

- Article I of the *Library Bill of Rights* states that "Materials should not be excluded because of the origin, background, or views of those contributing to their creation." The Association affirms that books and other materials coming from gay presses, gay, lesbian, or bisexual authors or other creators, and materials dealing with gay lifestyles are protected by the *Library Bill of Rights.* Librarians are obligated by the *Library Bill of Rights* to endeavor to select materials without regard to the gender or sexual orientation of their creators by using the criteria identified in their written, approved selection policies. (ALA policy 53.1.5).
- Article II maintains that "Libraries should provide materials and information presenting all points of view on current and historical issues. Materials should not be proscribed or removed because of partisan or doctrinal disapproval." Library services, materials, and programs representing diverse points of view on gender or sexual orientation should be considered for purchase and inclusion in library collections and programs. (ALA policies 53.1.1, 53.1.9, and 53.1.11). The Association affirms that attempts to proscribe or remove materials dealing with gay or lesbian life without regard to the written, approved selection policy violate this tenet and constitute censorship.
- Articles III and IV mandate that libraries "challenge censorship" and cooperate with those "resisting abridgement of free expression and free access to ideas."
- Article V holds that "A person's right to use a library should not be denied or abridged because of origin, age, background, or views." In the *Library Bill of Rights* and all its Interpretations, it is intended that: "origin" encompasses all the characteristics of individuals that are inherent in the circumstances of their birth; "age" encompasses all the characteristics of individuals that are inherent in their levels of development and maturity; "background" encompasses all the characteristics of individuals that are a result of their life experiences; and "views" encompasses all the opinions and beliefs held and expressed by individuals.

Therefore, Article V of the *Library Bill of Rights* mandates that library services, materials, and programs be available to all members of the community the library serves, without regard to gender or sexual orientation.

- Article VI maintains that "Libraries which make exhibit spaces and meeting rooms available to the public they serve should make such facilities available on an equitable basis, regardless of the beliefs or affiliations of individuals or groups requesting their use." This protection extends to all groups and members of the community the library serves, without regard to gender or sexual orientation.

The American Library Association holds that any attempt, be it legal or extra-legal, to regulate or suppress library services, materials, or programs must be resisted in order that protected expression is not abridged. Librarians have a professional obligation to ensure that all library users have free and equal access to the entire range of library services, materials, and programs. Therefore, the Association strongly opposes any effort to limit access to information and ideas. The Association also encourages librarians to proactively support the First Amendment rights of all library users, including gays, lesbians, and bisexuals.

Adopted by the ALA Council, June 30, 1993.

Access to Resources and Services in the School Library Media Program

An Interpretation of the *Library Bill of Rights*

The school library media program plays a unique role in promoting intellectual freedom. It serves as a point of voluntary access to information and ideas and as a learning laboratory for students as they acquire critical thinking and problem solving skills needed in a pluralistic society. Although the educational level and program of the school necessarily shapes the resources and services of a school library media program, the principles of the *Library Bill of Rights* apply equally to all libraries, including school library media programs.

School library media professionals assume a leadership role in promoting the principles of intellectual freedom within the school by providing resources and services that create and sustain an atmosphere of free inquiry. School library media professionals work closely with teachers to integrate instructional activities in classroom units designed to equip students to locate, evaluate, and use a broad range of ideas effectively. Through resources, programming, and educational processes, students and teachers experience the free and robust debate characteristic of a democratic society.

School library media professionals cooperate with other individuals in building collections of resources appropriate to the developmental and maturity levels of students. These collections provide resources which support the curriculum and are consistent with the philosophy, goals, and objectives of the school district. Resources in school library media collections represent diverse points of view on current as well as historical issues.

While English is, by history and tradition, the customary language of the United States, the languages in use in any given community may vary. Schools serving communities in which other languages are used make efforts to accommodate the needs of students for whom English is a second language. To support these efforts, and to ensure equal access to resources and services, the school library media program provides resources which reflect the linguistic pluralism of the community.

Members of the school community involved in the collection development process employ educational criteria to select resources unfettered by their personal, political, social, or religious views. Students and educators served by the school library media program have access to resources and services free of constraints resulting from personal, partisan, or doctrinal disapproval. School library media professionals resist efforts by individuals to define what is appropriate for all students or teachers to read, view, or hear.

Major barriers between students and resources include: imposing age or grade level restrictions on the use of resources, limiting the use of interlibrary loan and access to electronic information, charging fees for information in specific formats, requiring permissions from parents or teachers, establishing restricted shelves or closed collections, and labeling. Policies, procedures, and rules related to the use of resources and services support free and open access to information.

The school board adopts policies that guarantee students access to a broad range of ideas. These include policies on collection development and procedures for the review of resources about which concerns have been raised. Such policies, developed by persons in the school community, provide for a timely and fair hearing and assure that procedures are applied equitably to all expressions of concern. School library media professionals implement district policies and procedures in the school.

Adopted July 2, 1986; amended January 10, 1990, by the ALA Council.

Challenged Materials

An Interpretation of the *Library Bill of Rights*

The American Library Association declares as a matter of firm principle that it is the responsibility of every library to have a clearly defined materials selection policy in written form which reflects the *Library Bill of Rights*, and which is approved by the appropriate governing authority.

Challenged materials which meet the criteria for selection in the materials selection policy of the library should not be removed under any legal or extra-legal pressure. The *Library Bill of Rights* states in Article I that "Materials should not be excluded because of the origin, background, or views of those contributing to their creation," and in Article II, that "Materials should not be proscribed or removed because of partisan or doctrinal disapproval." Freedom of expression is protected by the Constitution of the United States, but constitutionally protected expression is often separated from unprotected expression only by a dim and uncertain line. The Constitution requires a procedure designed to focus searchingly on challenged expression before it can be suppressed. An adversary hearing is a part of this procedure.

Therefore, any attempt, be it legal or extra-legal, to regulate or suppress materials in libraries must be closely scrutinized to the end that protected expression is not abridged.

Adopted June 25, 1971; amended July 1, 1981; amended January 10, 1990, by the ALA Council.

Diversity in Collection Development

An Interpretation of the *Library Bill of Rights*

Throughout history, the focus of censorship has fluctuated from generation to generation. Books and other materials have not been selected or have been removed from library collections for many reasons, among which are prejudicial language and ideas, political content, economic theory, social philosophies, religious beliefs, sexual forms of expression, and other topics of a potentially controversial nature.

Some examples of censorship may include removing or not selecting materials because they are considered by some as racist or sexist; not purchasing conservative religious materials; not selecting materials about or by minorities because it is thought these groups or interests are not represented in a community; or not providing information on or materials from non-mainstream political entities.

Librarians may seek to increase user awareness of materials on various social concerns by many means, including, but not limited to, issuing bibliographies and presenting exhibits and programs.

Librarians have a professional responsibility to be inclusive, not exclusive, in collection development and in the provision of interlibrary loan.

Access to all materials legally obtainable should be assured to the user, and policies should not unjustly exclude materials even if they are offensive to the librarian or the user. Collection development should reflect the philosophy inherent in Article II of the *Library Bill of Rights:* "Libraries should provide materials and information presenting all points of view on current and historical issues. Materials should not be proscribed or removed because of partisan or doctrinal disapproval." A balanced collection reflects a diversity of materials, not an equality of numbers. Collection development responsibilities include selecting materials in the languages in common use in the community which the library serves. Collection development and the selection of materials should be done according to professional standards and established selection and review procedures.

There are many complex facets to any issue, and variations of context in which issues may be expressed, discussed, or interpreted. Librarians have a professional responsibility to be fair, just, and equitable and to give all library users equal protection in guarding against violation of the library patron's right to read, view, or listen to materials and resources protected by the First Amendment, no matter what the viewpoint of the author, creator, or selector. Librarians have an obligation to protect library collections from removal of materials based on personal bias or prejudice, and to select and support the access to materials on all subjects that meet, as closely as possible, the needs and interests of all persons in the community which the library serves. This includes materials that reflect political, economic, religious, social, minority, and sexual issues.

Intellectual freedom, the essence of equitable library services, provides for free access to all expressions of ideas through which any and all sides of a question, cause, or movement may be explored. Toleration is meaningless without tolerance for what some may consider detestable. Librarians cannot justly permit their own preferences to limit their degree of tolerance in collection development, because freedom is indivisible.

Adopted July 14, 1982; amended January 10, 1990, by the ALA Council.

Economic Barriers to Information Access

An Interpretation of the *Library Bill of Rights*

A democracy presupposes an informed citizenry. The First Amendment mandates the right of all persons to free expression, and the corollary right to receive the constitutionally protected expression of others. The publicly supported library provides free and equal access to information for all people of the community the library serves. While the roles, goals and objectives of publicly supported libraries may differ, they share this common mission.

The library's essential mission must remain the first consideration for librarians and governing bodies faced with economic pressures and competition for funding.

In support of this mission, the American Library Association has enumerated certain principles of library services in the *Library Bill of Rights.*

PRINCIPLES GOVERNING FINES, FEES, AND USER CHARGES

Article I of the *Library Bill of Rights* states: "Books and other library resources should be provided for the interest, information, and enlightenment of all people of the community the library serves."

Article V of the *Library Bill of Rights* states: "A person's right to use a library should not be denied or abridged because of origin, age, background, or views."

The American Library Association opposes the charging of user fees for the provision of information by all libraries and information services that receive their major support from public funds. All information resources that are provided directly or indirectly by the library, regardless of technology, format, or methods of delivery, should be readily, equally, and equitably accessible to all library users.

Libraries that adhere to these principles systematically monitor their programs of service for potential barriers to access and strive to eliminate such barriers when they occur. All library policies and procedures, particularly those involving fines, fees, or other user charges, should be scrutinized for potential barriers to access. All services should be designed and implemented with care, so as not to infringe on or interfere with the provision or delivery of information and resources for all users. Services should be re-evaluated on a regular basis to ensure that the library's basic mission remains uncompromised.

Librarians and governing bodies should look for alternative models and methods of library administration that minimize distinctions among users based on their economic status or financial condition. They should resist the temptation to impose user fees to alleviate financial pressures, at long-term cost to institutional integrity and public confidence in libraries.

Library services that involve the provision of information, regardless of format, technology, or method of delivery, should be made available to all library users on an equal and equitable basis. Charging fees for the use of library collections, services, programs, or facilities that were purchased with public funds raises barriers to access. Such fees effectively abridge or deny access for some members of the community because they reinforce distinctions among users based on their ability and willingness to pay.

PRINCIPLES GOVERNING CONDITIONS OF FUNDING

Article II of the *Library Bill of Rights* states: "Materials should not be proscribed or removed because of partisan or doctrinal disapproval."

Article III of the *Library Bill of Rights* states: "Libraries should challenge censorship in the fulfillment of their responsibility to provide information and enlightenment."

Article IV of the *Library Bill of Rights* states: "Libraries should cooperate with all persons and groups concerned with resisting abridgment of free expression and free access to ideas."

The American Library Association opposes any legislative or regulatory attempt to impose content restrictions on library resources, or to limit user access to information, as a condition of funding for publicly supported libraries and information services.

The First Amendment guarantee of freedom of expression is violated when the right to receive that expression is subject to arbitrary restrictions based on content.

Librarians and governing bodies should examine carefully any terms or conditions attached to library funding and should oppose attempts to limit through such conditions full and equal access to information because of content. This principle applies equally to private gifts or bequests and to public funds. In particular, librarians and governing bodies have an obligation to reject such restrictions when the effect of the restriction is to limit equal and equitable access to information.

Librarians and governing bodies should cooperate with all efforts to create a community consensus that publicly supported libraries require funding unfettered by restrictions. Such a consensus supports the library mission to provide the free and unrestricted exchange of information and ideas necessary to a functioning democracy.

The Association's historic position in this regard is stated clearly in a number of Association policies: 50.4, "Free Access to Information"; 50.9, "Financing of Libraries"; 51.2, "Equal Access to Library Service"; 51.3, "Intellectual Freedom"; 53, "Intellectual Freedom Policies"; 59.1, "Policy Objectives"; and 60, "Library Services for the Poor."

Adopted by the ALA Council, June 30, 1993.

Evaluating Library Collections

An Interpretation of the *Library Bill of Rights*

The continuous review of library materials is necessary as a means of maintaining an active library collection of current interest to users. In the process, materials may be added and physically deteriorated or obsolete materials may be replaced or removed in accordance with the collection maintenance policy of a given library and the needs of the community it serves. Continued evaluation is closely related to the goals and responsibilities of libraries and is a valuable tool of collection development. This procedure is not to be used as a convenient means to remove materials presumed to be controversial or disapproved of by segments of the community. Such abuse of the evaluation function violates the principles of intellectual freedom and is in opposition to the Preamble and Articles I and II of the *Library Bill of Rights*, which state:

The American Library Association affirms that all libraries are forums for information and ideas, and that the following basic policies should guide their services.

I. Books and other library resources should be provided for the interest, information, and enlightenment of all people of the community the library serves. Materials should not be excluded because of the origin, background, or views of those contributing to their creation.

II. Libraries should provide materials and information presenting all points of view on current and historical issues. Materials should not be proscribed or removed because of partisan or doctrinal disapproval.

The American Library Association opposes such "silent censorship" and strongly urges that libraries adopt guidelines setting forth the positive purposes and principles of evaluation of materials in library collections.

Adopted February 2, 1973; amended July 1, 1981, by the ALA Council.

Exhibit Spaces and Bulletin Boards

An Interpretation of the *Library Bill of Rights*

Libraries often provide exhibit spaces and bulletin boards. The uses made of these spaces should conform to the *Library Bill of Rights:* Article I states, "Materials should not be excluded because of the origin, background, or views of those contributing to their creation." Article II states, "Materials should not be proscribed or removed because of partisan or doctrinal disapproval." Article VI maintains that exhibit space should be made available "on an equitable basis, regardless of the beliefs or affiliations of individuals or groups requesting their use."

In developing library exhibits, staff members should endeavor to present a broad spectrum of opinion and a variety of viewpoints. Libraries should not shrink from developing exhibits because of controversial content or because of the beliefs or affiliations of those whose work is represented. Just as libraries do not endorse the viewpoints of those whose works are represented in their collections, libraries also do not endorse the beliefs or viewpoints of topics which may be the subject of library exhibits.

Exhibit areas often are made available for use by community groups. Libraries should formulate a written policy for the use of these exhibit areas to assure that space is provided on an equitable basis to all groups which request it.

Written policies for exhibit space use should be stated in inclusive rather than exclusive terms. For example, a policy that the library's exhibit space is open "to organizations engaged in educational, cultural, intellectual, or charitable activities" is an inclusive statement of the limited uses of the exhibit space. This defined limitation would permit religious groups to use the exhibit space because they engage in intellectual activities, but would exclude most commercial uses of the exhibit space.

A publicly supported library may limit use of its exhibit space to strictly "library-related" activities, provided that the limitation is clearly circumscribed and is viewpoint neutral.

Libraries may include in this policy rules regarding the time, place, and manner of use of the exhibit space, so long as the rules are content-neutral and are applied in the same manner to all groups wishing to use the space. A library may wish to limit access to exhibit space to groups within the community served by the library. This practice is acceptable provided that the same rules and regulations apply to everyone, and that exclusion is not made on the basis of the doctrinal, religious, or political beliefs of the potential users.

The library should not censor or remove an exhibit because some members of the community may disagree with its content. Those who object to the content of any exhibit held at the library should be able to submit their complaint and/or their own exhibit proposal to be judged according to the policies established by the library.

Libraries may wish to post a permanent notice near the exhibit area stating that the library does not advocate or endorse the viewpoints of exhibits or exhibitors.

Libraries which make bulletin boards available to public groups for posting notices of public interest should develop criteria for the use of these spaces based on the same considerations as those outlined above.

Libraries may wish to develop criteria regarding the size of material to be displayed, the length of time materials may remain on the bulletin board, the frequency with which material may be posted for the same group, and the geographic area from which notices will be accepted.

Adopted July 2, 1991, by the ALA Council.

Expurgation of Library Materials

An Interpretation of the *Library Bill of Rights*

Expurgating library materials is a violation of the *Library Bill of Rights*. Expurgation as defined by this Interpretation includes any deletion, excision, alteration, editing, or obliteration of any part(s) of books or other library resources by the library, its agent, or its parent institution (if any). By such expurgation, the library is in effect denying access to the complete work and the entire spectrum of ideas that the work intended to express. Such action stands in violation of Articles I, II, and III of the *Library Bill of Rights*, which state that "Materials should not be excluded because of the origin, background, or views of those contributing to their creation," that "Materials should not be proscribed or removed because of partisan or doctrinal disapproval," and that "Libraries should challenge censorship in the fulfillment of their responsibility to provide information and enlightenment."

The act of expurgation has serious implications. It involves a determination that it is necessary to restrict access to the complete work. This is censorship. When a work is expurgated, under the assumption that certain portions of that work would be harmful to minors, the situation is no less serious.

Expurgation of any books or other library resources imposes a restriction, without regard to the rights and desires of all library users, by limiting access to ideas and information.

Further, expurgation without written permission from the holder of the copyright on the material may violate the copyright provisions of the United States Code.

Adopted February 2, 1973; amended July 1, 1981; amended January 10, 1990, by the ALA Council.

Free Access to Libraries for Minors

An Interpretation of the *Library Bill of Rights*

Library policies and procedures which effectively deny minors equal access to all library resources available to other users violate the *Library Bill of Rights.* The American Library Association opposes all attempts to restrict access to library services, materials, and facilities based on the age of library users.

Article V of the *Library Bill of Rights* states, "A person's right to use a library should not be denied or abridged because of origin, age, background, or views." The "right to use a library" includes free access to, and unrestricted use of, all the services, materials, and facilities the library has to offer. Every restriction on access to, and use of, library resources, based solely on the chronological age, educational level, or legal emancipation of users violates Article V.

Libraries are charged with the mission of developing resources to meet the diverse information needs and interests of the communities they serve. Services, materials, and facilities which fulfill the needs and interests of library users at different stages in their personal development are a necessary part of library resources. The needs and interests of each library user, and resources appropriate to meet those needs and interests, must be determined on an individual basis. Librarians cannot predict what resources will best fulfill the needs and interests of any individual user based on a single criterion such as chronological age, level of education, or legal emancipation.

The selection and development of library resources should not be diluted because of minors having the same access to library resources as adult users. Institutional self-censorship diminishes the credibility of the library in the community, and restricts access for all library users.

Librarians and governing bodies should not resort to age restrictions on access to library resources in an effort to avoid actual or anticipated objections from parents or anyone else. The mission, goals, and objectives of libraries do not authorize librarians or governing bodies to assume, abrogate, or overrule the rights and responsibilities of parents or legal guardians. Librarians and governing bodies should maintain that parents—and only parents—have the right and the responsibility to restrict the access of their children—and only their children—to library resources. Parents or legal guardians who do not want their children to have access to certain library services, materials or facilities, should so advise their children. Librarians and governing bodies cannot assume the role of parents or the functions of parental authority in the private relationship between parent and child. Librarians and governing bodies have a public and professional obligation to provide equal access to all library resources for all library users.

Librarians have a professional commitment to ensure that all members of the community they serve have free and equal access to the entire range of library resources regardless of content, approach, format, or amount of detail. This principle of library service applies equally to all users, minors as well as adults. Librarians and governing bodies must uphold this principle in order to provide adequate and effective service to minors.

Adopted June 30, 1972; amended July 1, 1981; July 3, 1991, by the ALA Council.

Library-Initiated Programs as a Resource

An Interpretation of the *Library Bill of Rights*

Library-initiated programs support the mission of the library by providing users with additional opportunities for information, education, and recreation. Article I of the *Library Bill of Rights* states: "Books and other library resources should be provided for the interest, information, and enlightenment of all people of the community the library serves."

Library-initiated programs take advantage of library staff expertise, collections, services, and facilities to increase access to information and information resources. Library-initiated programs introduce users and potential users to the resources of the library and to the library's primary function as a facilitator of information access. The library may participate in cooperative or joint programs with other agencies, organizations, institutions, or individuals as part of its own effort to address information needs and to facilitate information access in the community the library serves.

Library-initiated programs on site and in other locations include, but are not limited to, speeches, community forums, discussion groups, demonstrations, displays, and live or media presentations.

Libraries serving multilingual or multicultural communities make efforts to accommodate the information needs of those for whom English is a second language. Library-initiated programs across language and cultural barriers introduce otherwise unserved populations to the resources of the library and provide access to information.

Library-initiated programs "should not be proscribed or removed (or canceled) because of partisan or doctrinal disapproval" of the contents of the program or the views expressed by the participants, as stated in Article II of the *Library Bill of Rights*. Library sponsorship of a program does not constitute an endorsement of the content of the program or the views expressed by the participants, any more than the purchase of material for the library collection constitutes an endorsement of the contents of the material or the views of its creator.

Library-initiated programs are a library resource, and as such, are developed in accordance with written guidelines, as approved and adopted by the library's policy-making body. These guidelines include an endorsement of the *Library Bill of Rights* and set forth the library's commitment to free and open access to information and ideas for all users.

Library staff select topics, speakers and resource materials for library-initiated programs based on the interests and information needs of the community. Topics, speakers and resource materials are not excluded from library-initiated programs because of possible controversy. Concerns, questions or complaints about library-initiated program[s] are handled according to the same written policy and procedures which govern reconsiderations of other library resources.

Library-initiated programs are offered free of charge and are open to all. Article V of the *Library Bill of Rights* states: "A person's right to use a library should not be denied or abridged because of origin, age, background, or views."

The "right to use a library" encompasses all of the resources the library offers, including the right to attend library-initiated programs. Libraries do not deny or abridge access to library resources, including library-initiated programs, based on an individual's economic background and ability to pay.

Adopted January 27, 1982. Amended June 26, 1990, by the ALA Council.

Meeting Rooms

An Interpretation of the *Library Bill of Rights*

Many libraries provide meeting rooms for individuals and groups as part of a program of service. Article VI of the *Library Bill of Rights* states that such facilities should be made available to the public served by the given library "on an equitable basis, regardless of the beliefs or affiliations of individuals or groups requesting their use."

Libraries maintaining meeting room facilities should develop and publish policy statements governing use. These statements can properly define time, place, or manner of use; such qualifications should not pertain to the content of a meeting or to the beliefs or affiliations of the sponsors.

These statements should be made available in any commonly used language within the community served.

If meeting rooms in libraries supported by public funds are made available to the general public for nonlibrary sponsored events, the library may not exclude any group based on the subject matter to be discussed or based on the ideas that the group advocates. For example, if a library allows charities and sports clubs to discuss their activities in library meeting rooms, then the library should not exclude partisan political or religious groups from discussing their activities in the same facilities. If a library opens its meeting rooms to a wide variety of civic organizations, then the library may not deny access to a religious organization. Libraries may wish to post a permanent notice near the meeting room stating that the library does not advocate or endorse the viewpoints of meetings or meeting room users.

Written policies for meeting room use should be stated in inclusive rather than exclusive terms. For example, a policy that the library's facilities are open "to organizations engaged in educational, cultural, intellectual, or charitable activities" is an inclusive statement of the limited uses to which the facilities may be put. This defined limitation would permit religious groups to use the facilities because they engage in intellectual activities, but would exclude most commercial uses of the facility.

A publicly supported library may limit use of its meeting rooms to strictly "library-related" activities, provided that the limitation is clearly circumscribed and is viewpoint neutral.

Written policies may include limitations on frequency of use, and whether or not meetings held in library meeting rooms must be open to the public. If state and local laws permit private as well as public sessions of meetings in libraries, libraries may choose to offer both options. The same standard should be applicable to all.

If meetings are open to the public, libraries should include in their meeting room policy statement a section which addresses admission fees. If admission fees are permitted, libraries shall seek to make it possible that these fees do not limit access to individuals who may be unable to pay, but who wish to attend the meeting. Article V of the *Library Bill of Rights* states that "a person's right to use a library should not be denied or abridged because of origin, age, background, or views." It is inconsistent with Article V to restrict indirectly access to library meeting rooms based on an individual's or group's ability to pay for that access.

Adopted July 2, 1991, by the ALA Council.

Restricted Access to Library Materials

An Interpretation of the *Library Bill of Rights*

Libraries are a traditional forum for the open exchange of information. Attempts to restrict access to library materials violate the basic tenets of the *Library Bill of Rights.*

Historically, attempts have been made to limit access by relegating materials into segregated collections. These attempts are in violation of established policy. Such collections are often referred to by a variety of names, including "closed shelf," "locked case," "adults only," "restricted shelf," or "high demand." Access to some materials also may require a monetary fee or financial deposit. In any situation which restricts access to certain materials, a barrier is placed between the patron and those materials. That barrier may be age related, linguistic, economic, or psychological in nature.

Because materials placed in restricted collections often deal with controversial, unusual, or "sensitive" subjects, having to ask a librarian or circulation clerk for them may be embarrassing or inhibiting for patrons desiring the materials. Needing to ask for materials may pose a language barrier or a staff service barrier. Because restricted collections often are composed of materials which some library patrons consider "objectionable," the potential user may be predisposed to think of the materials as "objectionable" and, therefore, are reluctant to ask for them.

Barriers between the materials and the patron which are psychological, or are affected by language skills, are nonetheless limitations on access to information. Even when a title is listed in the catalog with a reference to its restricted status, a barrier is placed between the patron and the publication. (See also "Statement on Labeling.")

There may be, however, countervailing factors to establish policies to protect library materials—specifically, for reasons of physical preservation including protection from theft or mutilation. Any such policies must be carefully formulated and administered with extreme attention to the principles of intellectual freedom. This caution is also in keeping with ALA policies, such as "Evaluating Library Collections," "Free Access to Libraries for Minors," and the "Preservation Policy."

Finally, in keeping with the "Joint Statement on Access" of the American Library Association and Society of American Archivists, restrictions that result from donor agreements or contracts for special collections materials must be similarly circumscribed. Permanent exclusions are not acceptable. The overriding impetus must be to work for free and unfettered access to all documentary heritage.

Adopted February 2, 1973; amended July 1, 1981; July 3, 1991, by the ALA Council.

Statement on Labeling

An Interpretation of the *Library Bill of Rights*

Labeling is the practice of describing or designating materials by affixing a prejudicial label and/or segregating them by a prejudicial system. The American Library Association opposes these means of predisposing people's attitudes toward library materials for the following reasons:

1. Labeling is an attempt to prejudice attitudes and as such, it is a censor's tool.
2. Some find it easy and even proper, according to their ethics, to establish criteria for judging publications as objectionable. However, injustice and ignorance rather than justice and enlightenment result from such practices, and the American Library Association opposes the establishment of such criteria.
3. Libraries do not advocate the ideas found in their collections. The presence of books and other resources in a library does not indicate endorsement of their contents by the library.

A variety of private organizations promulgate rating systems and/or review materials as a means of advising either their members or the general public concerning their opinions of the contents and suitability or appropriate age for use of certain books, films, recordings, or other materials. For the library to adopt or enforce any of these private systems, to attach such ratings to library materials, to include them in bibliographic records, library catalogs, or other finding aids, or otherwise to endorse them would violate the *Library Bill of Rights.*

While some attempts have been made to adopt these systems into law, the constitutionality of such measures is extremely questionable. If such legislation is passed which applies within a library's jurisdiction, the library should seek competent legal advice concerning its applicability to library operations.

Publishers, industry groups, and distributors sometimes add ratings to material or include them as part of their packaging. Librarians should not endorse such practices. However, removing or obliterating such ratings—if placed there by or with permission of the copyright holder—could constitute expurgation, which is also unacceptable.

The American Library Association opposes efforts which aim at closing any path to knowledge. This statement, however, does not exclude the adoption of organizational schemes designed as directional aids or to facilitate access to materials.

Adopted July 13, 1951; amended June 25, 1971; July 1, 1981; June 26, 1990, by the ALA Council.

The Universal Right to Free Expression

An Interpretation of the *Library Bill of Rights*

Freedom of expression is an inalienable human right and the foundation for self-government. Freedom of expression encompasses the freedoms of speech, press, religion, assembly, and association, and the corollary right to receive information.

The American Library Association endorses this principle, which is also set forth in the Universal Declaration of Human Rights, adopted by the United Nations General Assembly. The Preamble of this document states that ". . . recognition of the inherent dignity and of the equal and inalienable rights of all members of the human family is the foundation of freedom, justice, and peace in the world . . ." and ". . . the advent of a world in which human beings shall enjoy freedom of speech and belief and freedom from fear and want has been proclaimed as the highest aspiration of the common people. . . ."

Article 18 of this document states:

> Everyone has the right to freedom of thought, conscience, and religion; this right includes freedom to change his religion or belief, and freedom, either alone or in community with others and in public or private, to manifest his religion or belief in teaching, practice, worship, and observance.

Article 19 states:

> Everyone has the right to freedom of opinion and expression; this right includes freedom to hold opinions without interference and to seek, receive and impart information and ideas through any media regardless of frontiers.

Article 20 states:

> 1. Everyone has the right to freedom of peaceful assembly and association.
> 2. No one may be compelled to belong to an association.

We affirm our belief that these are inalienable rights of every person, regardless of origin, age, background, or views. We embody our professional commitment to these principles in the *Library Bill of Rights* and *Code of Ethics*, as adopted by the American Library Association.

We maintain that these are universal principles and should be applied by libraries and librarians throughout the world. The American Library Association's policy on International Relations reflects these objectives: ". . . to encourage the exchange, dissemination, and access to information and the unrestricted flow of library materials in all formats throughout the world."

We know that censorship, ignorance, and limitations on the free flow of information are the tools of tyranny and oppression. We believe that ideas and information topple the walls of hate and fear and build bridges of cooperation and understanding far more effectively than weapons and armies.

The American Library Association is unswerving in its commitment to human rights and intellectual freedom; the two are inseparably linked and inextricably entwined. Freedom of opinion and expression is not derived from or dependent on any form of government or political power. This right is inherent in every individual. It cannot be surrendered, nor can it be denied. True justice comes from the exercise of this right.

We recognize the power of information and ideas to inspire justice, to restore freedom and dignity to the oppressed, and to change the hearts and minds of the oppressors.

Courageous men and women, in difficult and dangerous circumstances throughout human history, have demonstrated that freedom lives in the human heart and cries out for justice even in the face of threats, enslavement, imprisonment, torture, exile, and death. We draw inspiration from their example. They challenge us to remain steadfast in our most basic professional responsibility to promote and defend the right of free expression.

There is no good censorship. Any effort to restrict free expression and the free flow of information aids the oppressor. Fighting oppression with censorship is self-defeating.

Threats to the freedom of expression of any person anywhere are threats to the freedom of all people everywhere. Violations of human rights and the right of free expression have been recorded in virtually every country and society across the globe.

In response to these violations, we affirm these principles:

> The American Library Association opposes any use of governmental prerogative that leads to the intimidation of individuals which prevents them from exercising their rights to hold opinions without interference, and to seek, receive, and impart information and ideas. We urge libraries and librarians everywhere to resist such abuse of governmental power, and to support those against whom such governmental power has been employed.
>
> The American Library Association condemns any governmental effort to involve libraries and librarians in restrictions on the right of any individual to hold opinions without interference, and to seek, receive, and impart information and ideas. Such restrictions pervert the function of the library and violate the professional responsibilities of librarians.
>
> The American Library Association rejects censorship in any form. Any action which denies the inalienable human rights of individuals only damages the will to resist oppression, strengthens the hand of the oppressor, and undermines the cause of justice.
>
> The American Library Association will not abrogate these principles. We believe that censorship corrupts the cause of justice, and contributes to the demise of freedom.

Adopted by the ALA Council, January 16, 1991.

APPENDIX D

Article 19 of the Universal Declaration of Human Rights

Proclaimed in 1948 by the United Nations General Assembly, Article 19 states:

> Everyone has the right to freedom of opinion and expression; this right includes freedom to hold opinions without interference and to seek, receive and impart information and ideas through any media regardless of frontiers.

This is not a binding treaty, but has been incorporated into many national constitutions.

INTERNATIONAL FEDERATION OF LIBRARY ASSOCIATIONS AND INSTITUTIONS (IFLA)

STATEMENT ON LIBRARIES AND INTELLECTUAL FREEDOM

IFLA (The International Federation of Library Associations and Institutions) supports, defends and promotes intellectual freedom as defined in the United Nations Universal Declaration of Human Rights.

IFLA declares that human beings have a fundamental right to access to expressions of knowledge, creative thought and intellectual activity, and to express their views publicly.

IFLA believes that the right to know and freedom of expression are two aspects of the same principle. The right to know is a requirement for freedom of thought and conscience; freedom of thought and freedom of expression are necessary conditions for freedom of access to information.

IFLA asserts that a commitment to intellectual freedom is a core responsibility for the library and information profession.

IFLA therefore calls upon libraries and library staff to adhere to the principles of intellectual freedom, uninhibited access to information and freedom of expression and to recognize the privacy of library user.

IFLA urges its members activity to promote the acceptance and realization of these principles. In doing so, IFLA affirms that:

- Libraries provide access to information, ideas and works of imagination. They serve as gateways to knowledge, thought and culture.
- Libraries provide essential support for lifelong learning, independent decision-making and cultural development for both individuals and groups.
- Libraries contribute to the development and maintenance of intellectual freedom and help to safeguard basic democratic values and universal civil rights.

- Libraries have a responsibility both to guarantee and to facilitate access to expressions of knowledge and intellectual activity. To this end, libraries shall acquire, preserve and make available the widest variety of materials, reflecting the plurality and diversity of society.
- Libraries shall ensure that the selection and availability of library materials and services is governed by professional considerations and not by political, moral and religious views.
- Libraries shall acquire, organize and disseminate information freely and oppose any form of censorship.
- Libraries shall make materials, facilities and services equally accessible to all users. There shall be no discrimination due to race, creed, gender, age or for any other reason.
- Library users shall have the right to personal privacy and anonymity. Librarians and other library staff shall not disclose the identity of users or the materials they use to a third party.
- Libraries funded from public sources and to which the public have access shall uphold the principles of intellectual freedom.
- Librarians and other employees in such libraries have a duty to uphold those principles.
- Librarians and other professional libraries staff shall fulfil their responsibilities both to their employer and to their users. In cases of conflict between those responsibilities, the duty towards the user shall take precedence.

Statement prepared by IFLA/FAIFE and approved by The Executive Board of IFLA 25 March 1999, The Hague, Netherlands

APPENDIX E

American Library Association Code of Ethics

As members of the American Library Association, we recognize the importance of codifying and making known to the profession and to the general public the ethical principles that guide the work of librarians, other professionals providing information services, library trustees and library staffs.

Ethical dilemmas occur when values are in conflict. The American Library Association Code of Ethics states the values to which we are committed, and embodies the ethical responsibilities of the profession in this changing information environment.

We significantly influence or control the selection, organization, preservation, and dissemination of information. In a political system grounded in an informed citizenry, we are members of a profession explicitly committed to intellectual freedom and the freedom of access to information. We have a special obligation to ensure the free flow of information and ideas to present and future generations.

The principles of this Code are expressed in broad statements to guide ethical decision making. These statements provide a framework; they cannot and do not dictate conduct to cover particular situations.

I. We provide the highest level of service to all library users through appropriate and usefully organized resources; equitable service policies; equitable access; and accurate, unbiased, and courteous responses to all requests.

II. We uphold the principles of intellectual freedom and resist all efforts to censor library resources.

III. We protect each library user's right to privacy and confidentiality with respect to information sought or received and resources consulted, borrowed, acquired or transmitted.

IV. We recognize and respect intellectual property rights.

V. We treat co-workers and other colleagues with respect, fairness and good faith, and advocate conditions of employment that safeguard the rights and welfare of all employees of our institutions.

VI. We do not advance private interests at the expense of library users, colleagues, or our employing institutions.

VII. We distinguish between our personal convictions and professional duties and do not allow our personal beliefs to interfere with fair representation of the aims of our institutions or the provision of access to their information resources.

VIII. We strive for excellence in the profession by maintaining and enhancing our own knowledge and skills, by encouraging the professional development of co-workers, and by fostering the aspirations of potential members of the profession.

Adopted by the ALA Council, June 28, 1995.

APPENDIX F

The Freedom to Read

The freedom to read is essential to our democracy. It is continuously under attack. Private groups and public authorities in various parts of the country are working to remove books from sale, to censor textbooks, to label "controversial" books, to distribute lists of "objectionable" books or authors, and to purge libraries. These actions apparently rise from a view that our national tradition of free expression is no longer valid; that censorship and suppression are needed to avoid the subversion of politics and the corruption of morals. We, as citizens devoted to the use of books and as librarians and publishers responsible for disseminating them, wish to assert the public interest in the preservation of the freedom to read.

We are deeply concerned about these attempts at suppression. Most such attempts rest on a denial of the fundamental premise of democracy: that the ordinary citizen, by exercising critical judgment, will accept the good and reject the bad. The censors, public and private, assume that they should determine what is good and what is bad for their fellow citizens.

We trust Americans to recognize propaganda, and to reject it. We do not believe they need the help of censors to assist them in this task. We do not believe they are prepared to sacrifice their heritage of a free press in order to be "protected" against what others think may be bad for them. We believe they still favor free enterprise in ideas and expression.

We are aware, of course, that books are not alone in being subjected to efforts at suppression. We are aware that these efforts are related to a larger pattern of pressures being brought against education, the press, films, radio and television. The problem is not only one of actual censorship. The shadow of fear cast by these pressures leads, we suspect, to an even larger voluntary curtailment of expression by those who seek to avoid controversy.

Such pressure toward conformity is perhaps natural to a time of uneasy change and pervading fear. Especially when so many of our apprehensions are directed against an ideology, the expression of a dissident idea becomes a thing feared in itself, and we tend to move against it as against a hostile deed, with suppression.

And yet suppression is never more dangerous than in such a time of social tension. Freedom has given the United States the elasticity to endure strain. Freedom keeps open the path of novel and creative solutions, and enables change to come by choice. Every silencing of a heresy, every enforcement of an orthodoxy, diminishes the toughness and resilience of our society and leaves it the less able to deal with stress.

Now as always in our history, books are among our greatest instruments of freedom. They are almost the only means for making generally available ideas or manners of expression that can initially command only a small audience. They are the natural medium for the new idea and the untried voice from which come the original contributions to social growth. They are essential to the extended discussion which serious thought requires, and to the accumulation of knowledge and ideas into organized collections.

We believe that free communication is essential to the preservation of a free society and a creative culture. We believe that these pressures towards conformity present the danger of limiting the range and variety of inquiry and expression on which our democracy and our culture depend. We believe that every American community must jealously guard the freedom to publish and to circulate, in order to preserve its own freedom to read. We believe that publishers and librarians have a profound responsibility to give validity to that freedom to read by making it possible for the readers to choose freely from a variety of offerings.

The freedom to read is guaranteed by the Constitution. Those with faith in free people will stand firm on these constitutional guarantees of essential rights and will exercise the responsibilities that accompany these rights.

We therefore affirm these propositions:

1. *It is in the public interest for publishers and librarians to make available the widest diversity of views and expressions, including those which are unorthodox or unpopular with the majority.*

Creative thought is by definition new, and what is new is different. The bearer of every new thought is a rebel until that idea is refined and tested. Totalitarian systems attempt to maintain themselves in power by the ruthless suppression of any concept which challenges the established orthodoxy. The power of a democratic system to adapt to change is vastly strengthened by the freedom of its citizens to choose widely from among conflicting opinions offered freely to them. To stifle every nonconformist idea at birth would mark the end of the democratic process. Furthermore, only through the constant activity of weighing and selecting can the democratic mind attain the strength demanded by times like these. We need to know not only what we believe but why we believe it.

2. *Publishers, librarians and booksellers do not need to endorse every idea or presentation contained in the books they make available. It would conflict with the public interest for them to establish their own political, moral, or aesthetic views as a standard for determining what books should be published or circulated.*

Publishers and librarians serve the educational process by helping to make available knowledge and ideas required for the growth of the mind and the increase of learning. They do not foster education by imposing as mentors the patterns of their own thought. The people should have the freedom to read and consider a broader range of ideas than those that may be held by any single librarian or publisher or government or church. It is wrong that what one can read should be confined to what another thinks proper.

3. *It is contrary to the public interest for publishers or librarians to determine the acceptability of a book on the basis of the personal history or political affiliations of the author.*

A book should be judged as a book. No art or literature can flourish if it is to be measured by the political views or private lives of its creators. No society of free people can flourish which draws up lists of writers to whom it will not listen, whatever they may have to say.

4. *There is no place in our society for efforts to coerce the taste of others, to confine adults to the reading matter deemed suitable for adolescents, or to inhibit the efforts of writers to achieve artistic expression.*

To some, much of modern literature is shocking. But is not much of life itself shocking? We cut off literature at the source if we prevent writers from dealing with the stuff of life. Parents and teachers have a responsibility to prepare the young to meet the diversity of experiences in life to which they will be exposed, as they have a responsibility to help them learn to think critically for themselves. These are affirmative responsibilities, not to be discharged simply by preventing them from reading works for which they are not yet prepared. In these matters taste differs, and taste cannot be legislated; nor can machinery be devised which will suit the demands of one group without limiting the freedom of others.

5. *It is not in the public interest to force a reader to accept with any book the prejudgment of a label characterizing the book or author as subversive or dangerous.*

The idea of labeling presupposes the existence of individuals or groups with wisdom to determine by authority what is good or bad for the citizen. It presupposes that individuals must be directed in making up their minds about the ideas they examine. But Americans do not need others to do their thinking for them.

6. *It is the responsibility of publishers and librarians, as guardians of the people's freedom to read, to contest encroachments upon that freedom by individuals or groups seeking to impose their own standards or tastes upon the community at large.*

It is inevitable in the give and take of the democratic process that the political, the moral, or the aesthetic concepts of an individual or group will occasionally collide with those of another individual or group. In a free society individuals are free to determine for themselves what they wish to read, and each group is free to determine what it will recommend to its freely associated members. But no group has the right to take the law into its own hands, and to impose its own concept of politics or morality upon other members of a democratic society. Freedom is no freedom if it is accorded only to the accepted and the inoffensive.

7. *It is the responsibility of publishers and librarians to give full meaning to the freedom to read by providing books that enrich the quality and diversity of thought and expression. By the exercise of this affirmative responsibility, they can demonstrate that the answer to a bad book is a good one, the answer to a bad idea is a good one.*

The freedom to read is of little consequence when expended on the trivial; it is frustrated when the reader cannot obtain matter fit for that reader's purpose. What is needed is not only the absence of restraint, but the positive provision of opportunity for the people to read the best that has been thought and said. Books are the major channel by which the intellectual inheritance is handed down, and the principal means of its testing and growth. The defense of their freedom and integrity, and the enlargement of their service to society, requires of all publishers and librarians the utmost of their faculties, and deserves of all citizens the fullest of their support.

We state these propositions neither lightly nor as easy generalizations. We here stake out a lofty claim for the value of books. We do so because we believe that they are good, possessed of enormous variety and usefulness, worthy of cherishing and keeping free. We realize that the application of these propositions may mean the dissemination of ideas and manners of expression that are repugnant to many persons. We do not state these propositions in the comfortable belief that what people read is unimportant. We believe rather that what people read is deeply important; that ideas can be dangerous; but that the suppression of ideas is fatal to a democratic society. Freedom itself is a dangerous way of life, but it is ours.

This statement was originally issued in May of 1953 by the Westchester Conference of the American Library Association and the American Book Publishers Council, which in 1970 consolidated with the American Educational Publishers Institute to become the Association of American Publishers.

Adopted June 25, 1953; revised January 28, 1972, January 16, 1991, by the ALA Council and the AAP Freedom to Read Committee.

A Joint Statement by
- American Library Association
- Association of American Publishers

Subsequently Endorsed by
- American Booksellers Association
- American Booksellers Foundation for Free Expression
- American Civil Liberties Union
- American Federation of Teachers AFL-CIO
- Anti-Defamation League of B'nai B'rith
- Association of American University Presses
- Children's Book Council
- Freedom to Read Foundation
- International Reading Association
- Thomas Jefferson Center for the Protection of Free Expression
- National Association of College Stores
- National Council of Teachers of English
- P.E.N.—American Center
- People for the American Way
- Periodical and Book Association of America
- Sex Information and Education Council of the U.S.
- Society of Professional Journalists
- Women's National Book Association
- YWCA of the U.S.A.

APPENDIX G

Development of a Materials Selection Policy

The primary purpose of a materials selection or collection development policy is to promote the development of a collection based on institutional goals and user needs. A secondary purpose is defending the principles of intellectual freedom.

The basis of a sound selection program is a materials selection statement, identifying specific criteria to be met for materials being added to the collection. Although a majority of professional librarians believe a materials selection statement is desirable, in too many instances the belief does not become reality. Librarians have given many reasons for not writing such a statement, but often two unmentioned ones are the most important: lack of knowledge about how to prepare one and lack of confidence in one's abilities to do so. Regardless of past failures and present difficulties, there is an absolute need for the firm foundation that a selection statement provides.

In virtually every case, it will be the librarian's task to prepare the materials selection statement. Although approval or official adoption of the statement rests with the institution's legally responsible governing body, it is the librarian who has the expertise and practical knowledge of the day-to-day activities of the library necessary for the development of useful and comprehensive selection and collection development criteria.

A materials selection statement must relate to concrete practices. It should provide guidelines for strengthening and adding to the library's collection. Furthermore, if the statement is to fulfill its secondary purpose, that of defending intellectual freedom, it must be a viable, working document that relates to the specific, day-to-day operations of the library or library system of which it is a part. In the case of very large libraries or even medium-sized institutions with highly sophisticated holdings, the librarian may prefer to prepare both an overarching policy or mission statement describing the philosophy of collection development that will guide selection decisions, and a separate list of specific procedures that staff will follow in carrying out the policy. Thus, the materials selection statement should reflect institutional policies, whereas a separate procedures manual should deal with the day-to-day applications of those policies.

A strong collection and intellectual freedom go hand in hand. It is less likely that problems will remain unresolved if the collection reflects the logical, coherent, and explicit statement from which it grows. In developing a materials selection statement, four basic factors must be considered: (1) service policy, (2) environmental characteristics, (3) collection specifications, and (4) current selection needs.

SERVICE POLICY

A service policy will provide practical operational guidelines to govern future collection development in accordance with the needs of the library's users and the goals of the library. In order to establish a service policy, it is necessary to determine what groups the library is striving to serve and what purposes it is attempting to achieve. To do so will entail a study of user-group characteristics and institutional objectives. Guidelines for such a study follow (fig. 1):

FIGURE 1 Guidelines for Establishing Service Policy

I. **User groups.** A materials selection statement must reflect the needs of the people the library will serve in trying to fulfill its objectives. To establish guidelines for collection development and related library activities, it is necessary to gather detailed information on various user groups.

A questionnaire to establish basic data can be prepared and completed by each staff member working with the public, or such information can be compiled on the basis of institutional statistics and records. After the library staff has been surveyed, users can be given questionnaires regarding their purposes in using the library, their library activities, and the like. It should be noted that certain sections of the prepared form can be used to determine the desired state of affairs as well.

A. Population characteristics
   1. Age
   2. Education
   3. Employment level
   4. Others

B. Size of each user group
C. Primary purpose of each group in using the library
D. Kinds of material used in accomplishing these purposes
E. Kinds of activities engaged in during the accomplishment of these purposes

II. **Institutional objectives.** The materials selection statement should define the library's goals and reason for existing. Institutional goals can be determined from at least two sources:

A. Statements of objectives are ideally available in a public document designed to inform all concerned persons.
   1. General need(s) the library is designated to fulfill
   2. Activities or standards most valued
   3. Distinction in some field of endeavor

B. Public documents and records, in lieu of a statement of objectives, may outline the institution's objectives and supplement statements of objectives.
   1. Annual reports of the institution
   2. Charter of the institution
   3. Published history of the institution
   4. Records of the governing body
   5. Budget (Because preparation of a budget usually demands a resolution of difficult questions of priorities in order to allocate scarce resources, this item should not be overlooked.)

ENVIRONMENTAL CHARACTERISTICS

The librarian should determine all aspects of the environment surrounding the institution that could possibly influence the development of the library collection and the library's related activities. A few such environmental factors and their implications follow (fig. 2):

FIGURE 2 Factors That Influence Development of the Library Collection

ENVIRONMENTAL FACTORS	PROVISIONS AFFECTED
Relative geographical isolation	Materials related to the cultural and recreational needs of users
Economic structure	Materials related to specific educational needs
Presence or absence of library resources external to the institution	Degree of self-sufficiency or completeness of materials
Presence or absence of postsecondary learning institutions	Scholarly and technical works
Relationship to local industries	Technical reports and business materials
Relationship to local professional and cultural groups	Specialized subcollections

COLLECTION SPECIFICATIONS

Specifications should be established for each subject area or area of concern. (The data gathered to determine service policy and environmental characteristics will show, in large measure, what the library requires.) For this section of the selection statement, each subject area should be carefully reviewed in order to determine the types of materials to be acquired in each and the depth in which materials are to be sought. Such a review is especially important in smaller libraries where funds are severely limited and the needs of the users potentially great. If possible, the following data should be collected for each area:

Number of library materials currently held

Total number of relevant materials available

Percent of total materials held

Distribution of current holdings by publication date

In addition, holdings should be rated by subject area in terms of specific user purposes:

Recreation

Self-help

Continuing education

Business

Finally, a desired acquisition level should be specified for each area.

The section of the selection statement dealing with collection specifications will no doubt be the largest and most detailed of all. It will specify the criteria to be used in selecting and reevaluating materials in terms of (1) types of materials (books, periodicals, newspapers, government publications, maps, records, films, etc.); (2) users' special needs by virtue of occupation, cultural interest, language, etc.; and (3) users' age groups. This section will also specify policies to be used in handling such matters as gifts and special bequests.

CURRENT SELECTION NEEDS

Current selection needs can be determined by the difference between the present collection and the collection specifications. In deciding what is currently needed, the desired state of affairs that may have been detailed under service policy should also be consulted. Once current needs are determined, other considerations come into play. Most prominent among these is the library's budget. Regardless of the amount of money available, the selection statement should indicate in as clear a manner as possible which materials are to be bought and which are not.

COMPONENTS OF A SELECTION POLICY

After full consideration of the aforementioned four factors—service policy, environmental characteristics, collection specifications, and current selection needs—the next step is to prepare a final draft of the selection (or collection development) statement itself for submission to the library's governing body. Taking into account the factors discussed above, the statement should relate to and include all materials and services offered by the library.

A good policy statement will first discuss the library's objectives in acquiring materials and maintaining services. It will state in succinct terms what the library is trying to accomplish in its program of services and the specific objectives in given areas of service.

The policy should derive from the library's mission statement. It is helpful if the role of the library in society (or in the parent institution) is spelled out in the policy and related to the objectives of selection, collection development, and maintenance. The overarching goal may be expressed in the broadest terms. For example, a policy for a public library should include reference to the traditional function of the library in the marketplace of ideas. It could include language like the following:

> The library serves a traditional role as a public forum for access to the full range of recorded information within the marketplace of ideas. Collection development shall be content neutral so that the library represents significant viewpoints on subjects of interest and does not favor any particular viewpoint.

A school library may declare that its main objective is to make available to faculty and students a collection of materials that will enrich and support the curriculum and meet the educational needs of the students and faculty served. Such a statement may then be divided into more specific objectives, such as to provide background materials to supplement classroom instruction, to provide access to classics of American and world literature, or to provide a broad range of materials on current issues of controversy to help students develop critical analytic skills.

The policy should precisely define responsibility for selection of all types of library materials. It should name, by professional position, those persons responsible in each area of selection. Although selection of materials will, of course, involve many people other than professionally trained librarians, ultimate responsibility should be delegated by the library's governing body to the professional staff. A public library's statement of responsibility might read thus:

> The elected Library Board shall delegate to the Head Librarian the authority and responsibility for selection of all print and nonprint materials. Responsibilities for actual selection shall rest with appropriate professionally trained personnel who shall discharge this obligation consistent with the Board's adopted selection criteria and procedures.

Depending upon the size and purpose of the library, the statement might continue by elaborating on any specialized selection responsibilities, the role of user input, and the like.

In terms of subject matter covered, the policy should include criteria, and the application of criteria, relevant to the library's stated objectives. These should include artistic or literary excellence, appropriateness to level of user, authenticity, interest, cost, and circumstances of use. Technical criteria, such as clarity of sound in audio materials, can be included as well. To guide the professional staff with responsibility for selection, criteria should be spelled out as specifically as possible. Bibliographies, reviewing journals, and other selection aids to be consulted should be listed. Special criteria to be applied in exceptional cases should be clearly stated. So, for example, a public library that regularly purchases all books on the *New York Times* best-seller list, even if these titles do not always meet other criteria, should state this clearly in the policy. There should be a section explaining how the library will treat donated materials and that such materials will be subject to the same selection criteria as materials the library purchases.

The policy should directly address problems associated with the acquisition of controversial materials. The document should include a statement on intellectual freedom and its importance to librarianship and an affirmation of the *Library Bill of Rights.* Some libraries also include the text of the First Amendment to the U.S. Constitution. A statement on intellectual freedom might read: "The library subscribes in principle to the statements of policy on library philosophy as expressed in the American Library Association *Library Bill of Rights,* a copy of which is appended to and made an integral part of this policy." The statement can also include the text of *The Freedom to Read* and the ALA "Policy on Confidentiality of Library Records," which states that circulation records and other records identifying the names of library users are considered confidential in nature.

The library's selection procedures should be described step-by-step from initial screening to final selection. The procedures should provide for coordination among departments and professional staff, for handling recommendations from library users, and for review of existing material. Any special procedures pertinent to collection development should be spelled out precisely in the materials selection statement. Some items to consider for treatment in the statement are sponsored materials, expensive or fragile materials, ephemeral materials, relations with jobbers and salespersons, distribution of free materials, and handling of special collections. The document should review procedures for collection maintenance.

Finally, occasional objections to materials will be made despite the quality of the selection process. The procedure for review of challenged materials in response to concerns of library users should be stated clearly. . . . The procedure should establish a fair framework for registering complaints, while defending the principles of intellectual freedom, the library user's right of access, and professional responsibility and integrity. Each specific step to be taken when a request for reconsideration is made, and all possible avenues of appeal, should be listed.

The final format and organization of the materials selection statement will depend, of course, on the particularities of the library concerned. One possible table of contents, however, might be outlined like this (fig. 3):

FIGURE 3 Materials Selection Considerations

PART 1: Selection of Library Materials

I. Statement of Policy

II. Objectives of Selection

III. Responsibility for Selection
  A. Delegation of Responsibility to Professional Staff
  B. Particular Responsibilities of Staff Members

IV. Selection Criteria
  A. General Selection Criteria
  B. Specific Selection Criteria

V. Policy on Controversial Materials
  A. General Statement
  B. *Library Bill of Rights*
  C. *Freedom to Read*

PART 2: Procedures for Selection of Library Materials

I. Procedures for Implementation
  A. Selection Aids
  B. Outside Recommendation Procedures
  C. Gifts
  D. Special Collections and Concerns

II. Collection Maintenance: Evaluation and Review of Existing Materials

III. Procedures for Dealing with Challenged Materials
  A. Request for Review
  B. The Review Committee
  C. Resolution and Appeal

It hardly need be said that preparation of a complete statement requires work—a great amount of it. And the work must be done before the censorship problem arises. Unfortunately, there are no shortcuts. The materials in this manual, including the texts of current ALA intellectual freedom policies, will be of some assistance. For school libraries, the American Association of School Librarians distributes a document entitled "Policies and Procedures for Selection of Instructional Materials." OIF distributes a "Workbook for Selection Policy Writing," with specific suggestions and examples of how to write a school library policy, the basic principles of which are also helpful in formulating policies for other libraries. The OIF and many state intellectual freedom committees have also collected sample selection statements that can serve as examples. It is, however, impossible simply to borrow a statement based on another institution's goals and needs: the statement must be a working document, a handbook for daily activities reflecting the specific needs of those who are to use it.

Reprinted from *Intellectual Freedom Manual*, 5th ed. (Chicago: ALA, 1996).

APPENDIX H

Statement on Library Use of Filtering Software

On June 26, 1997, the United States Supreme Court issued a sweeping re-affirmation of core First Amendment principles and held that communications over the Internet deserve the highest level of Constitutional protection.

The Court's most fundamental holding is that communications on the Internet deserve the same level of Constitutional protection as books, magazines, newspapers, and speakers on a street corner soapbox. The Court found that the Internet "constitutes a vast platform from which to address and hear from a worldwide audience of millions of readers, viewers, researchers, and buyers," and that "any person with a phone line can become a town crier with a voice that resonates farther than it could from any soapbox."

For libraries, the most critical holding of the Supreme Court is that libraries that make content available on the Internet can continue to do so with the same Constitutional protections that apply to the books on libraries' shelves. The Court's conclusion that "the vast democratic fora of the Internet" merit full Constitutional protection will also serve to protect libraries that provide their patrons with access to the Internet. The Court recognized the importance of enabling individuals to receive speech from the entire world and to speak to the entire world. Libraries provide those opportunities to many who would not otherwise have them. The Supreme Court's decision will protect that access.

The use in libraries of software filters which block constitutionally protected speech is inconsistent with the United States Constitution and federal law and may lead to legal exposure for the library and its governing authorities. The American Library Association affirms that the use of filtering software by libraries to block access to constitutionally protected speech violates the *Library Bill of Rights.*

WHAT IS BLOCKING/FILTERING SOFTWARE?

Blocking/filtering software is a mechanism used to:

- restrict access to Internet content, based on an internal database of the product, or;
- restrict access to Internet content through a database maintained external to the product itself, or;
- restrict access to Internet content to certain ratings assigned to those sites by a third party, or;
- restrict access to Internet content by scanning content, based on a keyword, phrase or text string, or;
- restrict access to Internet content based on the source of the information.

PROBLEMS WITH THE USE OF BLOCKING/FILTERING SOFTWARE IN LIBRARIES

- Publicly supported libraries are governmental institutions subject to the First Amendment, which forbids them from restricting information based on viewpoint or content discrimination.
- Libraries are places of inclusion rather than exclusion. Current blocking/filtering software prevents not only access to what some may consider "objectionable" material, but also blocks information protected by the First Amendment. The result is that legal and useful material will inevitably be blocked. Examples of sites that have been blocked by popular commercial blocking/filtering products include those on breast cancer, AIDS, women's rights, and animal rights.
- Filters can impose the producer's viewpoint on the community.
- Producers do not generally reveal what is being blocked, or provide methods for users to reach sites that were inadvertently blocked.
- Criteria used to block content are vaguely defined and subjectively applied.

- The vast majority of Internet sites are informative and useful. Blocking/filtering software often blocks access to materials it is not designed to block.
- Most blocking/filtering software is designed for the home market. Filters are intended to respond to the preferences of parents making decisions for their own children. Libraries are responsible for serving a broad and diverse community with different preferences and views. Blocking Internet sites is antithetical to library missions because it requires the library to limit information access.
- In a library setting, filtering today is a one-size-fits-all "solution," which cannot adapt to the varying ages and maturity levels of individual users.
- A role of librarians is to advise and assist users in selecting information resources. Parents and only parents have the right and responsibility to restrict their own children's access—and only their own children's access—to library resources, including the Internet. Librarians do not serve *in loco parentis.*
- Library use of blocking/filtering software creates an implied contract with parents that their children ***will not*** be able to access material on the Internet that they do not wish their children [to] read or view. Libraries will be unable to fulfill this implied contract, due to the technological limitations of the software, thus exposing themselves to possible legal liability and litigation.
- Laws prohibiting the production or distribution of child pornography and obscenity apply to the Internet. These laws provide protection for libraries and their users.

WHAT CAN YOUR LIBRARY DO TO PROMOTE ACCESS TO THE INTERNET?

- Educate yourself, your staff, library board, governing bodies, community leaders, parents, elected officials, etc., about the Internet and how best to take advantage of the wealth of information available. For examples of what other libraries have done, contact the ALA Public Information Office at 800-545-2433, ext. 5044 or pio@ala.org.
- Uphold the First Amendment by establishing and implementing written guidelines and policies on Internet use in your library in keeping with your library's overall policies on access to library

materials. For information on and copies of the *Library Bill of Rights* and its *Interpretation on Electronic Information, Services and Networks*, contact the ALA Office for Intellectual Freedom at 800/545-2433, ext. 4223.
- Promote Internet use by facilitating user access to Web sites that satisfy user interest and needs.
- Create and promote library Web pages designed both for general use and for use by children. These pages should point to sites that have been reviewed by library staff.
- Consider using privacy screens or arranging terminals away from public view to protect a user's confidentiality.
- Provide information and training for parents and minors that remind users of time, place and manner restrictions on Internet use.
- Establish and implement user behavior policies.

For further information on this topic, contact the Office for Intellectual Freedom at 800/545-2433, ext. 4223, by fax at (312) 280-4227, or by e-mail at oif@ala.org.

American Library Association Intellectual Freedom Committee.

APPENDIX I

Guidelines for the Development and Implementation of Policies, Regulations and Procedures Affecting Access to Library Materials, Services and Facilities

INTRODUCTION

Publicly supported libraries exist within the context of a body of law derived from the United States Constitution and appropriate state constitutions, defined by statute, and implemented by regulations, policies and procedures established by their governing bodies and administrations. These regulations, policies and procedures establish the mission of the library, define its functions, services and operations and ascertain the rights and responsibilities of the clientele served by the library.

Publicly supported library service is based upon the First Amendment right of free expression. The publicly supported library provides free and equal access to information for all people of the community it serves. Thus, publicly supported libraries are governmental agencies designated as limited public forums for access to information. Libraries that make meeting rooms, exhibit spaces and/or bulletin boards available for public use are also designated as limited public forums for the exchange of information.

Many libraries adopt administrative policies and procedures regulating the organization and use of library materials, services and facilities. These policies and procedures affect access and may have the effect of restricting, denying or creating barriers to access to the library as a public forum, including the library's resources, facilities and services. Library policies and procedures that impinge upon First Amendment rights are subject to a higher standard of review than may be required in the policies of other public services and facilities.

Policies, procedures or regulations that may result in denying, restricting or creating physical or economic barriers to access to the library's public forum must be based on a compelling government interest. However, library governing authorities may place reasonable and narrowly drawn restrictions on the time, place or manner of access to library resources, services or facilities, provided that such restrictions are not based upon arbitrary distinctions between individuals or classes of individuals.

The American Library Association has adopted the *Library Bill of Rights* and Interpretations of the *Library Bill of Rights* to provide library governing authorities, librarians and other library staff and library users with guidelines on how constitutional principles apply to libraries in the United States of America.

The American Library Association's Intellectual Freedom Committee recommends that publicly supported libraries use the following guidelines, based on constitutional principles, to develop policies, regulations and procedures.

GUIDELINES

All library policies, regulations and procedures should be carefully examined to determine if they may result in denying, restricting or creating barriers to access. If they may result in such restrictions, they:

1. should be developed and implemented within the legal framework that applies to the library. This includes: the United States Constitution, including the First and Fourteenth Amendments, due process and equal treatment under the law; the applicable state constitution; federal and state civil rights legislation; all other applicable federal, state and local legislation; and applicable case law;
2. should cite statutes or ordinances upon which the authority to make that policy is based, when appropriate;
3. should be developed and implemented within the framework of the *Library Bill of Rights* and its Interpretations;
4. should be based upon the library's mission and objectives;
5. should only impose restrictions on the access to, or use of library resources, services or facilities when those restrictions are necessary to achieve the library's mission and objectives;
6. should narrowly tailor prohibitions or restrictions, in the rare instances when they are required, so they are not more restrictive than needed to serve their objectives;
7. should attempt to balance competing interests and avoid favoring the majority at the expense of individual rights, or allowing individual

users' rights to interfere materially with the majority's rights to free and equal access to library resources, services and facilities;

8. should avoid arbitrary distinctions between individuals or classes of users, and should not have the effect of denying or abridging a person's right to use library resources, services, or facilities based upon arbitrary distinctions such as origin, age, background or views;

In the *Library Bill of Rights* and all of its Interpretations, it is intended that: "origin" encompasses all the characteristics of individuals that are inherent in the circumstances of their birth; "age" encompasses all the characteristics of individuals that are inherent in their levels of development and maturity; "background" encompasses all the characteristics of individuals that are a result of their life experiences; and "views" encompasses all the opinions and beliefs held and expressed by individuals;

9. should not target specific users or groups of users based upon an assumption or expectation that such users might engage in behavior that will materially interfere with the achievement of substantial library objectives;
10. must be clearly stated so that a reasonably intelligent person will have fair warning of what is expected;
11. must provide a means of appeal;
12. must be reviewed regularly by the library's governing authority and by its legal counsel;
13. must be communicated clearly and made available in an effective manner to all library users;
14. must be enforced evenhandedly, and not in a manner intended to benefit or disfavor any person or group in an arbitrary or capricious manner;

Libraries should develop an ongoing staff training program designed to foster the understanding of the legal framework and principles underlying library policies and to assist staff in gaining the skill and ability to respond to potentially difficult circumstances in a timely, direct and open manner. This program should include training to develop empathy and understanding of the social and economic problems of some library users;

15. should, if reasonably possible, provide adequate alternative means of access to information for those whose behavior results in the denial or restriction of access to any library resource, service or facility.

GLOSSARY

Below are definitions of some of the terms used in the Guidelines to assist in understanding the applicable standards:

Arbitrary distinctions Inappropriate categorizations of persons, classes of persons, conduct, or things based upon criteria irrelevant to the purpose for which the distinctions are made. For example, a rule intended to regulate the length of time an item may be borrowed should not be based on an irrelevant consideration (arbitrary distinction) such as a personal characteristic of the borrower (height or age).

Compelling government interest A term often used by courts when assessing the burden of government regulation or action upon a fundamental right such as freedom of speech. For such a rule to withstand constitutional challenge, the government must show more than a merely important reason—the reason for the rule must be *compelling*—so important that it outweighs even the most valued and basic freedom it negatively impacts.

Limited public forum A public place designated by the government, or established through tradition, as a place dedicated to a particular type of expression. As in a public forum, only reasonable time, place and manner restrictions on speech within the scope of the designated purpose of the forum, may be imposed. The government may exclude entire categories of speech which do not fall within the designated purpose of the forum, but may not discriminate against particular viewpoints on subjects appropriate to the forum.

Materially interfere A term used by courts to describe the necessary level of intrusion, inconvenience or disruption of an accepted or protected activity caused by certain conduct in order to justify regulation of that conduct. A material interference is much more than mere annoyance—it must be an *actual obstacle* to the exercise of a right.

Substantial objectives Goals related to the fundamental mission of a government institution, and not merely incidental to the performance of that mission. Providing free and unrestricted access to a broad selection of materials representing various points of view is a substantial objective of a public library. Having spotless white carpeting is not.

Adopted June 28, 1994, by the ALA Intellectual Freedom Committee.

APPENDIX J

ALA Policies on Confidentiality

Suggested Procedures for Implementing "Policy on Confidentiality of Library Records"

When drafting local policies, libraries should consult with their legal counsel to insure these policies are based upon and consistent with applicable federal, state, and local law concerning the confidentiality of library records, the disclosure of public records, and the protection of individual privacy.

Suggested procedures include the following:

1. The library staff member receiving the request to examine or obtain information relating to circulation or other records identifying the names of library users will immediately refer the person making the request to the responsible officer of the institution, who shall explain the confidentiality policy.
2. The director, upon receipt of such process, order, or subpoena, shall consult with the appropriate legal officer assigned to the institution to determine if such process, order, or subpoena is in good form and if there is a showing of good cause for its issuance.
3. If the process, order, or subpoena is not in proper form or if good cause has not been shown, insistence shall be made that such defects be cured before any records are released. (The legal process requiring the production of circulation or other library records shall ordinarily be in the form of *subpoena duces tecum* [bring your records] requiring the responsible officer to attend court or the taking of his/her deposition and may require him/her

to bring along certain designated circulation or other specified records.)

4. Any threats or unauthorized demands (i.e., those not supported by a process, order, or subpoena) concerning circulation and other records identifying the names of library users shall be reported to the appropriate legal officer of the institution.
5. Any problems relating to the privacy of circulation and other records identifying the names of library users which are not provided for above shall be referred to the responsible officer.

Adopted by the ALA Intellectual Freedom Committee, January 9, 1983; revised January 11, 1988.

Policy concerning Confidentiality of Personally Identifiable Information about Library Users

The ethical responsibilities of librarians, as well as statutes in most states and the District of Columbia, protect the privacy of library users. Confidentiality extends to "information sought or received, and materials consulted, borrowed or acquired," and includes database search records, reference interviews, circulation records, interlibrary loan records, and other personally identifiable uses of library materials, facilities, or services.

The First Amendment's guarantee of freedom of speech and of the press requires that the corresponding rights to hear what is spoken and read what is written be preserved, free from fear of government intrusion, intimidation, or reprisal. The American Library Association reaffirms its opposition to "any use of government prerogatives which lead to the intimidation of the individual or the citizenry from the exercise of free expression . . . [and] encourages resistance to such abuse of government power. . . ." (ALA Policy 53.4). In seeking access or in the pursuit of information, confidentiality is the primary means of providing the privacy that will free the individual from fear of intimidation or retaliation.

Libraries are one of the great bulwarks of democracy. They are living embodiments of the First Amendment because their collections include voices of dissent as well as assent. Libraries are impartial resources providing information on all points of view, available to all persons regardless of age, race, religion, national origin, social or political views, economic status, or any other characteristic. The role of libraries as such a resource must not be compromised by an erosion of the privacy rights of library users.

The American Library Association regularly receives reports of visits by agents of federal, state, and local law enforcement agencies to libraries, where it is alleged they have asked for personally identifiable information about library users. These visits, whether under the rubric of simply informing libraries of agency concerns or for some other reason, reflect an insensitivity to the legal and ethical bases for confidentiality, and the role it plays in the preservation of First Amendment rights, rights also extended to foreign nationals while in the United States. The government's interest in library use reflects a dangerous and fallacious equation of what a person reads with what that person believes or how that person is likely to behave. Such a presumption can and does threaten the freedom of access to information. It also is a threat to a crucial aspect of First Amendment rights: that freedom of speech and of the press include the freedom to hold, disseminate, and receive unpopular, minority, "extreme," or even "dangerous" ideas.

The American Library Association recognizes that, under limited circumstances, access to certain information might be restricted due to a legitimate "national security" concern. However, there has been no showing of a plausible probability that national security will be compromised by any use made of *unclassified* information available in libraries. Thus, the right of access to this information by individuals, including foreign nationals, must be recognized as part of the librarian's legal and ethical responsibility to protect the confidentiality of the library user.

The American Library Association also recognizes that law enforcement agencies and officers may occasionally believe that library records contain information which would be helpful to the investigation of criminal activity. If there is a reasonable basis to believe such records are *necessary* to the progress of an investigation or prosecution, the American judicial system provides the mechanism for seeking release of such confidential records: the issuance of a court order, following a showing of *good cause* based on *specific facts*, by a court of competent jurisdiction.

Adopted July 2, 1991, by the ALA Council.

Policy on Confidentiality of Library Records

The Council of the American Library Association strongly recommends that the responsible officers of each library, cooperative system, and consortium in the United States:

1. Formally adopt a policy which specifically recognizes its circulation records and other records identifying the names of library users to be confidential in nature.*
2. Advise all librarians and library employees that such records shall not be made available to any agency of state, federal, or local government except pursuant to such process, order, or subpoena as may be authorized under the authority of, and pursuant to, federal, state, or local law relating to civil, criminal, or administrative discovery procedures or legislative investigative power.
3. Resist the issuance or enforcement of any such process, order, or subpoena until such time as a proper showing of good cause has been made in a court of competent jurisdiction.**

*Note: See also ALA "Code of Ethics," point III: "We protect each library user's right to privacy and confidentiality with respect to information sought or received and materials consulted, borrowed, acquired or transmitted."

**Note: Point 3, above, means that upon receipt of such process, order, or subpoena, the library's officers will consult with their legal counsel to determine if such process, order, or subpoena is in proper form and if there is a showing of good cause for its issuance; if the process, order, or subpoena is not in proper form or if good cause has not been shown, they will insist that such defects be cured.

Adopted January 20, 1971; revised July 4, 1975, and July 2, 1986, by the ALA Council.

APPENDIX K

ACRL/IFC *Intellectual Freedom Principles for Academic Libraries*

Introduction

A strong intellectual freedom perspective is critical to the development of academic library collections and services that dispassionately meet the education and research needs of a college or university community. The purpose of this statement is to provide an interpretation of general intellectual freedom principles in an academic library setting and, in the process, raise consciousness of the intellectual freedom context within which academic librarians work. These principles should be reflected in all relevant library policy documents.

The Principles

1. The general principles set forth in the *Library Bill of Rights* form an indispensable framework for building collections, services, and policies that serve the entire academic community.
2. The privacy of library users is and must be inviolable. Policies should be in place that maintain confidentiality of library borrowing records and of other information relating to personal use of library information and services.
3. The development of library collections in support of an institution's instruction and research programs should transcend the personal values of the selector. In the interests of research and learning, it is essential that collections contain materials representing a variety of perspectives on subjects that may be considered controversial.

4. Preservation and replacement efforts should ensure that balance in library materials is maintained and that controversial materials are not removed from the collections through theft, loss, mutilation, or normal wear and tear. There should be alertness to efforts by special interest groups to bias a collection through systematic theft or mutilation.
5. Licensing agreements should be consistent with the *Library Bill of Rights*, and should maximize access.
6. Open and unfiltered access to the Internet should be conveniently available to the academic community in a college or university library. Content filtering devices and content-based restrictions are a contradiction of the academic library mission to further research and learning through exposure to the broadest possible range of ideas and information. Such restrictions are a fundamental violation of intellectual freedom in academic libraries.
7. Freedom of information and of creative expression should be reflected in library exhibits and in all relevant library policy documents.
8. Library meeting rooms, research carrels, exhibit spaces, and other facilities should be available to the academic community regardless of research being pursued or subject being discussed. Any restrictions made necessary because of limited availability of space should be based on need, as reflected in library policy, rather than on content of research or discussion.
9. Whenever possible, library services should be available without charge in order to encourage inquiry. Where charges are necessary, a free or low-cost alternative (e.g., downloading to disc rather than printing) should be available when possible.
10. A service philosophy should be promoted that affords equal access to information for all in the academic community with no discrimination on the basis of race, values, gender, sexual orientation, cultural or ethnic background, physical or learning disability, economic status, religious beliefs, or views.
11. A procedure ensuring due process should be in place to deal with requests by those within and outside the academic community for removal or addition of library resources, exhibits, or services.
12. It is recommended that this statement of principle be endorsed by appropriate institutional governing bodies, including the faculty senate or similar instrument of faculty governance.

Adopted by ACRL Intellectual Freedom Committee on June 28, 1999. Approved by ACRL Board of Directors on June 29, 1999.

BIBLIOGRAPHY

Abbott, Andrew. *The System of Professions: An Essay on the Division of Expert Labor.* Chicago: University of Chicago Pr., 1988.

Access Denied: The Impact of Filtering Software on the Lesbian and Gay Community. Washington, D.C.: Gay and Lesbian Alliance against Defamation, 1997.

Achbar, Mark, and Peter Wintonick, dir. *Manufacturing Consent: Noam Chomsky and the Media.* Montreal: Zeitgeist Films, 1992, 2 videocassettes.

American Library Association, Office for Intellectual Freedom. *Confidentiality in Libraries: An Intellectual Freedom Modular Education Program.* Chicago: American Library Association, 1993.

———. *Intellectual Freedom Manual.* 5th ed. Chicago: American Library Association, 1996.

Berman, Sanford. *Prejudices and Antipathies: A Tract on the LC Subject Heads concerning People.* Metuchen, N.J.: Scarecrow, 1971.

Bernal, Martin. *Black Athena,* 2 vols. New Brunswick, N.J.: Rutgers University Pr., 1987.

Bloom, Allan. *The Closing of the American Mind.* New York: Simon & Schuster, 1987.

Boyle, James. *Shamans, Software, and Spleens: Law and the Construction of the Information Society.* Cambridge, Mass.: Harvard University Pr., 1996.

Branscomb, Anne Wells. *Who Owns Information? From Privacy to Public Access.* New York: Basic Books, 1994.

Buschman, John. "A House Divided against Itself: ACRL Leadership, Academic Freedom, and Electronic Resources." *Progressive Librarian* 12/13 (1997): 7–17; http://www.libr.org/PL/html.

———. *Cyberguide for Kids and Parents.* Chicago: Illinois Library Association, 1997; ila@ila.org.

Cervantes Saavadra, Miguel de. *Don Quijote.* Trans. Burton Raffel. New York: Norton, 1995.

"Controversial Materials in the Jewish Library." *Judaica Librarianship* 3 (1986–87): 49–57.

Downs, Donald A. "Public Forum Doctrine." In *The Oxford Companion to the Supreme Court of the United States*, ed. Kermit L. Hall. New York: Oxford University Pr., 1992, pp. 692–93.

Doyle, Robert. "Update." *Illinois Library Association Reporter* (June 1997): 1, 8–9, 11–12.

D'Souza, Dinesh. *Illiberal Education: The Politics of Race and Sex on Campus.* New York: Free Pr., 1991.

Eaton, Judith S. "'PC' or Not 'PC': That Is Not the Question." *Educational Record* (winter 1992): 25–29.

Edwards, Marcy, et al. *Freedom of Speech in the Public Workplace: A Legal and Practical Guide to Issues Affecting Public Employment.* Chicago: American Bar Association, 1998.

Emerson, Thomas. "The Affirmative Side of the First Amendment." *Georgia Law Review* 15 (1981): 795–849.

———. *The System of Freedom of Expression.* New York: Random House, 1970.

Fogel, Robert, and Stanley Engerman. *Time on the Cross: The Economics of American Negro Slavery.* New York: Norton, 1989.

Gates, Henry Louis, Jr. "To 'Deprave and Corrupt.'" *The Nation* (June 29, 1992): 903.

Giacoma, Pete. *The Fee or Free Decision: Legal, Economic, Political, and Ethical Perspectives for Public Libraries.* New York: Neal-Schuman, 1989.

Godwin, Mike. *CyberRights: Defending Free Speech in the Digital Age.* New York: Random House, 1998.

Guernsey, Lisa. "Off-Campus Users Swamp College Libraries, Seeking Access to Web and E-Mail." *The Chronicle of Higher Education* 44 (July 31, 1998): A17.

Habermas, Jurgen. *The Structural Transformation of the Public Sphere: An Inquiry into a Category of Bourgeois Society*, trans. Thomas Burger. Cambridge, Mass.: MIT Pr., 1989.

Harris, Roma M. *Librarianship: The Erosion of a Woman's Profession.* Norwood, N.J.: Ablex, 1992.

Himmel, Ethel, and William James Wilson. *Planning for Results: A Public Library Transformation Process.* Chicago: American Library Association, 1998.

Hunter, James D. *Culture Wars: The Struggle to Define America.* New York: Basic Books, 1991.

Jenner & Block, Attorneys at Law. Legal memoranda presented to Freedom to Read Foundation, various dates.

Jones, Barbara M. "Should Libraries Post Suspect Notices? A First Amendment Perspective." In *Symposium on Identifying Cultural Property Protection Needs for the Twenty-first Century*, sponsored by the Smithsonian Institution, Arlington, Va., 1995, from published proceedings, pp. 77–82.

Kalman, Laura. *Legal Realism at Yale, 1927–1960.* Chapel Hill: University of North Carolina Pr., 1986.

Kalven, Harry. "The Concept of the Public Forum." *Supreme Court Review* (1965): 1–32.

Katsh, M. Ethan. *Law in a Digital World.* New York: Oxford University Pr., 1995.

Kennedy, Caroline, and Ellen Alderman. *The Right to Privacy.* New York: Knopf, 1995.

Kranich, Nancy C. *Staking a Claim in Cyberspace: Ensuring Public Places on the Info Highway.* Westfield, N.J.: Open Magazine Pamphlet Series, 1996.

Lefkowitz, Mary, and Guy M. Rogers, eds. *Black Athena Revisited.* Chapel Hill: University of North Carolina Pr., 1996.

Lindsey, Jonathan A., and Ann E. Prentice. *Professional Ethics and Librarians.* Phoenix: Oryx Pr., 1985.

McCormack, Thelma. "Making Sense of Research on Pornography." In *Women Against Censorship.* Ed. Varda Burstyn. Vancouver: Douglas & McIntyre, 1985.

MacKinnon, Catharine. *Feminism Unmodified.* Cambridge: Harvard University Pr., 1987.

Martin, Murray, and Betsy Park. *Charging and Collecting Fees and Fines: A Handbook for Libraries.* New York: Neal-Schuman, 1998.

Mass Communication Law: Cases and Comment. 5th ed. Ed. Donald Gillmor et al. St. Paul: West, 1990.

Menand, Louis, ed. *The Future of Academic Freedom.* Chicago: University of Chicago Pr., 1996.

Nash, Gary, Charlotte Crabtree, and R. Dunn. *History on Trial: Culture Wars and the Teaching of the Past.* New York: Knopf, 1997.

Olsen, Tillie. *Silences.* New York: Delacorte, 1978.

O'Neil, Robert. "Protecting Free Expression in Electronic Communications." *EDUCOM Review* 31 (May/June 1996): 16–20.

Peck, Robert S. *The Bill of Rights and the Politics of Interpretation.* St. Paul: West, 1992.

Platt, Charles. *Anarchy Online: Net Crime, Net Sex.* New York: Harper, 1997.

Powell, Judith. *Peoplework: Communications Dynamics for Librarians.* Chicago: American Library Association, 1979.

Pungitore, Verna. *Innovation and the Library: The Adoption of New Ideas in Public Libraries.* Westport, Conn.: Greenwood Pr., 1995.

Rheingold, Howard. *The Virtual Community: Homesteading on the Electronic Frontier.* Reading, Mass.: Addison-Wesley, 1993.

Roszak, Theodore. *The Cult of Information: A Neo-Luddite Treatise on High Tech, Artificial Intelligence, and the True Art of Thinking.* Berkeley: University of California Pr., 1994.

Schmidt, Benno. "The University and Freedom." *Educational Record* (winter 1992): 14–18.

Schneider, Karen. *A Practical Guide to Internet Filters.* New York: Neal-Schuman, 1997.

Shenk, David. *Datasmog: Surviving the Information Glut.* Rev. ed. New York: HarperCollins, 1997.

Shiell, Timothy C. *Campus Hate Speech on Trial.* Lawrence: University Press of Kansas, 1998.

Smolla, Rodney A. "Freedom of Speech for Libraries and Librarians." *Law Library Journal* 85 (1993): 71–79.

Smolla and Nimmer on Freedom of Speech. 3d ed. 2 vols. Deerfield, Ill.: Clark, Boardman, and Callaghan, 1996.

Snyder, Herbert, and Elizabeth Davenport. *Costing and Pricing in the Digital Age.* New York: Neal-Schuman, 1997.

Stoll, Clifford. *Silicon Snake Oil: Second Thoughts along the Information Highway.* New York: Doubleday, 1995.

Swanson, Rick A. "Regaining Lost Ground: Toward a Public Forum Doctrine under the Illinois Constitution." *Southern Illinois University Law Journal* 18 (1993–94): 453–80.

Symons, Ann K., and Carla J. Stoffle. "When Values Conflict." *American Libraries* (May 1998): 56–58.

University Libraries and Scholarly Communication: A Study Prepared for the Andrew W. Mellon Foundation. Washington, D.C.: Association for Research Libraries, 1992.

Van Horn, Carl E., Donald C. Baumer, and William T. Gormley Jr. *Politics and Public Policy.* 2d ed. Washington, D.C.: Congressional Quarterly Pr., 1992.

Wallace, Jonathan, and Mark Mangan. *Sex, Laws, and Cyberspace.* New York: Holt, 1997.

Warren, Samuel D., and Louis D. Brandeis. "The Right to Privacy." *Harvard Law Review* 4 (1890): 193–220.

Wells, Donald T., and Chris R. Hamilton. *The Policy Puzzle: Finding Solutions in the Diverse American System.* Upper Saddle River, N.J.: Prentice-Hall, 1996.

White, Herbert S. "Teaching Professional Ethics to Students of Library and Information Science." In *Ethics and the Librarian*, ed. F. W. Lancaster. Urbana: University of Illinois Graduate School of Library and Information Science, 1989.

Wilson, Allan. "The Hierarchy of Belief: Ideological Tendentiousness in Universal Classification." In *Classification Research for Knowledge Representation and Organization.* Proceedings. Fifth International Study Conference on Classification Research, 1991. Amsterdam: Elsevier, 1992, pp. 389–97.

Winter, Michael F. *The Culture and Control of Expertise.* New York: Greenwood Pr., 1988.

Wolfson, Nicholas. *Hate Speech, Sex Speech, Free Speech.* London: Praeger, 1997.

INDEX

Barbara M. Jones chose intellectual freedom as her primary professional interest early in her career. Since the 1980s, she has served one term as chair of ALA's Intellectual Freedom Round Table, two terms as a member of the Intellectual Freedom Committee and a member of the state intellectual freedom committees in Iowa and Minnesota. She was the first chair of the recently created ACRL Intellectual Freedom Committee. Jones has spoken to library, general academic, legislative and community groups about the First Amendment in libraries of all types. Her writing on intellectual freedom culminated in her Ph.D. in United States history from the University of Minnesota in 1995, with a focus on legal history.

She is currently Coordinator of the Special Collections Division and Rare Book and Special Collections Librarian at the University of Illinois at Urbana-Champaign. Her current project focuses on the expansion and description of the Baskette Freedom of Expression Collection at UIUC.